GOD'S WORDS

by the same author

'Fundamentalism' and the Word of God
The thirty-nine articles
Evangelism and the sovereignty of God
Our Lord's understanding of the law of God
Keep yourselves from idols
God has spoken
The Gospel in the Prayer Book
Tomorrow's worship
The Spirit within you (with A. M. Stibbs)
The thirty-nine articles today
Knowing God
I want to be a Christian
For man's sake
The evangelical Anglican identity problem
Under God's Word
Freedom and authority
A kind of Noah's ark?

GOD'S WORDS

Studies of key Bible themes

J. I. Packer

Inter-Varsity Press

Inter-Varsity Press
38 De Montfort Street, Leicester LE1 7GP, England

First published 1981

British Library Cataloguing in Publication Data
Packer, J. I.
   God's Words.
   1. Theology, Doctrinal
   I. Title
   230   BT77.3

ISBN 0–85110–434–7

Set in 10/11 Times.
Phototypeset in Great Britain by Nuprint Services Ltd, Harpenden, Herts
Printed in Great Britain by ©ollins, Glasgow

*Inter-Varsity Press is the publishing division of the Universities and Colleges
Christian Fellowship (formerly the Inter-Varsity Fellowship), a student
movement linking Christian Unions in universities and colleges throughout
the British Isles, and a member movement of the International Fellowship of
Evangelical Students. For information about local and national activities in
Great Britain write to UCCF 38 De Montfort Street, Leicester LE1 7GP.*

CONTENTS

For

RUTH, NAOMI and MARTIN

with their father's prayers
that they will make their own
all that I have written about here

FOREWORD

Much of the following material first appeared in the now-defunct magazine *Inter-Varsity*. It comes from an era in which biblical word-study was in its hey-day of popularity as a way into theological and spiritual understanding. Today such study is somewhat out of fashion, its reputation tarnished by mistakes of method which some of its pioneer practitioners are seen to have made. Yet its value remains great if it is properly done. Preparing this material for its reappearance, I felt the need to write an introduction setting out what seem to me to be proper principles for biblical word-study, and marking off some of the pitfalls. But because I fear it is harder reading than the rest of the book, I invite readers who would rather skip it to do just that. And because its opening section touches on some semantic technicalities, it is printed in smaller type to show that it is more skippable than the rest.

Biblical references in the studies themselves are not, however, skippable; they are part of the argument, and are meant to be looked up.

I love pregnant brevity, and some of my material is, I know, packed tight (Packer by name, packer by nature). I ask my readers' pardon if they find obscurity due to my over-indulging this love of mine.

J. I. PACKER

ABBREVIATIONS

Books of the Old Testament
Gn., Ex., Lv., Nu., Dt., Jos., Jdg., Ru., 1, 2 Sa., 1, 2
Ki., 1, 2 Ch., Ezr., Ne., Est., Jb., Ps. (Pss.), Pr., Ec.,
Song, Is., Je., La., Ezk., Dn., Ho., Joel, Am., Ob.,
Jon., Mi., Na., Hab., Zp., Hg., Zc., Mal.

Books of the New Testament
Mt., Mk., Lk., Jn., Acts, Rom., 1, 2 Cor., Gal., Eph.,
Phil., Col., 1, 2 Thes., 1, 2 Tim., Tit., Phm., Heb.,
Jas., 1, 2 Pet., 1, 2, 3 Jn., Jude, Rev.

AV	Authorized, or King James, Version (1611)
cf.	compare
JB	Jerusalem Bible (1966)
LB	Living Bible (1971)
mg.	margin
Moffatt	James Moffatt's translation of the Bible (NT 1913, OT 1924)
NEB	New English Bible (1970)
NIV	New International Version (1978)
RSV	Revised Standard Version (1952, 1971)
RV	Revised Version (1885)

Biblical quotations are from RSV unless otherwise stated.

INTRODUCTION:
OF BIBLICAL WORDS
AND THEMES

Keys open doors; keywords open minds, and through minds hearts. This book takes keywords from the Bible – terms, we may truly say, from God's own vocabulary – and spells out in a practical way some of the main thoughts linked with them. The goal is understanding, faith and wisdom. Since the words themselves are our starting-point, I begin by asking you to brood with me for a moment on word study.

'What do you read, my lord?' asked Polonius, that classic compound of senile sententiousness and servile stupidity. Hamlet's reply – 'Words, words, words' – was meant as an insulting non-answer, a put-down and brush-off for a prize specimen of the *genus*, tedious old fools. Of course we read words! – but we do so for the sake of their subject-matter, and may never notice how the words are used to convey it. Yet in fact the reading of words as words, the particular words which this or that writer chose in preference to any other in order to express his meaning, can be both fascinating and enriching. Some who travel by train are interested only in reaching their destination; some, however, like the present writer, are interested in trains too, and so get more knowledge about their journeys, and more pleasure from them, than do others. In the same way, some read literature just to get the message or story, while others savour the style and vocabulary as well, and the latter are likely to end up understanding what has been said more adequately than the former (hence the teaching of literary appreciation in schools and colleges). Nowhere is this truer than in the case of Holy Scripture.

Pitfalls with words
Granted, there are pitfalls. To start with, we must not let words mesmerize us, even if they are words in the Bible. 'Words', said

Hobbes, 'are the counters of wise men; they do reckon by them; but they are the coinage of fools.' To assume that a thing can be said only in the words in which we first learnt it and would ourselves express it, or in words in which the Bible says it, is a foolish though frequent mistake. Words are not magic. They are the raw material of language, God-given tools for conceptualizing and communicating. They convey meaning, reveal minds, evoke moods and stir thoughts. Their importance lies in the freight they carry and the jobs they do. To be sure, hearing, reading and speaking familiar words has a comforting and supportive effect, as all familiar things have; coming home to the familiar is like a return to the womb. But to be so tied to particular words as to think that no other words could possibly express the same meaning is superstition. Focusing on words must not be allowed to bog us down in that.

Then, second, we need to be clear on how to see what words mean. Words signify what they are used to signify in the particular linguistic circles (nations, tribes, families, gangs, interest groups) that use them. Thus they gain recognized public meaning, which dictionaries record. To use words in private senses without saying so would be perverse, because communication would then break down. Lewis Carroll makes Humpty Dumpty sneer at Alice for her protest at finding that by 'glory' he meant 'a nice knock-down argument'. 'When I use a word,' said he scornfully, 'it means just what I choose it to mean – neither more nor less.' We laugh, because this is outrageous; but we would not laugh if our friends acted that way, nor would they laugh if we did. Linguistic good manners require the listener to expect words to be used in the accepted way, and the speaker so to use them.

This leads to a further point. We must realize how perverse it is when construing others' words to take derivation rather than use as the clue to their meaning. Just as knowing that 'dandelion' was originally *dent de lion* ('lion's tooth' in French) does not prepare you to recognize the yellow flower that goes by that name, so knowing that *ekklēsia,* the New Testament Greek word for 'church', has an etymological form that suggests *calling out of* somewhere (*ek-klēsis,* from *ek-kaleō*) is no preparation for understanding what it means in use, which is just a gathering, assembly or congregation. In the Bible, as in ordinary life, words mean what they are used to mean – neither more nor less; and to import from etymology extra notions which the writer did not demonstrably have in mind is to mislead oneself by finding in his statement what isn't there. Much word study, both secular and sacred, has erred here, assuming that a word's history must be part of the user's meaning every time. But ask yourself how you use words like 'dandelion', 'church', 'prevent' (which etymologically means 'precede', from the Latin *prae-venio,* and is used in that sense in the King James Version and the 1662 Prayer Book), and you will see that, as the song says, it ain't necessarily so.

Thirdly, we have to remember that words (apart from publicly defined technical terms) are regularly flexible, and gain their precise meaning each time they appear only as part of larger units of sense – sentences, paragraphs, lines of argument, chapters, books. Most words carry a cluster of possible meanings and nuances (see the dictionaries), so that you have to check the context each time to see which precisely is meant. To treat as technical terms, having a single standard significance, everyday words which convey different shades of meaning and may indeed be systematically ambiguous (like 'bat', which means both a hitting tool in cricket and a small twittering winged mammal that comes out at night; or 'pig', which some use to mean not the source of pork and bacon but a policeman viewed as an old meanie) is a major mistake. Technical terms (*e.g.,* computer, subjunctive, diminuendo, wok, tort, mulch) have universally accepted meanings within single frames of reference, so that their presence has a defining effect on the meaning of other words linked with them. The precise sense of such other words – ordinary everyday words, as we would call them – is fixed by the verbal flow of which they are part. Their range of possible meaning may be known to us from the start, but their specific significance each time they are used will only be discerned accurately through understanding the sentence and line of thought to which they belong. (For an example of what I mean, look at the ambiguous words 'range', 'sentence' and 'line' in that last sentence.) Many books on words, both secular and sacred, have been flawed by failure to observe how close particular words come to being used technically, or how far from that they are (how in Paul, for instance, 'justify' is more like a technical term than 'lead', 'holy' than 'good', and so on).

We need not dwell on the mistakes that Bible students have made through overlooking the fact that words in the Bible work the same way as they do outside it. Suffice it to note that echoing biblical language is no index of spiritual depth and that statements explaining the meaning of biblical words from their derivation, along with statements beginning 'in scripture this word always means...' are more likely to be wrong than right. You have been warned!

Light from words

But having said that, we may well extol word study – study, that is, of usage and meanings – as an avenue of insight into men's minds; which in the case of the 40-odd biblical writers means insight into the mind of God who spoke to and through them. Some keywords in the Bible – cultic terms, for instance – seem to have been at least semi-technical from the start (e.g., covenant, holy, sacrifice, worship, prayer, sin, wisdom, redeem); it is fascinating to watch their meaning broaden and deepen as God's historical self-disclosure by word and deed proceeds. Other keywords seem to have started with a 'this-worldly' reference and to have acquired theological meaning through being taken up by one and another as pictures, models and analogies of God's work and its fruits (e.g., light, life, word, power, death, faith, hope, blood, peace, kingdom, father, world, spirit, people, judge); it is fascinating to trace this process and reflect on why this or that word should have come to mean so much theologically and spiritually to this or that writer. While such study must always take its place as a handmaid to exegesis rather than a substitute for it, it has an interest all its own and sometimes, like an undulating footpath alongside a main road, it shows you views which those who stick to the exegetical highway never see.

In our time Christian teachers have been vividly aware of this and much good word study has been done, on a scale ranging from Kittel's mammoth *Theological Dictionary of the New Testament* (9 volumes, over 8,000 pages) and Colin Brown's *New International Dictionary of New Testament Theology*

(3 volumes, over 3,000 pages) to Julian Charley's slim volume *50 Key Words: The Bible* (69 pages). This book, however, does not strictly belong in that league, for though it starts with words it is both less and more than a wordbook. It is as untechnical as possible; it focuses not on words as such but on the realities to which they point; and though it is a biblical word which announces the theme of each chapter, the treatment of material is integrative and theological rather than analytical and 'biblicist'. My selection of themes reflects a purpose of spelling out the gospel which is the Bible's central message; therefore my style is expository and applicatory rather than exegetical and historical. Yet this book builds on the technical work of others, without which it could hardly have been written.

Biblical and theological words

It is worth stopping here to note that our present-day Christian vocabulary contains two classes of words: those found in Scripture, and those coined or borrowed since New Testament times. Class two words—Trinity, incarnation, person, nature, satisfaction, aseity, hierarchy, transcendence, omniscience, for example – should be seen as technical terms, introduced as vocal shorthand to express particular biblical thoughts and therefore defined with precision at the outset. Some of them have lost their precision in our theologically wayward age, but they all had it once, and it is a good rule to use them only in their classical sense and to espouse them only if you can show that their classical meaning is just crystallized biblical thinking. Today, traditional theological language is slippery and different people bend it different ways; one should not risk adding to the confusion.

Would it not then help us to think more biblically if we ditched all class two words and used biblical words only? Alas, the suggestion is specious and the objections to it seem unanswerable.

First, the proposal is *stultifying*. It would rob us of clarity. No science – that is, no department of tested and digested knowledge – can do without technical terms; they are needed for precision of thought and speech. Without appropriate technical terms communication would become unmanageably clumsy and progress in crystallizing truth would hardly be possible. This is as true in theology as in, say, astrophysics or ophthalmology.

Second, the proposal is *impoverishing*. It would rob us of truth. Technical terms that have been well defined and tested embody and transmit in capsule form much accurate knowledge and many correct decisions about matters that were once in debate. Thus they act as a bulwark against error. The stage of church history is littered with the corpses of those who, having given up the technical terms *trinity* and *incarnation*, promptly fell into the errors that those words were defined to exclude.

In any case, we cannot today use biblical words with just the meaning they had for biblical writers, neither more nor less. Why not? Because they come to us loaded with associations and feeling-tones which they have picked up during the Christian centuries and which cling to them like coats of paint that cannot be burned off. Thus, when we use biblical words like predestinate, election, justification, perfect, sin, world, faith, grace, authority, devil, church, the associations in our minds which shape our interest and determine our questions are drawn from the world of post-biblical controversy – the world in which Augustine fought Pelagius and the Reformers fought Rome and the Calvinists fought the Arminians and the conservatives fought the liberals, each debating what the Bible as a whole really tells us about this or that. And in fact, the only worthwhile way for us to explore the themes which words like these designate is in explicit relation to our own latter-day questions and interests, asking how biblical thought and teaching touches them, and how in general it engages with the lives of twentieth-century men and women. Anything less would be mere biblical antiquarianism, a solemn but ultimately trivial game. Our goal must be to think biblically, not just about Bible writers' problems, but about our own.

In the chapters which follow, biblical words announce the themes and biblical material builds them up, but technical terms are freely used and the angle of approach is contemporary. I try to think through the material in the light of today's perplexities, and to show how what biblical writers said in response to questions of their day can speak to questions of ours. Readers will form their own opinions as to how far I succeed.

The Spirit and the Scriptures

My hope is that the effect of this set of studies will correspond to what I take to be the Holy Spirit's dual purpose in relation to the Bible. In form, as I think we all know, Scripture is historical witness to God's work of redemption which climaxed initially in the incarnation, immolation, resurrection and exaltation of the Son of God who is Jesus, and which will climax finally in the eucatastrophe (to borrow Tolkien's recondite but happy word) of Jesus' return in shattering glory to make all things perfectly new. Viewed from this standpoint (as view it we must, else we shall misunderstand it) Scripture is often written off as odd and remote, because its message does not square with what modern man thinks he knows. But in its essential nature, which unhappily not all seem to appreciate, Scripture is quite simply God communicating, God talking, God teaching, God preaching: God telling you – yes, you, with me and all other Bible-readers and Bible-hearers everywhere – things about himself which call here and now for faith, worship and obedience; prayer, praise and practice; devoting, denying and disciplining ourselves in order to serve God; in short, our complete conversion and our total commitment.

Viewed from this standpoint, Scripture is the most up-to-date and relevant reading that ever comes my way. Three hours ago, for instance, I was reading the letter to the Hebrews, and by it God was telling me all over again of the finality and sufficiency of Jesus Christ to keep me in a joyful relationship with him, with men, with circumstances and with myself. And whenever I read Ecclesiastes (I am something of an Ecclesiastes man) God teaches me afresh that trustful acceptance of life as it comes, and keeping on doing what I should, are the two keys to happiness both here and hereafter – wisdom which, for me at least, is always in season. And so on, and so on. Such is the Bible, the timeliest book in the world for you or me or anyone; and the Holy Spirit, who inspired it and who gives us understanding of it, leads us two ways when we allow him to open and apply it to us.

On the one hand, the God-given organism of Scripture (66 books in all, 39 making the Old Testament and 27 the New) has a centre, what Calvin called a *scopus* – that is, a focal point set in view, a target aimed at and a reference point for everything. That *scopus* is the Lord Jesus Christ himself, whom the prophets proclaim as the Messiah who should come and the apostles as the Messiah who has come and is coming again. The Spirit leads us to focus on him and on our need of him. We find Scripture acting both as the mirror in which we see ourselves as guilty, vile and helpless sinners who need saving, and also as the searchlight which shows us the living Saviour – the Christ who is *there,* and there *for us;* or, better, the Christ who is *here,* and here *for me.* The Spirit puts us out of doubt as to Jesus' reality and brings us to know and trust him as our own Deliverer from sin, from self and from the dark and painful emptiness here and hereafter for which hell – gehenna, the burning place – is the apt name. (Scripture calls this trustful knowledge *faith.*) Thus we prove for ourselves the truth of Paul's statement that 'the sacred writings... are able to instruct you for salvation through faith in Christ Jesus' (2 Tim. 3:15). This is the first thing that it means to be taught by God (*cf.* Jn. 6:45); one learns to cry with Charles Wesley

> Jesus! the name to sinners dear,
> The name to sinners given;
> It scatters all their guilty fear,
> It turns their hell to heaven.
>
> O that the world might taste and see
> The riches of his grace;
> The arms of love that compass me
> Would all mankind embrace.
>
> His only righteousness I show,
> His saving grace proclaim;
> 'Tis all my business here below
> To cry: Behold the Lamb!

Happy, if with my latest breath
I might but gasp his name;
Preach him to all, and cry in death:
Behold, behold the Lamb!

No Christian can aim higher, or desire better, than that; and to set and keep us aiming and desiring so is one side of the Spirit's constant ministry to us through the Scriptures.

But there is another side too. With Christ at its centre, the Bible is like a huge circle embracing the whole of every man's life. Those who, in C. S. Lewis' figure, look *along* the Bible, as along the ray of a flashlight in the attic, find that all they are is weighed and judged by the light of the teaching, narratives and states of affairs that the Bible sets before us. The Spirit of God leads us to make the judgment on our lives that he himself makes. He leads us to measure ourselves by what Scripture shows us of right and wrong ways of being a parent, a child, a politician or citizen, a spouse, a single or bereaved person, a homemaker, a manager, a workman or employee, a neighbour, a teacher or student, an invalid, a rich man or whatever, and also by what we learn from scriptural precepts and examples (Christ, Abraham, Paul, Elijah, all the heroes of faith) of what true godliness involves. Regularly, when we thus weigh ourselves, we find ourselves wanting; and then the Spirit leads us to change our ways in accordance with that self-measurement. (Scripture calls this clear-sighted change *repentance*.) Thus we prove for ourselves the truth of Paul's further statement that all Scripture, being God-breathed, is 'profitable for teaching, for reproof, for correction, and for training in righteousness, that the man of God may be complete, equipped for every good work' (2 Tim. 3:16 f.). This is the second thing that it means to be taught|by God.

I hope that the following sketches of biblical themes (they are no more) will subserve the Spirit's double purpose of constantly leading us to love and adore the Christ of the Scriptures, and to amend our lives by their light. I have no interest in any study of biblical material that does not seek these biblical ends.

1
REVELATION

The English word 'reveal' comes from the Latin *revelo*, which means 'unveil' or 'uncover'. This is exactly the idea expressed by the Hebrew and Greek words which are translated 'reveal' in the Bible. 'Reveal' is a picture-word (as, indeed, all theological words are), and the picture is of *God unveiling* – God showing us things which were previously hidden from us, God bringing into the open things which before were out of our sight, God causing and enabling us to see what hitherto we could not see. God takes us into his confidence and shares his secrets with us; God finds us ignorant, and gives us knowledge. That is what revelation means.

The very picture itself answers three basic questions straight away. First, what need is there of revelation? Answer: certain vital things are hidden from us, veiled from our eyes, till God discloses them. Secondly, what is the aim of revelation? Answer: to give us knowledge of these things. God wants to share them with us. Thirdly, what should our attitude be in face of revelation? Answer: we should attend respectfully, and thankfully receive all that God imparts to us. When he speaks, man must be ready to listen, to learn, and to respond.

Personal and propositional revelation

What does God reveal? Older Protestant theologians replied: truths about himself which we could not otherwise have known. Modern Protestant theologians, on the whole, prefer to say simply: God reveals himself. But these two answers are complementary, not contradictory. It is true that revelation is essentially self-disclosure on God's part, and that its goal is to make men 'know the Lord', in personal fellowship with a personal God. But how does God make himself known to us? In the same way in which you would make yourself known to me, or I to you: by talking. Talking is always a revelation of the talker, and God discloses himself to us by talking to us about himself, and about ourselves as he sees us. He tells us of his own past achievements, how he has created, judged, redeemed, raised up men to serve him, and created a people for himself. He tells us of his present work: how he orders and governs all things for the fulfilling of his purposes. He tells us his future plans, sketching for us in mysterious but glowing terms the coming climax of history and the final destiny of his people. He tells us what he thinks about human life, and the different ways in which men live it. He gives us directions, and counsel, and makes promises and announces warnings. He teaches us his own scale of values, detailing for us the things that he approves and the things that he hates. Thus, by talking, he reveals himself. He discloses himself by telling us about himself. His revelation is *personal* just because it is *propositional;* for it is precisely by making true statements about himself to us that God makes himself known to us, and if he did not speak in this way we could never know him at all. To affirm, as some do, that man can discover and know God without God speaking to him is really to deny that God is personal. Persons cannot be known unless in some way they speak to reveal themselves.

Old and New Testament revelation
The core of the Bible is its story of God speaking to men. The Old Testament tells us how he spoke directly to Adam and Eve in the garden, and to Cain, and Noah, and Abraham, and Isaac, and Jacob. He spoke directly also to Moses and the prophets. Through Moses as his mouthpiece, he spoke to all Israel in the wilderness, setting before them the promises and laws of his covenant. Through the later prophets (for Moses the lawgiver was, as God's spokesman, a prophet: Dt. 18:15; 34:10), he continued to speak to his people, enforcing the law, explaining his purposes of judgment and mercy in history, appealing for repentance and exhorting to a life of faith in himself.

All direct revelation of God's will and purposes throughout the Old Covenant dispensation was given through prophets. The psalmists and wisdom writers meditated with inspired insight on religion and life in the light of this revelation, as they knew it, but the prophets were the persons through whom the revelation itself was made at each stage. There are two Hebrew words for prophet, one meaning *seer* and one meaning *spokesman,* and together they indicate the nature of the prophet's calling. First, it was his privilege, as a seer, to receive revelation. God, so to speak, took the prophets into his confidence and showed them his plans. 'Surely', declared Amos, 'the Lord GOD does nothing, without revealing his secret to his servants the prophets' (Am. 3:7). The prophet stood 'in the council of the LORD to perceive and to hear his word' (Je. 23:18). Then, second, it was his responsibility, as spokesman, to proclaim the word of revelation that he had received. 'I have put my words in your mouth,' said God to Jeremiah; 'whatever I command you you shall speak' (Je. 1:9, 7). 'You shall say to them, "Thus says the Lord GOD." ... you shall speak my words to them,' was God's commission to Ezekiel (Ezk. 2:4, 7; *cf.* 1 Ki. 22:14; Nu. 22:18, 20, 35, 38). The formula 'Thus says the LORD', which introduces prophetic oracles 359 times in the Old Testament, was a witness to the reality of revelation – a witness, that is, to the fact that the prophet did not originate his own message, but spoke as God's mouthpiece, so that what he said was to be received, not as man's guesswork, or speculation, or wishful thinking, but as God's utterance, and therefore as infallible truth. We can understand the horror which Jeremiah felt when, on the one hand, false prophets declared in God's name messages of their own devising (Je. 14:14 ff.; 23:9–40), and, on the other hand, the words of true prophets like himself were shrugged off and disregarded (Je. 20:7 f.; 25:3 ff.).

The New Testament message about revelation is crystallized in the opening words of the letter to the Hebrews. 'God, having of old time spoken unto the fathers in the prophets by divers portions and in divers manners, hath at the end of these days spoken unto us in his Son' (Heb.

1:1 f., RV). The Lord Jesus Christ fulfilled the ministry of a prophet, inasmuch as he spoke those words, and those only, which the Father had given him to speak (Jn. 7:16; 8:28; 12:49 f.; *cf.* Heb. 2:3f.). But he did more. He revealed the Father, not only by what he said, but by what he was, and what he did; for he, as the Son, is the image of the Father, and all the many-sided fullness of the character of the invisible God was made visible in his incarnate life (Col. 1:15, 19; 2:9; Heb. 1:3). Thus he could say: 'He who has seen me has seen the Father' (Jn. 14:9). And John could write: 'No one has ever seen God; the only Son, who is in the bosom of the Father, he has made him known [lit., expounded, elucidated him]' (Jn. 1:18).

Nor is this all. Christ promised his disciples the Holy Spirit, to reveal to them the full truth concerning himself and to enable them to bear witness of it (Jn. 14:26; 15:26; 16:13 ff.). Thus, in effect, he designated them for a properly prophetic ministry. After Pentecost we find them fulfilling such a ministry. On the one hand, they received revelation through the Holy Spirit. Paul makes much of the 'mystery' of God's plan of salvation in Christ, long hidden, but now 'revealed to his holy apostles and prophets by the Spirit' (Eph. 3:5; *cf.* vv. 3–11; 1:9 ff.; 1 Cor. 2:7 ff.; Rom. 16:25 f.). On the other hand, they declared what had been shown them in a Spirit-taught, authoritative way, as the word of God (1 Cor. 2:1 ff., 13 ff.; 1 Thes. 2:13). They ministered and taught as Christ's representatives, authorized and equipped by him. Thus the witness of the apostles is an integral part of the great complex divine utterance that is covered by the phrase: 'God...has...spoken...in his Son.' The teaching of Christ and the apostles forms a unity, and that unity, embodied in our New Testament, is God's last word to man.

If, now, we ask what in a nutshell was God revealing in the biblical period, several things must be said together.

First, God was revealing *himself*. He was showing his 'eternal power and deity' (Rom. 1:20) as maker and master, and with that his character and his ways with men (see Ex. 34:6 f.; Dt. 5:9 f.; Je. 9:24; 1 Jn. 1:5; 4:7–10), so that he might be acknowledged and worshipped for all that he is and does and gives. Viewed from this standpoint, revelation reached its climactic point in the incarnate life of God's Son.

Second, God was revealing *his kingdom*. He was showing the reality of his universal kingship (note how prophet after prophet saw visions of God's *throne*, 1 Ki. 22:19; Is. 6:1 ff.; Ezk. 1:26; Dn. 7:9; Rev. 4:2, and how psalmist after psalmist celebrated God's *reign*, Pss. 93:1 f.; 96:10; 97:1; 99:1; *cf.* 1 Ch. 16:31; Is. 52:7; Rev. 19:6). He was showing too how he moves history on to the final form that his kingship takes, namely the saving reign of Jesus the Messiah, who is already the world's true Lord (*cf.* Mt. 28:18; Heb. 1:3, 8 f., 13) and who will come one day in glory to bring all persons and powers that deny his rule to an ignominious end (1 Cor. 15:24 ff.; Phil. 2:9–11).

Third, God was revealing *his covenant*. This was and is an imposed relationship: God pledges himself to men, to bless them, and they pledge themselves to him, to serve him. 'I will be your God, and you shall be my people' is the relational commitment which God repeats for each new stage of covenant blessing (Gn. 17:7–14; Ex. 19:4–6; Lv. 26:12; Dt. 7:6; 14:2; Je. 11:3 f.; 30:22; 31:33; Ezk. 11:20; 36:28; Zc. 8:8; 2 Cor. 6:16; Rev. 21:3; *etc.*); it is the covenant slogan throughout the Bible. The new covenant that was made known through Jesus its mediator was better than its predecessor in many ways (see Heb. 8–10), but God's undertaking to bless both here and hereafter, which is the covenant relationship itself, was the same throughout. The essence of the covenant in all forms of its administration is that God says '*my* people' and those addressed say in response to him, and of him, '*our* God', '*my* God'. Luther was entirely right to describe Christianity as a matter of personal pronouns. God's covenant people – faithful Israelites under the Old Testament, disciples of Christ worldwide under the New – are those of whom it can be said, 'you have come to know God, or rather to be known by God' (Gal. 4:9). To them are fulfilled God's 'precious and very great promises' (2 Pet. 1:4). Such is the revealed covenant relationship.

Fourth, God was revealing *his law,* which is his will for all men but which comes as *torah* (authoritative paternal instruction) to his own people. 'He declares his word to Jacob, his statutes and ordinances to Israel. He has not dealt thus with any other nation' (Ps. 147:19 f.). In Old Testament times God identified himself as Father of his people corporately (Ex. 4:22 f.; Mal. 1:6); under the New Testament all who receive God's 'one and only' Son (so the NIV perceptively paraphrases 'only-begotten', a term implying affection) become Jesus' brothers by adoption and new birth (Jn. 1:12 f.; 20:17; Gal. 4:4–7); and God's *torah,* in its dual form of commands and wisdom, was spelt out under both Testaments (by Moses and the prophets under the Old, and by Christ and his apostles under the New) so that God's children might learn to honour their Father by maintaining the family standards and thus displaying the family likeness.

Fifth, God was revealing *his salvation*: that is, his work of rescuing folk from whatever threatens to destroy them – Egyptian captivity (Ex. 14:13; 15:2), Babylonian captivity (Is. 51:5–6, 8), national foes and personal troubles (the Psalms, dozens of times), sin and Satan (the New Testament, dozens of times). From this standpoint, revelation reached its climax when God gave the word of the gospel (*cf.* Gal. 1:11 f.), which sets forth the finished work of Christ and the continuing work of Christ's Spirit (*cf.* Rom. 1:16; Eph. 1:13).

Put these themes together, and you have the core content of revelation.

Past and present revelation

Our review of the biblical message leads on to the next point. God's speaking, as we saw, began in Eden and ended with the apostolic age. It is thus very much a matter of past history. Does this mean that for nineteen centuries now God has not been speaking to man at all? No, it does not mean that. It is true that since the apostolic age God has said nothing new to men, for he has in fact no more to say to us than he said then. But it is also true that God has not

23

ceased to say to man all that he said then. Mr Gladstone is not still saying what he said to the nation a hundred years ago, for Mr Gladstone is dead: but the living God is still saying to mankind what he said in and through his Son nineteen centuries ago. Which means that when we read, or hear read or expounded, the biblical record of what God said in Old or New Testament times, we are as truly confronted by a word of revelation addressed by God to us, and demanding a response from us, as were the Jewish congregations who listened to Jeremiah or Ezekiel, or Peter, or Christ, or the Gentile congregations who listened to the sermons of the apostle Paul.

General and special revelation

The Bible records the words that God has spoken in history about his work of redemption in history. But one of the things which the Bible reveals is that God also reveals himself apart from the Bible, and in a way not dependant upon the revelation of his saving purpose. The latter revelation was given through a particular sequence of events, to particular men at particular times in particular places; but this other form of revelation is given everywhere and at all times, to all men, through the ordinary experience of being alive in God's world. It is given through all created things. Psalm 19:1–4 affirms that celestial phenomena, simply by being what they are, proclaim their Maker's glory in unmistakable 'speech' to the ends of the earth. Paul lays it down in general terms that 'the things that have been made' convey knowledge of God's 'eternal power and deity' – *i.e.*, reveal that he is almighty God, and ought to be worshipped, and so make men inexcusable if they fail to acknowledge him (Rom. 1:20 f.). Paul's indictment of the Gentile world in Romans 1:18 – 2:16 is based on this truth.

Again, this revelation is given through God's ordinary providence, which affords manifold proofs of his goodness. In Acts 14:16 f., Paul declares that though God permitted apostate Gentile nations to 'walk in their own ways', he 'did not leave himself without witness, for he did good and gave you from heaven rains and fruitful seasons, satisfying your hearts with food and gladness' (*cf*. Mt. 5:45; Ps.145: 9). Thus God shows men his kindness, and the greatness of the debt of thanks that they owe him.

Also, this revelation is mediated through the voice of conscience, which speaks as God's monitor, telling every man something, at least, of the demands of his law (Rom. 2:14 f.) and assuring even the most hardened of judgment and condemnation to come (Rom. 1:32).

Because this revelation is conveyed through the ordinary course of the created order, it is called 'natural' in contrast with the 'supernatural' revelation given through God's particular redemptive utterances in history. Because it is universally given, it is called 'general' in contrast with the 'special' revelation recorded in the Bible, which comes only to those who read or hear God's Word, and which never reaches many men.

What is the difference between the content of general and special revelation? Basically, this: that general revelation carries no redemptive message. It speaks only to the needs of unfallen man. It tells sinners no more than it told Adam in innocence. It gives no hint that God, who is merciless to sin, may be merciful to those who break his law. It assures transgressors of their condemnation, but offers no hope of forgiveness; it preaches the law, but not the gospel. Only special revelation, given since the fall, and carrying a message of redemption through Christ, can speak to the needs of sinners. General revelation can bring about condemnation if it is neglected or denied, but it cannot provide the condemned with a way of restoration. If fallen man received the witness of general revelation, and took it seriously, it would drive him to despair. In fact, however, he does not. Men 'suppress ('stifle', NEB) the truth' (Rom. 1:18); they deny and pervert general revelation, so that only flashes of its light break through, and their knowledge of their Maker takes the form of willed negation or ignorance of him, as Paul goes on to explain (see verses 19–32; Acts 17:22–28).

This leads to our next point.

Objective and subjective revelation

'The unspiritual man does not receive the gifts [better, 'things' as AV or 'thoughts' as LB] of the Spirit of God... he is not able to understand them, because they are spiritually discerned' (1 Cor. 2:14). 'The god of this world has blinded the minds of the unbelievers, to keep them from seeing the light of the gospel of the glory of Christ...' (2 Cor. 4:4). It is not enough for God to unveil his secrets and make plain his mysteries before the sight of fallen men, for they are blind. The Jews, says Paul, could not understand the Old Testament (God's objective revelation to them), because there was a veil on their minds (2 Cor. 3:15). The same is true when any part of God's truth is presented to any child of Adam. Man in sin is incapable of apprehending either general or special revelation rightly, because his capacity for spiritual discernment has been so largely destroyed. And if revelation, objectively given, is ever to be received and responded to, God must take the veil from our hearts by restoring our spiritual sight. This is the operation to which Paul refers in 2 Corinthians 4:6: 'God who said, "Let light shine out of darkness," has shone in our hearts to give the light of the knowledge of the glory of God in the face of Christ.' It is the work of subjective revelation which Paul describes in his own case by saying that God 'was pleased to reveal his Son in me' (Gal. 1:15–16, RSV mg.) – *in, i.e.* by an act of illumination within the heart – and which Christ acknowledges when he tells Peter that it was the Father who 'revealed' to him that Jesus was the Christ, the Son of God (Mt. 16:17). The process of objective manifestation must be complemented by one of inward enlightenment if ever man is to come to a knowledge of God. Two veils must be taken away: that which hides God's mind, and that which clouds our heart. God in his mercy removes both. Thus our knowledge of God, first to last, is his gracious gift.

Present and future revelation

We saw that in one sense revelation is ended: God has no more to say to the world in this age than he says in the Scriptures, which were completed by the writing of the

New Testament in the first century AD. In another sense, however, the clearest and fullest revelation is yet to come. The unimaginable yet certain event of Christ's public return, when for weal or woe every eye shall see him and every human being that ever was or will be – millions of millions – shall stand before him, each for personal judgment, will be a disclosure surpassing anything we have been shown of Christ to date. It will be precisely, as Peter says, 'the *revelation* of Jesus Christ' (1 Pet. 1:7). It will usher in for God's people an eternity of fellowship with the one whom already 'without having seen...you love' (verse 8), and one aspect of that fellowship is pictured for us thus: 'They shall see *his face*' (Rev. 22:4); 'We shall see him *as he is*' (1 Jn. 3:2).

The heavenly vision of God, of which being 'with the Lord (Jesus)' to see his face is part (*cf.* 1 Thes. 4:17), has always been viewed by the church as man's highest good (*summum bonum*) – and rightly. Paul contrasts present and future knowledge of God by saying that now we see 'in a mirror dimly' (1 Cor. 13:12), whereas then it will be face to face. Ancient mirrors were of beaten and polished metal and were not very good, and part of what Paul is saying is that this present indirectness of knowledge involves inadequacy. The NIV brings this out by paraphrasing: 'Now we see *but a poor reflection*; then we shall see face to face. Now I know in part; then I shall know fully, even as I am fully known.' At this moment you cannot see me, the writer of this paragraph. My words are a mirror of sorts into my mind and heart, but you do not know me 'through and through', as we say, just by reading them. God also is invisible to you; his revealed Word truly reflects his mind and heart, but not in a way adequate to the reality. When Christ comes again, however, we shall know the divine mind and heart as fully and directly as ours are known now. When I am away from home and my wife writes or talks to me on the phone, my feelings are a mixture of pleasure at the contact and discontent at her remoteness; at such times I want to be home, to see her and be with her. So Christians, who hear from their Lord through the Bible which he opens and applies to them, find themselves eager for the closer and fuller revelation that is to come.

Once I stood on top of Ben Nevis, Britain's highest point, with grey mist everywhere, so that I could not see a thing. (It had been like that all the way up.) But when I raised my head the mist above me gleamed so bright that it hurt my eyes. Clearly there were only a few feet of it between me and the sun. The intensity of my longing in that moment that the mist might roll away was painful. (Alas, it didn't; I shall have to climb Ben Nevis again.) Some of Scripture's achingly beautiful pictures of heaven stir Christian hearts in a similar way: like the glowing mist, they give a sense of the nearness of the sun that you cannot see (which in this case is the Son) and arouse the wish to be fully in the brightness beyond the mist (which in this case is the picture). 'His servants shall worship him; they shall see his face, and his name shall be on their foreheads. And night shall be no more; they need no light of lamp or sun, for the Lord God will be their light' (Rev. 22:3 ff.). On Ben Nevis I wanted to see the sun; on earth the Christians hope with strong desire for the day when they will see their Lord.

> When by his grace I shall look on his face,
> That will be glory, be glory for me.

Yes – and it will be revelation, too.

Revelation given and received

Do you want to know God? Then do as notices at open level crossings tell you to do – stop, look and listen.

Stop trying to discover God by pursuing thoughts, fancies and feelings of your own, in disregard of God's revelation. Our knowledge of him and his revelation to us are correlative realities; you do not have the first without the second.

Look at what God has revealed. The Bible is the window through which you may look to see it, and there are many Christians and guide books (this is one) that can help you to see what you are looking at and pick out what is important. As London is the centre of England, put first in their itinerary by tourists from overseas, wherever else they plan to go, so Jesus Christ the Lord, who died and is alive for evermore, is the centre of Scripture. Whatever else in the Bible catches your eye, do not let it distract you from him.

Listen to what the Bible tells you about him, and about our need of him (which means, your need of him). The Bible in which you see him is itself God's communication to you about him. Learn from God about the Son of God; respond to all that you are shown. Do that, and one day you will be saying with Paul and many millions more, 'God... has shone in our hearts to give the light of the knowledge of the glory of God in the face of Christ' (2 Cor. 4:6). You will be saying with the once-blind man of Jerusalem, 'One thing I know, that though I was blind, now I see' (Jn. 9:25). You will know revelation in the only way that finally counts – namely, from the inside; and in so knowing it you will know God.

2
SCRIPTURE

This study has to do with the volume whose cover, as it stands on your shelf, bears the legend Holy Bible.

'Bible' comes from the Greek word for 'book'. 'The Holy Bible' means just 'the holy book'. But the title is surely an odd one. For when you open the Bible, you find that it is really an omnibus volume. It contains sixty-six separate books, written originally in three languages (Hebrew, Greek, and a few bits in Aramaic) over a period of a thousand years and more. The books themselves are a very mixed bag. There are history books, sermon books, letters, a hymn book, and a love song. They include geographical surveys, architects' specifications, travel diaries, population statistics, family trees, inventories, and legal documents of all sorts. 'The library of Hebrew-Christian memoirs and remains' might seem a more suitable title. Yet the Christian church treats this miscellany as a single book, and calls it the Holy Bible. Why? What makes the collection 'holy'? And on what principle do these sixty-six items make a unity – 'the Bible'?

Biblical authority
Other questions arise too. There is the problem of biblical authority. The church has always regarded the Bible as authoritative in some sense, but there is disagreement today as to how biblical authority should be understood. What sort of authority belongs to the Bible? It is a human book – is its authority therefore a species of human authority? Should we think of it as the authority of a group of religious experts, whose words are to be respected just because they are the words of experts in that particular field? Or is it the same sort of authority as the best primary source has for the

historian – the sort of authority that the statements of Thucydides have for students of the Peloponnesian War? Both these views are widely held today. But it should be noted that both ascribe to the Bible an authority that is merely relative and provisional, not absolute and final. Experts can be wrong, and even Thucydides can trip up on his facts. Both views, therefore, allow for the possibility that Bible students may sometimes need to put the Bible right. But Christians of an earlier day would have scouted this idea as blasphemous, for they regarded the authority of Scripture statements as infallible, because divine. Were they right? What sort of authority has the Bible?

We shall seek answers to these questions in the Bible itself. Nor – to forestall an obvious objection – is this reasoning in a circle. We are not assuming the truth and authority of the Bible in order to prove the truth and authority of the Bible. We are simply going to the Bible for information. The Bible gives us the views of various people about the subject of our enquiry. Among them are Jesus Christ, of whose teaching we have four near-contemporary accounts; the prophets and psalmists of the Old Testament; and the apostles of the New. We want to see what views they hold. Whether we accept these views, once we have discovered them, will depend on our estimate of the trustworthiness of the teachers whose views they are.

Revelation and Scripture

'Bible' is not a biblical word. The New Testament (referring, of course, to the Old) speaks instead of 'Scripture', or 'the Scriptures'. The Greek word is *graphē,* which means 'writing'. German reproduces this; where we speak of 'the Holy Bible', German says 'die Heilige Schrift' – the holy *writing.* Sometimes also the New Testament calls the Old 'the law' (the term can cover not only the Pentateuch, but also the prophets and the Psalms – see Jn. 10:34–35; 15:25, quoting Pss. 82:6 and 35:19, and 1 Cor. 14:21, quoting Is. 28:11–12). 'Law' represents the Hebrew *torah,* which has a broader meaning than formal legal enactments and expresses the thought of authoritative instruction in any form.

Writing which is authoritative instruction from God – writing that can properly be described, as it is in Psalm 119, as God's 'word', 'words', 'statutes', 'precepts', 'testimonies', 'commandments' – that is the conception of Scripture which Christ, and the apostles, and the prophets, and the psalmists, teach.

One can sum up this view in two propositions.

1. *The Scriptures are a historical record of revelation.* They tell us what God has been saying and doing down the centuries to make himself known to sinful men as their Lord, their Judge and their ·Saviour. Starting from the creation and the fall, the Scriptures trace the story of the acts of God from his first promise, that the woman's seed should bruise the serpent's head, through all that he did, or caused to be done, to bring about its fulfilment. The Old Testament tells us of the call of Abraham, God's dealings with the patriarchs, the exodus from Egypt, the giving of the law, the conquest of Canaan, the raising up of the judges, the founding of the monarchy, the splitting of the kingdom, the sending of the prophets, the promising of Christ, the repeated judging and restoring of Israel, and the making, wrecking and rebuilding of the temple to which the Lord was to come. The New Testament completes the story by telling us of the awakening ministry of John the Baptist, the Messianic work of Jesus as prophet, priest and king, his rising from the dead and outpouring of the Spirit, and the apostolic preaching of the gospel. Thus the Bible is the written record of the drama of redemption. The historical books relate it, as far as the apostolic age; the sermons of the prophets and the letters of the apostles explain and apply it, and point forward to the future climax of the drama, when Christ comes again; the Psalms meditate on it, praise God for it, and pray in terms of it; the wisdom writings, Job, Proverbs and Ecclesiastes, look at life from various angles in the light of it. Such is the theme of the Bible; and the first reason why its sixty-six books do in fact make one book is because they all deal harmoniously with this common subject.

This partly explains why the apostles were so sure that the

Old Testament was a book written for Christian believers (*cf.* Rom. 4:23f.; 15:4; 1 Cor. 10:11; 2 Tim. 3:15 ff.; 1 Pet. 1:10 ff.). They saw that the Old Testament is the first part of the story which their own message completes. Just as the Old Testament without the Christian gospel is a foundation without a building, so the gospel without the Old Testament is a building without a foundation. The apostles therefore took care to ensure that the first Gentile Christians took over and used the Old Testament as Christian Scripture.

So far, so good: few Christian theologians would disagree. But now we must complement our first proposition with a second, the force of which modern theology is less ready to recognize.

2. *The Scriptures are a revelation in the form of a historical record.* They are 'the oracles of God' (Rom. 3:2), the disclosure, direct or indirect, of his mind and will. Scripture is divine writing. 'All scripture (or 'every text of scripture') is inspired by God' (2 Tim. 3:16). This reference to inspiration, let it be said at once, has no psychological overtones. It does not imply that the biblical authors all wrote in a state of ecstasy, or abnormally heightened consciousness, nor yet that they wrote as automata, in some trance-state in which the normal functioning of their minds was suspended. Some maybe did, some plainly didn't, but that is not the issue. 'Inspired by God' translates a single Greek word, *theopneustos,* meaning 'breathed out from God' – *ex*spired, in fact, rather than *in*spired. And it is not the writers, but their writings, of which the word is predicated. Thus, the statement means simply that all that comes in the category of Scripture came from God, and should therefore be received as instruction from God. Accordingly, inspiration, in its theological sense, is to be defined as the work of the Holy Spirit (God's 'breath': 'Spirit' means 'breath') ensuring that men wrote precisely what God wanted written for the communication of his mind to men. It is that 'bearing along' by the Holy Spirit in virtue of which 'men spoke from God' (2 Pet. 1:21, NIV) – and wrote from God too, for it is the *written* 'prophetic word made more sure' (verse 19) of

which Peter is speaking. Inspiration is the activity which ensures that what is written is in truth the Word of God. Thus, inspired Scripture is written revelation.

The reliability of Scripture

In other words, Scripture has a double authorship. Men wrote it, and God wrote it through those men. The Scriptures are as truly divine writing as they are human writing. Scripture is not only human witness to God, it is also divine self-testimony. The words of Scripture are in the final analysis the words of God bearing witness to himself. Their immediate authors were men, but their ultimate Author was God the Holy Spirit. Hence Scripture statements can be quoted either as what the human author said (*e.g.* Moses, David, Isaiah: see Rom. 10:5; 11:9; 10:20, *etc.*), or as what God said through the human author (*e.g.* Acts 4:25; 28:25), or as what the Holy Spirit says (Heb. 3:7; 10:15). Moreover, Old Testament statements, not made by God in their context, can be quoted as words of God, just because they are written in the Old Testament (*cf.* Mt. 19:4 f.; Heb. 3:7; Acts 4:24 f.; 13:34 f.; quoting Gn. 2:24; Pss. 95:7; 2:1; Is. 55:3 respectively). Also, Paul can refer to God's promise to Abraham and his threat to Pharaoh, both spoken long before the biblical record of them was written, as words which *Scripture* spoke to these two men (Gal. 3:8; Rom. 9:17). This shows how completely in his mind he identified the words of Scripture with the utterance of God.

It is clear, then, that to Christ and his apostles, what Scripture said, God said. Their conviction was that all Scripture is prophetic, in the primary sense of that word: *i.e.*, that the biblical writers were God's pens in the same sense that the prophets, when they preached, were God's voices, so that all that was written could be introduced with the same formula that introduced the prophets' sermons – 'thus says the LORD'. This is the deepest reason why the biblical writings are 'holy' (*cf.* 2 Tim. 3:15): not just because they deal with holy things, but because the Holy God is their true Author. Such is the nature of Scripture; and the second reason why these sixty-six books do in fact make one book is because they have all proceeded from a single mind – the mind of God the Holy Spirit.

This is not, of course, to deny that God accommodated himself to the outlook, temperament, language and style of those whom he used as his penmen. It is clear that he did – though we are told that sometimes he moved the prophets to speak of things which they did not fully understand (1 Pet. 1:10–12). Nor is it to deny that God's penmen were in themselves fallible and imperfect, and naturally prone to error. But it is to assert that in the writing of Holy Scripture God did in fact keep them from error, so that they neither falsified facts, nor misrepresented God's purpose and character. It is to assert that, while what a particular passage teaches may not be the whole truth on the subject under discussion, it is always right and true as far as it goes. This follows from the fact that Scripture is the written testimony of God, who can neither lie nor deceive (Nu. 23:19; Tit. 1:2). The veracity of God guarantees the trustworthiness of Scripture. And this trustworthiness is presupposed in all the New Testament handling of the Old. Christ and his apostles assume the truth of Old Testament history, and the permanent validity of Old Testament teaching as expressing God's mind and will. Hence they argue from Scripture, for 'Scripture cannot be broken' (Jn. 10:35; *cf.* Mt. 5:18; Lk. 16:17). 'It is written' was to them the end of the argument; there could be no appeal against the verdict of Scripture, for that would be to appeal against the judgment of God himself. Such was their estimate of Scripture; such was the divine authority which they ascribed to their Bible. If we think that the Son of God and his Spirit-endued representatives knew what they were talking about when they spoke of spiritual realities, we shall accept their estimate, just as we accept their word on all other matters relating to faith and practice.

Corollaries of inspiration

We shall now draw out some corollaries of what we have said.

    1. *Canonicity* rests on inspiration. 'Canon' means 'rule',

and a 'canonical' book is one that forms part of the rule of faith and life. But the only valid rule of faith and life is the word of God. To be canonical, therefore, a book must be inspired, *i.e.* must be God's word in writing. The Church's task, therefore, in settling the limits of the canon of Scripture is simply to discern which books are inspired, *i.e.* have the nature of Scripture. The Church does not confer authority on a set of books which had a merely human origin, but recognizes the authority inherent in those books which had a divine origin. The Christian Church inherited a fixed Old Testament canon, and knew that the apostles had been equipped with the Holy Spirit, according to Christ's promise (Jn. 14:26; 15:26; 16:13 ff.), so that their teaching was inspired in exactly the same sense as the Old Testament Scriptures had been (1 Cor. 2:12 f.; 14:37; 1 Thes. 2:13). Accordingly, the fixing of the New Testament canon (a work which was almost finished within a century of the apostolic age) was in essence a matter of finding out by historical enquiry which books were authentically apostolic, *i.e.* were written or sanctioned by apostles, or came from the inner circle where revelation operated through prophets and apostles (*cf.* Eph. 3:5), and demonstrably taught apostolic doctrine. (Examples of books not written by apostles or their agents, yet evidently coming from the inner circle and teaching apostolic doctrine, are Hebrews, James, Jude and Revelation if John the apostle is not its author – learned opinion, as is well known, differs on that.)

The question whether our New Testament has in it too many or too few books bothers some. We cannot discuss the matter properly here, but it should suffice to say:

(i) There is enough external and internal evidence to justify both accepting as authentic and inspired all twenty-seven New Testament books, and rejecting as unauthentic and uninspired all other books that have come down to us bearing apostolic names or dealing with alleged dominical or apostolic doings.

(ii) Repeated demonstrations of the inner unity of our New Testament, plus the church's historic experience of hearing the Lord's voice in all the New Testament books without exception, leave us in no position to challenge the limits of the canon by querying this or that book at this late date. The fact that Luther could query James, Revelation, Hebrews and Jude (basing his doubts on what most regard as a misunderstanding of their contents), and that clever individuals today can query whether Matthew, John, Ephesians, the Pastorals and John's letters are by the apostles whose names they bear, need not daunt us. The doubts are honest and the scholars who voice them reputable, but I venture to affirm that they are neither necessary nor even, on a disciplined approach to the evidence, natural. To those who may wish to test that statement I recommend Donald Guthrie's *New Testament Introduction* and the articles on New Testament books in *The New Bible Dictionary* and *The Illustrated Bible Dictionary*.

2. *Biblical authority* rests on inspiration. Many today regard Scripture as man's witness to God, and resolve its authority into the authority of the divine words and deeds to which (more or less adequately) witness is borne. But this is only half the truth. Scripture is also, and fundamentally, God's witness to himself, and its authority rests ultimately on the fact that it is his Word. Why ought we to believe biblical history, and accept biblical teaching, and confide in Scripture promises, and be governed by Scripture commands? Because Scripture is the written speech of our Creator. 'Thus says *the Lord*.' The life of faith and obedience is thus founded on the recognition that what Scripture says, God says. And Christ is not truly Lord in a man's heart till Scripture has been made lord of his mind and conscience. If you would honour Christ and his Father, therefore, bow before Holy Scripture, in which the Father through the Spirit bears witness of his Son. To do this is not superstitious bibliolatry. It is pure and true religion. It is mere Christianity.

3. *Biblical interpretation* rests on inspiration. Interpretation, biblically understood, means discovering the relevance of Scripture for us today; but those who see Scripture simply as the religious self-expression of ancient

midEasterners of whom we can only say that they held their beliefs in good faith, can never tell us how to find in it God's message for ourselves. Most of Protestant Christendom for the past century has been at sixes and sevens (and still is, in some ways worse than ever) over this question. But once we acknowledge Scripture as God's teaching and recall that neither God nor Christ, nor human nature and need, nor repentance, faith and godliness have changed since the Bible was put together, we shall have no basic problem of principle or method in seeking to hear God's word to us through analysis and application of what is written. We shall see the task as comparable to learning the law of the land from a study of what has been said and decided in the courts: from reviewing those particular decisions and seeing how principles were applied to reach them, we begin to see how the law applies to us where we are now, and in a similar way the Bible student will see from God's dealings with his servants in Bible times what is God's mind and will regarding himself. The only problem will be to do this accurately, not missing what we most need to notice. For success here we need to rely utterly on the light and help of the Holy Spirit, our divine teacher (cf. 1 Jn. 2:20, 27). It is his special ministry through sermons, scholarship and personal prayerful study to make us aware of our needs and what God through the text is saying to us about them.

To interpret Scripture well we must be clear on two things on which minds have sometimes been hazy. The first is *the jobs words do for us*: a matter much studied today at technical level in the world of linguistics, semantics, philosophical analysis and what is sometimes called deep grammar. Words in Scripture as elsewhere combine in sentences to inform (*e.g.* 'God reigns'), to command and direct (*e.g.* 'Rejoice always'), to create a state of affairs (*e.g.* 'I make a covenant'), to produce an imaginative existential awareness of what was previously known, if at all, only in flat formulae (*e.g.* Christ's parables), to evoke attitudes and reactions (trust, love, faith, fear, repentance, hope, joy, awe, adoration, *etc.*), and to reveal persons to each other (*e.g.* 'I love you'). Biblical sentences are meant to function in all these ways in relation to us, just as they were in relation to those to whom they were first directed. We must not imagine *either* that they are only meant to give us information and orders, *or* that because they are meant to do much more than that the information and orders they give are of secondary importance, and we can sit loose to them. Both ideas are mistakes, and bad ones.

The second thing we must be clear on is *the way God speaks to us*. This is essentially by making us judge ourselves and our situations as he himself judges them. What he does is to lead us, whether discursively over a period of time or in a sudden flash of insight (both occur), to see how biblical truth bears on this or that aspect of our own and others' lives. The New Testament directs Christians to get their guidance on faith and life from apostolic teaching backed by the Old Testament – that is, in effect, from the Bible we have – rather than from any non-rational, out-of-the-blue illuminations, and Paul is very hard on the person who rests his faith on visions (see Col. 2:18). While it is not for us to forbid God to reveal things apart from Scripture, or to do anything else (he is God, after all!), we may properly insist that the New Testament discourages Christians from expecting to receive God's word to them by any other channel than that of attentive application to themselves of what is given to us twentieth-century Christians in Holy Scripture. Which leads into our final point.

Our need of Scripture

'Thy word is a lamp to my feet and a light to my path' (Ps. 119:105). See the psalmist's picture. He has to travel. (Scripture regularly pictures life as a journey.) He was in the dark, unable to see the way to go and bound to get lost and hurt if he advanced blindly. (This pictures our natural ignorance of God's will for our lives, our inability to guess it and the certainty in practice of our missing it.) But a lamp (think of a flashlight) has been handed to him. Now he can pick out the path before him, step by step, and stick to it, though darkness still surrounds him. (This pictures what God's word does for us, showing us how to live.) The psalmist's cry is one of praise, thanks, admonition, testimony and confidence – praise that God glorifies his grace by giving men so precious a gift as his word; thanks because he knows how much he himself needed it, and how lost he was without it; admonition to himself and any who might read his psalm always to value God's word at its true worth and to make full use of it for the purpose for which it was given; testimony to the fact that already in his experience it had proved its power; and confidence that this would continue.

The psalmist would have committed to memory the Pentateuch, the law of Moses in its narrative context, and in his meditations would be working from that. We are privileged to have the entire Bible available to us in printed form. How well do we know it? How much do we love it? Happy are we if we have learned, in defiance of modern scepticism, to make the psalmist's words and meaning our own.

Some 170 of the psalm's 176 verses celebrate the ministry of God's revealed word in the godly man's life as his source of guidance, hope, strength, correction, humility, purity and joy. Psalm 19:7–14 and 2 Timothy 3:15–17 more briefly do the same thing. Do we know anything of what Paul and the psalmists knew of the power of Scripture to reshape, redirect and renew disordered lives?

Why does contact with God's scriptural word transform some people while leaving others cold? First, some let the written word lead them to the living Word, Jesus Christ, to whom it constantly points us; others don't. Second, not all come to the Bible hungry and expectant, conscious of daily need to hear God speak. 'Open your mouth wide, and I will fill it,' says God (Ps. 81:10). The open mouth is a gesture of hunger and dependence. 'With open mouth I pant, because I long for thy commandments,' says the psalmist (Ps. 119:131). Desire for God, springing from a sense of our need of him, is the factor that decides how much or how little impact scripture will make upon us. Bible reader, check your heart!

What Bishop J. C. Ryle wrote in a tract over a century ago remains wholly relevant:

You live in a world where your soul is in constant danger. Enemies are round you on every side. Your own heart is deceitful. Bad examples are numerous. Satan is always labouring to lead you astray. Above all false doctrine and false teachers of every kind abound. This is your great danger.

To be safe you must be well armed. You must provide yourself with the weapons which God has given you for your help. You must store your mind with Holy Scripture. This is to be well armed.

Arm yourself with a thorough knowledge of the written word of God. Read your Bible regularly. Become familiar with your Bible.... Neglect your Bible and nothing that I know of can prevent you from error if a plausible advocate of false teaching shall happen to meet you. Make it a rule to believe nothing except it can be proved from Scripture. The Bible alone is infallible .... Do you really use your Bible as much as you ought?

There are many today, who believe the Bible, yet read it very little. Does your conscience tell you that you are one of these persons?

If so, you are the man that is likely to get little help from the Bible in time of need. Trial is a sifting experience .... Your store of Bible consolations may one day run very low.

If so, you are the man that is unlikely to become established in the truth. I shall not be surprised to hear that you are troubled with doubts and questions about assurance, grace, faith, perseverance, etc. The devil is an old and cunning enemy. He can quote Scripture readily enough when he pleases. Now you are not sufficiently ready with your weapons to fight a good fight with him.... Your sword is held loosely in your hand.

If so, you are the man that is likely to make mistakes in life. I shall not wonder if I am told that you have problems in your marriage, problems with your children, problems about the conduct of your family and about the company you keep. The world you steer through is full of rocks, shoals and sandbanks. You are not sufficiently familiar either with lighthouses or charts.

If so, you are the man who is likely to be carried away by some false teacher for a time. It will not surprise me if I hear that one of these clever eloquent men who can make a convincing presentation is leading you into error. You are in need of ballast (truth); no wonder if you are tossed to and fro like a cork on the waves.

All these are uncomfortable situations. I want you to escape them all. Take the advice I offer you today. Do not merely read your Bible a little – but read it a great deal....Remember your many enemies. Be armed!

3

THE LORD

Is the doctrine of the Holy Trinity in the Bible? I was once
challenged by a Jehovah's Witness heckler to find it there,
so I had a go along this line: Jesus

(i) endorsed Old Testament monotheism (Mk. 12:29), yet

(ii) regarded himself as 'the Son' in a unique sense (Mt.
11:27; Mk. 12:1-12; 13:32), and prescribed and accepted
worship of himself as Son of God, treating this as a proper
expression of faith (Jn. 5:23; 9:35–38; 20:28); and

(iii) promised the Holy Spirit as 'another Comforter' in
succession to himself, to carry on his own many-sided
ministering role (Jn. 14:16); and

(iv) bracketed Father, Son and Spirit together as the
triune 'name' (singular, note, not plural) into which – that
is, into a relationship with which – future disciples were to
be baptized (Mt. 28:19).

Did this answer do the trick? Perhaps; there was no
come-back, and the next heckle was on a different subject,
church ownership of slum property in Paddington.

Jehovah's Witnesses deny that Scripture teaches the deity
of the Son and the Spirit; thus they reproduce fourth-
century Arianism. Mainstream Christians affirm the Trinity,
as formerly the whole church learned to do against the
Arians, but sometimes they nosedive in expressing it.
Illustrations are a plentiful source of stumbling. One will
picture the Godhead as a cloverleaf (three leaves making
one leaf) and then describe the Son and the Spirit as each a
'part' of God. Another will illustrate from the three forms
of water (ice, liquid, steam) or the different aspects of a
cube (one cube, several surfaces) and go on from this to
speak of the Son and the Spirit as two extra roles which the
one God plays in self-revelation. There are Christians today

who have real difficulty in thinking of Jesus and the Father as two distinct persons, and who regularly depersonalize the Holy Spirit by calling him 'it'. Popular among radical theologians is a unitarianism which sees Jesus as a God-filled man and Trinitarian talk as just an objectifying of our threefold experience of God above us, beside us and within us. Meantime the Mormons, the fastest-growing religious body in America, proclaim tritheism, seeing Father, Son and Spirit as three gods together. The scene is confused.

Many Christians dismiss the doctrine of God's triunity as a difficult and unimportant abstraction, a piece of antique theological lumber that is valueless today. They would agree with the late Emil Brunner that the Trinity is a 'theological defensive doctrine' developed in the early church and was no part of the original gospel. They do not see that it matters whether one prays to the Father, the Son or the Spirit (or whether, indeed, one jumps from one to another in a single prayer). They shift attention frequently from one person of the Godhead to another, but if you urge the importance of relating the divine three in your thinking they distrust you, as if there was something unspiritual and unfitting about such an intellectual endeavour in our time.

But the divine triunity is not an ecclesiastical formula whose biblical basis is doubtful. It is actually one of the most pervasive elements in the New Testament. Three of the Greek technical terms round which the classic fourth-century discussions revolved (*ousia,* essence; *homoousios,* of one substance with; *trias,* Trinity) are not in the New Testament at all, and a fourth (*hypostasis,* subsistence or person) is not there in its technical sense; but the tri-personality of the one God is there, plain and inescapable as part of the given form of New Testament thinking. Our tracing of the word 'Lord', as applied to the God of Israel, to Jesus Christ and to the Holy Spirit, will show us this. (Since, however, this tracing involves a fair amount of compressed detail, it may be appropriate to say to some of my readers that if you have not hitherto practised skim-reading this might be a very good time to start.).

The Lord God

In the Old Testament section of the English Bible, 'Lord' always has a capital when used of God, and three times out of every four it is printed 'LORD'. The reason is this. 'Lord' renders *adonai,* literally 'my lord', a regular title for God derived from the Hebrew *'adon,* which means governor or master (see Gn. 24:12; 45:8, for its secular use). The Greek Old Testament (the Septuagint) rendered *adonai* by *kurios,* a synonym of *adon. Kurios* was also applied from at least the first century BC to pagan deities. The Septuagint seems to date from the second century BC; probably this pagan theological use of *kurios* already existed when the translation was made. By this time the Jews had come to regard God's proper name, Yahweh, as too sacred to utter, and in worship (reading Scripture, preaching and prayer), as well as in ordinary speech, they regularly used *adonai* in its place. The Septuagint translators therefore did the equivalent: they made no attempt to render Yahweh in Greek, but simply put *kurios* instead. Of the 8,000 instances where *kurios* is used for God in the Septuagint, 6,700 are renderings of Yahweh. The Authorized Version followed this lead, using 'LORD' for the sacred name on all occasions except four (Ex. 6:3; Ps. 83:18; Is. 12:2; 26:4; *cf.* also the compound names of Gn. 22:14; Ex. 17:15; Jdg. 6:24). In these few cases, it rendered God's name as JEHOVAH, the time-honoured (though inaccurate) version of it which the church has used since the twelfth century. The RSV and NIV have however eliminated JEHOVAH everywhere.

In Exodus 3, where God commissions Moses to lead the Israelites out of Egypt, and again in Exodus 6, where Moses, having tackled Pharaoh as directed (4:22 f.; 5:1 ff.), with no result save a worsening of Israel's bondage (5:6-19) and the fall of his own personal stock to zero (5:20 f.), returns to God in despair (5:22 f.), God lays great stress on the meaning of his name Yahweh, as a revelation of his gracious sovereignty. The passages merit study.

At the burning bush, the speaker identified himself to Moses as the God (*elohim,* the superhuman, supernatural One) of the patriarchs, and of Moses' own father (3:6).

Moses, having heard God's commission and received the promise of his presence (verses 10–12), asked what he was to say if, when he told the Israelites that 'the God of your fathers has sent me to you', they should ask, 'What is his name?' (verse 13). Both the Hebrew grammar (see J. A. Motyer, *The Revelation of the Divine Name,* pp.17–21) and the context show that this question enshrines a request for some disclosure of God's nature which would, on the one hand, authenticate the Being who had spoken to Moses as truly Israel's God (*cf.* chapter 4:1–9), and, on the other, assure them of his ability to achieve for them this incredible-sounding deliverance that he was promising. (The idea of a name, not as a mere label, but as disclosing facts about its bearer, was already deeply rooted in Israelite tradition: see Gn. 16:11; 17:5, 15; 30:6–24: 32:28.) It was in this sense that God answered Moses' question, for he gave his 'name' as 'I AM WHO (or WHAT) I AM', 'I AM' for short (verse 14). It is probably right to render this, with the RV, RSV and NIV margin, as a future tense – 'what I will be, I will be'. In any case, the verb denotes a 'be'-ing that is dynamic and energetic, not static and frozen; God's 'be'-ing is a state, not of rest, but of activity. God's phrase-name is thus a proclamation of his sovereign self-sufficiency and self-consistency: he is free and independent; he acts as he pleases; he does what he wills; what he purposes and promises, that he also performs. Therefore Israel, to whom he extended this staggering promise of redemption, could rely on him absolutely to do as he had said. Because the God of the promise is almighty to fulfil his word, he is also utterly trustworthy, for he is absolutely invincible. As he declared through a later prophet, 'I work and who can hinder it?' (Is. 43:13). Here is the meaning of the reassuring 'name' that God gave Moses to announce to sceptical and diffident Israelites. 'Say this to the people of Israel, "I AM has sent me to you."'

Then God went on to show, by his next words, that this declaration of his almightiness in fulfilling his word actually expressed the real significance of his historic name Yahweh (itself derived, in some obscure way about which philologists

46

still differ, from the verb 'to be'). 'God also said to Moses, "Say this to the people of Israel, 'The LORD, the God of your fathers...has sent me to you': this is my name for ever..."' (verse 15). 'I AM' is here identified with 'Yahweh, the God of your fathers', the covenant God of Israel. That 'this' denotes the whole phrase, Yahweh-God-of-your-fathers, is clear from both this and the next verse. The composite name denotes both God's covenant pledge of himself to Israel and his power to bless within the covenant relationship. The force of the name, as a basis for faith and reliance, springs from the disclosure that 'Yahweh' signifies invincible, self-sufficient sovereignty. 'Yahweh', as a label for God, was known to the patriarchs (*cf.* Gn. 15:2) and was indeed used in worship in antediluvian days (Gn. 4:26, *cf.* 9:26); it appears in Genesis over a hundred times; but not till Exodus 3 was its meaning made plain. The meaning of 'Yahweh' is that which was symbolized by the flame in the bush which did not need to feed on the wood of the bush. 'Yahweh' signifies an inexhaustible ruler – God of limitless life and power – a God, therefore, whom it is safe to trust at all times and in all places. The 'LORD' of the English Bible is actually as good a rendering of 'Yahweh' as one could hope to have.

In Exodus 6:2 ff., God met Moses' complaints by declaring: 'I am the LORD. I appeared to Abraham, to Isaac, and to Jacob, as God Almighty (*El Shaddai*), but by my name the LORD (*Yahweh*) I did not make myself known to them. I also established my covenant with them, to give them the land of Canaan,...and I have remembered my covenant....' About the patriarchs' knowledge of himself, God was saying that though he announced himself to them as El Shaddai (to Abraham, Gn. 17:1, mg.; to Jacob, Gn. 35:11, mg.; for Isaac, *cf.* Gn. 26:24), linking his promises to them with this title as a basis for their trust, he never expounded to them the meaning of his name Yahweh as he did to Moses at the bush. (The common critical interpretation, that God meant that the very sound of the name Yahweh was unknown to the patriarchs, has been made the basis for both the J–E dissection of Genesis by the higher critics and the hypothesis held by many of them that Yahweh was a Kenite fire-and-storm God whom Moses introduced for the first time; but if anything is certain, it is that the author of Exodus 6:3 did not take God's recorded words that way.)

The phrase 'I am the LORD' is the leading theme of the paragraph (verses 2-8): it blazes out again and again like Siegfried's horn-call in Wagner's *Ring* (verses 2, 6, 7, 8;*cf.* 29; 7:5, 17; 8:22; 14:4, 18). God was teaching Moses, so that Moses might teach Israel, to trust his revealed name as guaranteeing the fulfilment of his promises. His answer to all Moses' 'buts' and 'oh dears' was simply, 'I am the LORD'. Verses 6–9 are the supreme manifesto of the Exodus. 'I am the LORD, and I will bring you out... I will deliver you from their bondage... I will redeem you... I will take you for my people... I will be your God; and you shall know that I am the LORD your God, who has brought you out... and I will bring you into the land... I will give it to you... I am the LORD.' In other words, 'I am the LORD – and this is my promise – and can my word fail?'

Such was Yahweh, God of Israel, the God whom the whole Old Testament extols as creator, ruler, saviour, judge, source and goal of all things that exist. Yahweh was the name that proclaimed his Godhood. Israel's theology and religion were avowedly monotheistic: 'Hear, O Israel: The LORD our God is one LORD (mg.: the LORD is one); and you shall love the LORD your God with all your heart, and with all your soul, and with all your might' (Dt. 6:4 f.). As the one and only God, his claim upon his people's loyalty and service is absolute and total. And Israel's thought about her God always started from the vast difference and contrast between Yahweh and man. Yahweh is creator, man is his creature; Yahweh is almighty, man is weak; man depends on Yahweh for everything – health, happiness, life itself – but Yahweh does not depend on man for anything; Yahweh is just and holy, man is sinful and crooked. Against this background of contrast, God taught Israel through prophets and psalmists to appreciate grace, and to see how amazing it really is that he, the high and holy One, should stoop to reclaim sinners and bring them into fellowship with himself. It was this one mighty God of grace, and him alone, that the word 'Lord' (Hebrew, *adonai;* Greek, *kurios;* Aramaic, *maran*) denoted in Jewish religious circles in the time of Christ.

The Lord Jesus

Jesus of Nazareth was an unorthodox wandering rabbi, whose three-year ministry was brought to a sudden end by judicial murder. His disciples claimed that he had risen from death, was alive for ever, was reigning over all the world as God's Messiah, and would some day be visibly manifested again on earth for the final judgment. They endorsed the Old Testament faith in one God, as Jesus himself had done (see Mt. 23:9; Mk. 10:18; 12:29; Jn. 5:44; 17:3; Rom. 3:30; 1 Cor. 8:4–6; Gal. 3:20; Eph. 4:6; 1 Tim. 1:17; 2:5; Jas. 2:19; 4:12; Jude 25). Yet – and this is really very remarkable – they used the word 'Lord' far more often of 'the Lord Jesus' than when referring to the One to whom Jesus had prayed as his Father.

Does this New Testament usage imply Jesus' personal deity? Not always. In the Gospels, 'Lord' as a form of address is simply 'sir', a polite way of talking to a rabbi (*e.g.* Lk. 7:6). Even on the disciples' lips, 'Lord' in the Gospels seems to mean no more than 'master, teacher' (see Jn. 13:13 f., *etc.*). Again, in the Acts and Epistles 'Lord' sometimes denotes simply the Messianic dominion which Jesus has exercised since his resurrection and ascension, ruling the world in his Father's name to compass the salvation of those for whom he died. Thus, in Acts 2:36, after citing Psalm 110:1 ('The LORD said to my Lord, Sit at my right hand') as a Messianic prophecy, Peter declares: 'Let all the house of Israel therefore know assuredly, that God has made him both Lord and Christ, this Jesus, whom you crucified.' 'Lord' and 'Christ' (Messiah; literally, 'anointed one') explain each other: the phrase is a hendiadys, two words expressing a single thought, that of Jesus' Messianic rule. Similarly, the 'name which is above every name' in Philippians 2:9–11 is the name 'Lord', denoting Jesus' universal dominion, which all must acknowledge.

Sometimes, however, 'Lord' as a title for Jesus implies personal deity quite unmistakably. This is most obvious when Old Testament prophecies concerning Yahweh are quoted as being fulfilled in Jesus. Thus, Joel 2:32, cited in Acts 2:21 and Romans 10:13 as 'everyone who calls upon the name of the Lord (Yahweh in the Hebrew) will be saved', is in the first passage probably and in the second certainly taken as a promise of salvation to those who call upon Jesus (see Acts 2:38 and Rom. 10:4–17). (Over and above this identification of Jesus with Yahweh, the verb 'call upon' denotes religious invocation and trust, which, as every Jew knew, was an attitude which could only be taken up with propriety towards God himself; one must not invoke a creature as one's saviour. So the New Testament use of Joel 2:32 actually contains a double demonstration that Jesus was viewed as divine.) Then again, John identifies Jesus as 'the Lord' whose arm is not revealed to unbelievers (Jn. 12:38, 41), and Matthew and Mark identify him as 'the Lord' whose way John the Baptist was sent to prepare (Mt. 3:3; Mk. 1:3). But in Isaiah 40:3 and 53:1, the Old Testament texts quoted, the Hebrew has Yahweh.

Another significant passage is 1 Corinthians 8:5 f., where to the 'gods' and 'lords' (*i.e.* gods called lords) of pagan polytheism Paul opposes 'one God, the Father' and 'one Lord Jesus Christ'. In this context, at any rate, 'Lord' implies deity, and a claim upon our worship. With this may be linked passages in which Jesus is invoked as 'Lord' in prayer (Acts 7:59; 1 Cor. 16:22 – *Maranatha* is Aramaic: 'Come, O Lord!' NEB; 2 Cor. 12:8; Rev. 22:20). Optative benedictions, which are really prayers, are given in his name (1 Thes. 3:11 f.; 2 Thes. 3:5, 16), and doxologies are addressed to him, either alone (Rom. 9:5, where AV, RV and NIV are right, as against RSV and NEB; 2 Tim. 4:18; 2 Pet. 3:18; Rev. 1:5 f.) or with the Father (Rev. 5:13; 7:10). Hebrews 1:6 says that God wills all the angels to worship Jesus.

Against this background of Christian worship of Jesus as Lord together with his Father, a worship which is set in conscious opposition to the worship of pagan 'lords', it is evident that when the gospel message is concentrated into a demand for confession that 'Jesus is Lord' (as it is in 1 Cor. 12:3; Rom. 10: 9; *cf.* Phil. 2:11) what is called for is an acknowledgment of Jesus, not merely as risen Saviour and reigning King, but as a Person to be invoked, trusted, known, praised and adored, as God the Father is – in other words, as divine.

After this, it is no surprise to find in the New Testament a number of passages in which, according to the natural grammatical reading (sometimes disputed, but not effectively), Jesus is explicitly declared to be *theos* (God): John 1:1, 18 (where the right reading is surely 'God only begotten', as RV and NIV margin); 20:28; Romans 9:5; Titus 2:13; Hebrews 1:8; 2 Peter 1:1.

We cannot fully discuss the evidence of our Lord's divinity here: that would take a book. But it is worth rounding off our survey of it by quoting two further lines of proof from Berkhof:

> [The New Testament] *ascribes to Him divine attributes,* such as eternal existence...Jn. 1:1, 2; Rev. 1:8; 22:13, omnipresence, Mt. 18:20; 28:20;...omniscience, Jn. 2:24, 25; 21:17; Rev. 2: 23, omnipotence,...Phil. 3:21; Rev. 1:8, immutability, Heb. 1:10–12; 13:8, and in general every attribute belonging to the Father, Col. 2:9; [and it] *speaks of Him as doing divine works,* as creation, Jn. 1:3, 10; Col. 1:16; Heb. 1:2, 10, providence, Lk. 10:22; Jn. 3:35; 17:2; Eph. 1:22; Col. 1:17; Heb. 1:3, the forgiveness of sins, Mt. 9:2–7; Mk. 2:7–10; Col. 3:13 [add Acts 5:31; Mt. 1:21], resurrection and judgment, Mt. 25:31, 32; Jn. 5:19–29; Acts 10:42; 17:31; Phil. 3:21; 2 Tim. 4:1 [add Jn. 6:39 f., 54; 11:24–26; 1 Cor. 15:45; Rom. 2:16; Rev. 19:15; 20:12], the final dissolution and renewal of all things, Heb. 1:10–12; Phil. 3:21; Rev. 21:5 (*Systematic Theology,* p.94).

All this goes further to show that the New Testament habit of calling Jesus 'Lord' is of a piece with its unambiguous overall witness to his deity.

That men brought up in Jewish monotheism should ever

affirm the deity of a fellow-man might seem incredible. To Judaism and Islam, Christian faith in Jesus as God seems a wild absurdity, a lapse into the paganism that deified Egyptian kings and Roman emperors. Theologically, it looks suicidal, for it involves three mind-blinding mysteries which when first stated sound quite fantastic: (i) that the one God consists of more than one Person; (ii) that one of the divine Persons, without ceasing to be what he was, became human and remains so; (iii) that while this Person was sharing the limitations of human life on earth as a baby in Bethlehem and a boy in Nazareth, then teaching in Palestine, sweating in Gethesemane, dying on Calvary, lying dead in Joseph's grave, he was also simultaneously keeping the universe together, 'upholding all things by the word of his power' (Col. 1:17; Heb. 1:3). Plainly, these were not beliefs to which Peter and Paul and John and the writer to the Hebrews could have come easily; equally plainly, they were driven to them by Jesus' own words, and the events of the forty days from his resurrection to his ascension, and visions such as Paul's on the Damascus road and John's in Patmos (Acts 9; Rev. 1), and the witness of Old Testament prophecy, and the light of the Holy Spirit convincing them that what they saw in Jesus' face was indeed the image and glory of God (2 Cor. 4:4–6).

The truth to which they were thus led remains, however, stranger than fiction – much stranger: it is as much an inexplicable mystery to theological minds as it is an inescapable implication of historical events.

The Lord the Spirit
We noticed above the remarkable fact that 'Lord', which in the Greek Old Testament, both as name and title, denotes the Godhood of God, is used chiefly in the New Testament not of the Father but of the Son. It is equally remarkable that 'holy', the regular Old Testament adjective for expressing the 'God-ness' of God, is mainly applied in the New Testament not to the Father or the Son, but to the Spirit.

The Holy Spirit is not spoken of in the Old Testament as a person distinct from the Father (see Ps. 51:11; Is. 63:10):

is he in the New? Jehovah's Witnesses say no, but the Bible is àgainst them. The Holy Spirit (Greek *pneuma*, neuter) has a masculine pronoun, against all the rules of grammar, in John 16:14, and a personal title (*paraklētos* – comforter, counsellor, advocate, helper) in John 14:26; 15:26; 16:7. He is shown to have intelligence (Jn. 14:26; 15:26; Rom. 8:27), will (Acts 16:7; 1 Cor. 12:11), and affections (Eph. 4:30). Most of the acts ascribed to him could only be performed by a personal agent: speaking (Acts 8:29; 13:2; Rev. 2:7, *etc.*; nearly twenty references altogether), deciding (Acts 15:28), forbidding (Acts 16:7), testifying (Acts 5:32, *etc.*), searching into secrets (1 Cor. 2:10 f.), showing the future (Jn. 16:13), sending out missionaries (Acts 13:4), interceding (Rom. 8:26 f.).

Granted that the New Testament views the Spirit as a person, does it depict him as a divine Person? In effect, yes (though it never actually calls him *theos*, God): for (i) Jesus links the Holy Spirit with Father and Son in the tri-personal name of God (Mt. 28:19); (ii) he is linked with Father and Son in prayer for, and pronouncement of, the blessing of God (2 Cor. 13:14; Rev. 1:4f., where the 'seven spirits' signify the Holy Spirit); (iii) he is linked with Father and Son as having the applicatory, and so completive, part in the work of salvation which the Father performs through the Son (1 Pet. 1:1 f.; 2 Thes. 2:13 f.; Eph. 1:3–14; 2:13–22; Rom. 8; *etc.*); and (iv) in 2 Corinthians 3:16–18 he, as being 'the Spirit of the Lord (Jesus)', is so closely linked with Jesus, as his agent for working in men, that Paul can actually say 'the Lord (Jesus) is the Spirit' and speak of 'the Lord who is the Spirit'; and this startling mode of speech would not have been possible for Paul had he not thought of the Spirit as one with Jesus in the unity of the Godhead.

In what sense does Paul mean us to gather that Christ and the Spirit are one? 'Not one and the same person,' writes Charles Hodge, commenting on the statement, 'but one and the same Being...It is an identity of essence and power ...where Christ is, there the Spirit is, and where the Spirit is, there is Christ....By turning unto Christ we become partakers of the Holy Spirit...because he and the Spirit are one, and Christ dwells in his people, redeeming them from the law and making them the children of God, by his Spirit.' So the phrase 'the Lord who is the Spirit' means 'the Lord who is one with the Spirit, the same in substance, equal in power and glory; who is where the Spirit is, and does what the Spirit does'. Paul's words thus do not assert the deity of the Spirit in terms, but – even more significantly – presuppose it in thought. Paul could never have said 'the Lord *is* the Spirit', meaning that the Lord works in men through the Spirit, had he not thought of Son and Spirit as coequal divine Beings. (He would never, for instance, have dreamed of saying 'the Lord *is* Paul' to express the thought that Christ worked through Paul!) The verses thus bear clear witness to the Spirit's place in the Godhead.

The gospel of the Trinity

So the Bible bequeaths to the church the doctrine of three divine Agents and one God: Father, Son, and Holy Spirit as the 'name' – as Karl Barth happily put it, the 'Christian name' – of the one Yahweh. As the Athanasian Creed states, 'the Father is Lord, the Son Lord: and the Holy Ghost Lord. And yet not three Lords: but one Lord.' Not one person impersonating two others in addition to himself; not a trio of separate deities; but a God who is really one, and yet within whose unity there are really three, the threeness and the oneness being each fundamental to the other. The three are 'in' each other (*cf.* Jn. 14:11, 20) without losing their personal distinctness, just as all three may be 'in' the Christian without him losing his personal identity and self-awareness (*cf.* Jn. 14:17, 23). They stand in definite and distinct mutual relations: the Father initiates, the Son is the Father's agent, the Spirit is the executive of both. Yet (the Athanasian Creed again) 'the Godhead of the Father, of the Son, and of the Holy Ghost, is all one: the Glory equal, the Majesty co-eternal. Such as the Father is, such is the Son: and such is the Holy Ghost.'

'So what?' says someone. 'Granted, Trinitarian thinking is biblical, but is it important? What is lost by not asserting the Trinity?'

54

What is lost is, quite simply, the gospel – or at least, the right to assert the gospel. Let me explain.

In following a path up a mountain, you concentrate on the path rather than the mountain. A single-minded person could hurry to the top without really noticing the mountain at all. I once climbed a mountain whose name I did not discover till four years afterwards. Now, when you state the gospel you take a path up a mountain: and the Trinity is both the name and the nature of the mountain you have under your feet the whole time.

In John 3:1–15 (and probably on to verse 21, as in NIV, NEB and JB) we see Jesus explaining to Nicodemus that the only way into God's kingdom is through faith in the Son whom the Father sent down to be 'lifted up' in sacrificial death, and through being born anew of the Spirit. Jesus is spelling out the gospel; and its substance, very obviously, is the combined action of the Triune God. Well did the Anglican Prayer Book select John 3:1–15 as the Gospel for Trinity Sunday! The Trinity is the basis of the gospel, and the gospel is a declaration of the Trinity in action.

To put it the other way round: the gospel says that there was in God from eternity mutuality of love and joy (Jn. 1:1 f.; 17:5, 24); that men were made to share this fellowship; that when sin had made this impossible, God came in person – the second Person, sent by the first Person and empowered by the third Person – to save us; that God-made-flesh died for us, lives for us, unites us to himself, brings us to God the Father now and will take us one day to share his glory; that a divine Guest, the Holy Spirit, indwells each Christian (there are over 800,000,000 of us alive today, leaving aside the faithful departed) to prompt prayer and transform our fallen nature; and that Jesus Christ is companion and friend to every single believer, giving him or her constant and undistracted attention. It is surely obvious that none of these marvellous, almost fantastic things could be said save on the supposition that Father, Son and Holy Spirit are God – in other words, that God is Father, Son and Holy Spirit. Those who deny the Trinity have to scale down the gospel – and do.

So we may well make it a matter of conscience to pray:

Almighty and everlasting God, who hast given unto us thy servants grace by the confession of a true faith to acknowledge the glory of the eternal Trinity, and in the power of the Divine Majesty to worship the Unity; We beseech thee, that thou wouldest keep us steadfast in this faith, and evermore defend us from all adversities, who livest and reignest, one God, world without end.

Book of Common Prayer
Collect for Trinity Sunday.

4

THE WORLD

When we use the word 'world', what we usually have in mind is the sum total of things and people around us. This general idea takes different forms in different contexts. The angle of our thought may, for instance, be physical and geographical: in that case, 'the world' means this planet, the Earth, with its chemical structure, climatic laws, population statistics, annual production of raw materials, and so forth. Or our thoughts may be racial and anthropological: then 'the world' means men of all nations. When we speak of world health, or world peace, or world opinion, we are clearly using the word in this sense. Or, again, our thought may be sociological and cultural. 'World' then signifies a particular outlook and pattern of communal life, as in the contrast which our grandfathers drew between the 'old' world and the 'new' world across the Atlantic, or the contrast which we ourselves draw between the 'Western world' and the 'Communist world'. There may also be a temporal contrast implied, 'the world' meaning things as they are as distinct from how they were, *e.g.* the 'modern' as contrasted with the 'ancient' world. Or, finally, our thought may be personal and subjective, and then 'world' denotes things in general as they appear to some one man from the vantage-point (or through the blinkers) of his own private knowledge and interests. Thus we say 'So-and-so lives in a world of his own'; and Thurber says 'My world and welcome to it'. But whatever form our idea of the world takes, one factor remains constant. The world of which we think is the world as man knows and sees it – *our* world, *his* world, *my* world. In our thoughts of the world, man is always at the centre.

The biblical idea of the world covers approximately the same area of meaning as our secular notion does. It, likewise, denotes this earth with its cosmic environment, and men upon it, or sometimes mankind alone. There are words in both Hebrew and Greek translated 'world' in the English Bible, which mean simply 'the habitable (or, inhabited) earth'. Yet the standpoint from which the Bible speaks of 'the world' is quite different from ours. For in the Bible 'world' is a theological word – a word, that is, which is defined in terms of God. 'The world' is always, and emphatically, *God's* world – the order of things which he made, which he owns, and which he rules, despite all his creatures' efforts to cast off his sway. The reference-point of the biblical idea of the world, therefore, is not man, but God. What we have to do now is to learn to think of the world God-centredly, as the Bible presents it – not always as it appears to human inspection, but as God sees it, and thinks of it. For the thoughts of God about it are the measure of what it really is.

The order of creation

The commonest word for 'world' in the New Testament (occurring about 150 times) is *kosmos*. *Kosmos* basically means 'order', and the thought of order – the harmonious integration of a variety of elements and energies – is in fact the key-thought in the biblical presentation of God's work as Creator. Note the layout of the first chapter of Genesis. Its stress is not on the fact that God made all things out of nothing (the doctrine of creation from nothing, though no doubt implicit in Gn. 1:1, derives rather from texts like Ps. 33:6; Jn. 1:3; Col. 1:16 f.; Heb. 11:3). What Genesis 1 emphasizes is the fact that God by his creative Word and Spirit (speech and breath) brought order out of a primeval chaos. 'The earth was without form and void, and darkness was upon the face of the deep; and the Spirit (breath) of God was moving over the face of the waters. And God said . . . and there was . . .' (Gn. 1:2 f.). The chapter goes on to tell us how God separated land from sea, established the regular rhythm of day and night and the round of the year, filled the dry land with vegetation, and populated it with birds, beasts, and human beings, each 'according to its kind'

58

(verses 11, 21, 24 ff.). Everywhere, God's creative work brought *order* out of a state of affairs which otherwise would have remained chaotic. This is the central truth about God the Creator that Genesis 1 is concerned to show us.

The producing of an ordered world involved the imposing of limits and boundaries in both space and time. Each thing must be kept in its place, so that there might be room for everything that God had planned. Accordingly, in space, God restrained the rain and the sea (Gn. 1:6–10; *cf.* Jb. 38:8 ff.; Ps. 104:9), so that all his purposes for life on dry land might be fulfilled. Similarly, when men multiplied, he allotted particular areas for each national group to inhabit (Dt. 32:8). Again, in time, God has set bounds, not only to the life of each living thing, and to the seasons of the year and the natural processes proper to each, like fruit-bearing and hibernation, but also to the successive eras of human history. We find Paul explaining to the Athenians these created, providential limits that God has imposed upon the life of mankind. 'He created every race of men of one stock, to inhabit the whole earth's surface. He fixed the epochs of their history and the limits of their territory' (Acts 17:26, NEB).

The AV translators were not, therefore, really wide of the mark when they rendered the Greek word *aiōn* some 30 times as 'world'. (Whenever the AV speaks of '*this* world', in contrast, implicit or explicit, with 'the world *to come*', and whenever it makes mention of the *end* of the world, the Greek word is always *aiōn*.) It is true that the dictionary meaning of *aiōn* is 'epoch', 'era', and that RV, RSV and NIV regularly change the AV rendering to 'age' (in the margin, if not in the text) in all these cases. But what *aiōn* in the New Testament actually refers to is the whole present state of things, viewed as limited in time and so as transitory; while *kosmos* denotes the same state of things, viewed as an integrated whole made up of spatially limited parts. Thus *aiōn* and *kosmos* are in fact complementary words, each expressing a different aspect of the same basic idea.

What God made at the beginning, then, was precisely a world-*order*. In the first chapter of the Bible he is the One

... whose almighty word
Chaos and darkness heard,
And took their flight.

It is natural to conclude from Genesis 1 that the goodness which God saw in each thing as he formed it, and in the entire finished work of creation before mankind fell (see verses 4, 10, 12, 18, 21, 25, 31), lay partly, at least, in the fact that each step in creation was a further step in the exclusion and banishment of chaos. The Creator is a God, not of confusion, but of order (*cf.* 1 Cor. 14:33).

We cannot dwell here on the relation between the biblical creation story (Gn. 1:1 – 2:4a, with 2:4b–25 supplementing 1:26–30 in the manner of a long footnote or appendix) and contemporary scientific thinking about origins. Suffice it to say that

(i) the narrative is a celebrating of the fact of creation and of the Creator's wisdom, power and goodness, rather than an observational monitoring of stages in the creative process;

(ii) the story focuses not on the cosmic system as a system, but on the Creator apart from whose will and word it would not at this moment exist;

(iii) the narrative method is imaginative, pictorial, poetic and doxological (glory-giving, in the style of worship) rather than clinically descriptive and coldly prosaic in the dead-pan scientific manner;

(iv) the Earth-centredness of the presentation reflects not scientific naïvety about the solar system and outer space, but theological interest in man's uniqueness and responsibility under God on this planet;

(v) the evident aim of the story is to show its readers their own place and calling in God's world, and the abiding significance of the sabbath as a memorial of creation, rather than to satisfy curiosity about the details of what happened long ago.

Within these perspectives various ways of understanding the six days of creation and relating the creative process to the shifting hypotheses of science are open. None is more than an educated guess; verification is not possible. All hypotheses that take note of the five points above should be judged legitimate, but none should ever expect to have the field to itself, and its sponsors will need to put it forward with modesty and tolerance towards other views.

Mankind was made to rule creation. This noblest of creatures was set at the head of the created order, and told to *subdue* it (Gn. 1:28); that is, to map and tap its resources, to bring out and utilize its latent possibilities, to put it to work for him, and thus to harness and develop all its powers for the enriching of his own life, in obedience to God. God gave us richly all things to enjoy (*cf.* 1 Tim. 6:17). He willed to be glorified through humanity's learning to appreciate and admire his wisdom and goodness as Creator. In other words, God commissioned mankind to build a culture and civilization. Some, with justice, call Genesis 1:28 the *cultural mandate*.

Right at the outset, God introduced Adam to the vocation appointed for him by putting him in charge of a *garden* (Gn. 2:15). Gardening is a perfect picture of the human cultural task. Adam was to learn to see the whole created order as, so to speak, the estate which he, as God's gardener, was responsible for cultivating. Man was not made to be a barbarian, nor to live in savagery, and 'back to nature' is never the road back to Eden. For mankind was made to rule nature, to master it and to enjoy its fruits, to the glory of God the Creator, according to the principle laid down in 1 Timothy 4:4: 'Everything created by God is good, and nothing is to be rejected if it is received with thanksgiving.' So the Psalmist writes: 'What is man that thou art mindful of him, and the son of man that thou dost care for him? Yet thou hast made him little less than God, and dost crown him with glory and honour. Thou hast given him dominion over the works of thy hands; thou hast put all things under his feet, (Ps. 8:4–6).

Clearly, God meant us to live in avowed acknowledgment of the goodness of what he has made. However conscious we may be of how God's creation is abused through human self-seeking, and how needful it is to eschew some of the forms of self-indulgence that folk around us have devised, we must never lose sight of the goodness of the created order itself, or we dishonour its Creator. The Manichean idea that the world of matter, physical life and sensory pleasure is valueless and indeed evil, so that the godly must be as detached from it as possible, has over sixteen centuries spawned many ugly things in the church: a false antithesis between the material and the spiritual; inhibitions and guilt about sex in marriage; glorifying dirt, seediness and barbarism, and contracting out of cultural endeavour; proud asceticism of the kind described in Colossians 2:20–23; negativity towards literature, the arts and all producing and enjoying of beauty ('unspiritual, you know'); and so on. Certainly, Christ may call us as individuals to renounce many good and pleasant things (a career in music, business or sport; marriage; home comforts; etc.), just as once he called upon the rich young ruler to reduce himself to poverty (Lk. 18:18–23), and we must be open to such possibilities (cf. Mt. 19:12). But we must never forget that what is given up in such cases is something good, not something evil.

The entry of sin cut across the Edenic pattern, but it did not cancel the cultural mandate, nor the principle that God is glorified when the good things of creation are received and enjoyed as his gifts, and men praise and thank him for them. These principles still have a decisive bearing on the Christian attitude to life in this world.

The disorder of rebellion

Adam's one transgression disrupted the entire order of things which God had made. First, and fundamentally, it disordered Adam's relationship with God. From being a relationship of communion and peace, it became one of guilt, shame, and evasion on man's side, and of inquisition, rebuke, and judgment on God's side (Gn. 3:8–19). Also, the first sin disordered Adam's own nature. Acts create habits, and Adam's soul was now set in the mould of lawless, faithless self-assertion against God which had been the essence of his fatal action. Now he bore the devil's image rather than God's, and it is in this warped image that all his descendants are born (*cf.* Gn. 5:3). This is the original sinfulness which we all inherit in virtue of Adam's original sin. Thus it is in all ages a universal truth that 'the mind that is set on the flesh [the mind of man in Adam] is hostile to God; it does not submit to God's law, indeed it cannot' (Rom. 8:7). By reason of this hereditary inner twistedness, mankind is always at one in opposing God's rule.

Hence in the New Testament the word 'world' (*kosmos*) is often used to denote sinful mankind in the mass, solidly given to unrighteousness and ungodliness and solidly hostile to the truth and the people of God (*cf.* Jn. 15:18 f.; 1 Cor. 1:21; 3:19). The 'world' in this sense is ruled by three evil influences – 'the lust of the flesh and the lust of the eyes and the pride of life' (1 Jn. 2:16): the pleasure, profit, power and promotion motives. Christians must not love the world (verse 15), nor allow themselves to grow like it (*cf.* Rom. 12:2: 'world' here is *aiōn*). To swim with the stream and be ruled by the spirit of the world is easy and tempting, but the Christian must on no account let himself do it, for worldliness is the starkest unfaithfulness to God. James states this in a very blunt way. 'Unfaithful creatures!' (literally, 'adulteresses': this to his Christian readers!) 'Do you not know that friendship with the world is enmity with God? Therefore whoever wishes to be a friend of the world makes himself an enemy of God' (Jas. 4:4).

From this we can see what the nature of worldliness is, and avoid the mistake of equating it with the use and enjoyment of created things, as such. Worldliness means yielding to the *spirit* that animates fallen mankind, the spirit of self-seeking and self-indulgence without regard for God. Whether a man is worldly thus depends, not on how much enjoyment he takes from the good and pleasant things of this life, but on the spirit in which he takes it. If he allows these things to enslave him (1 Cor. 6:12) and become a god – that is, an idol – in his heart (Col. 3:5), he is worldly. If, on the other hand, he is disciplined in his use of them, not indulging to the detriment of his own or others' edification (1 Cor. 10:23–33; 8:8–13) nor losing his heart to them, but receiving them gratefully as God's gifts and a means for showing forth his praise, thanking God for all pleasant occupations and all delightful experiences, and not letting the merely good elbow out the best, then he is not worldly, but godly. Again, it is not worldly to be praised; but it is worldly to live for men's compliments and applause, and to find one's highest happiness in the thought that one has gratified men, rather than in the knowledge that one has done God's will. Worldliness is the spirit which substitutes some earthly ideal, such as pleasure, or gain, or popularity, for life's true goal, which is in all things to praise and to please God.

The Bible points to a further aspect of disorder caused by sin. Human relations are now disrupted; man is against man. Cain kills Abel (Gn. 4:8); Lamech proclaims jungle law (Gn. 4:23 f.); men swindle each other for gain, and find pleasure in being violent and cruel; nations vie for supremacy, and go to war to gain it; and the social structures which men organize for mutual well-being break down, through lack of an adequate sense of social responsibility to sustain them. Science is put to serve selfish ambitions, and the fine arts used to undermine moral standards. In Romans 1:26–31, Paul describes this terrible pattern of disrupted human relations as he saw it in the pagan society of his time; but the pattern is a recurring one, and we can see it working out afresh today in our own post-Christian generation.

Scripture calls Satan the 'prince' and 'god' of the world as it now is (Jn. 12:31; 14:30; 2 Cor. 4:4). What this means is that Satan at present occupies the world and rules over it (Eph. 2:2; *cf.* 6:12). 'The whole godless world lies in the power of the evil one' (1 Jn. 5:19, NEB), who seeks to maintain it in a state of spiritual blindness and perversity (2 Cor. 4:4; Eph. 2:2; *cf.* 1 Jn. 4:1–6). But God over-rules both it and him, and Christ by his death has broken Satan's power over all God's children (Heb. 2:14 f.; 1 Jn. 4:4; *cf.* Lk. 11:17–22; Rev. 12 – 20).

The new order of redemption
Now we review what the New Testament says about the relation of Christ and of the Christian to the world of

humanity – *i.e.* the mass of ungodly mankind, enslaved to sin and needing salvation. John's Gospel and First Epistle are our main guides here.

In John's writings, Christ's redeeming work is related to the world in two apparently opposite ways. Sometimes, the world is its object. God, we are told, loved the world (Jn. 3:16) and sent his Son to save it (verse 17 and 12:47; *cf.* 2 Cor. 5:19); Christ is the light of the world (Jn. 8:12; 9:5) and its Saviour (4:42; 1 Jn. 4:14), the propitiation for its sins (1 Jn. 2:2; *cf.* Jn. 1:29), the One who gives it life (Jn. 6:33) by giving his life for it (verse 51). Elsewhere, however, the world is apparently excluded from redemption: the disciples are chosen out of it (17:6), and Christ declines either to pray for it (17:9), or to manifest himself to it (14:17, 22). Is there an inconsistency here? No; for John never uses the word 'world' in his writings in a statistical sense, though that is how we persistently take it. 'World' in John is never a synonym for 'every single person'. In a general and comprehensive sense, the word denotes people in the mass, of all sorts and nationalities, Jew and Gentile without distinction, but its numerical reference is always indefinite. The hard core of its meaning is not quantitative, but qualitative. It is not, as John uses it, a statistical, but a moral and spiritual term. 'The world', said B. B. Warfield preaching on John 3:16, 'is just the synonym of all that is evil and noisome and disgusting. There is nothing in it that can attract God's love ... the point of (the word's) employment (in this verse) is not to suggest that the world is so big that it takes a great deal of love to embrace it all, but that the world is so bad that it takes a great kind of love to love it at all, and much more to love it as God has loved it when He gave His Son for it' (*Biblical and Theological Studies,* Philadelphia, 1952, pp. 514 ff.). 'The world', in other words, is simply a synonym for *bad men everywhere,* both in this text and in the others quoted. Whether the precise reference is to bad people who are, or will be, saved, or to bad people who are not saved, or simply to bad people who need saving, must be determined in each case from the context.

What is to be the Christian's relation to the world? As a

65

Christian, he is not *of* it (Jn. 17:14, 16), but remains *in* it (verses 11, 15), to bear witness *to* it (Mt. 24:14). The world will oppose Christians (Jn. 15:18 ff.; 1 Jn. 3:13); it will not love them any more than it loves Christ; they must expect to be misunderstood and resented by their fellow-men. One proof, however, that they are Christians, born of God, is that they overcome the world, as their Master did (1 Jn. 5:4; Jn. 16:33): that is, they are not mastered by it, not 'conformed to this world' (Rom. 12:2), but persist in serving God, and maintain an unquenchable joy as they do so, despite all contrary influences from society and its members round about them. Living thus, they are 'the light of the world' (Mt. 5:14), 'holding forth the word of life' to it (Phil. 2:16, AV). So they go on, from strength to strength, looking for the day when 'the kingdom of the world' becomes 'the kingdom of our Lord and of his Christ' (Rev. 11:15); the day when the whole creation acknowledges Christ as King (Phil. 2:10 f.), and God is 'all in all' (1 Cor. 15:28).

The reordering of chaos

It is idle trying to fore-fancy the future from Scripture, for there God presents future events to us filtered through the exuberant, even lurid imaginations of ancient Orientals who were much more concerned to sense and express the glow and the glory of divine things than to describe them in a way that we could call objective or exact. J. N. Darby's dictum, 'prophecy is history written in advance,' is not false, but it is as misleading as any true statement could ever be. For it encourages us to read the details, including the numbers, in predictive prophecies (specially those couched in the idiom of Jewish apocalyptic, where numbers and fantastically imagined details abound: *e.g.*, Daniel and Revelation) as if they were matters of literal fact in the way that the contents of our history books are. But really these details are elements of symbolically expressed totalities which as wholes often prove to be conveying much less specific meaning than their plethora of detail might suggest, and in which all you can be sure of as regards each detail is its theological point. Example: Revelation 21:18–21 tells us that new Jerusalem will be built of gold with twelve gems in its foundations and twelve gates each made of one pearl. This detail certainly conveys the thought that new Jerusalem, whether located on this planet or not – exegetes differ – will be of supreme worth and beauty, but is it 'literal fact'? Verse 16 says that the city will be cubic, no less than 1,500 miles long, across and high: is that 'literal fact'? Surely such questions answer themselves: and we must acknowledge that reading predictive prophecy as if the theological images of inspired Oriental imagination could be matter-of-factly literalized is a bad mistake.

But having said that, we can go on to affirm that Scripture is clear and positive about the future hope for the world, both the world of nature and the world of humanity.

Note first Paul's teaching (Rom. 8:19–22) that through Adam's fall all creation was in some way 'subjected to futility' – *mataiotēs*, a Greek word meaning frustration in the sense of non-achievement of purpose. Paul is implying that creation (*i.e.*, nature) went back some way towards chaos. Whether 'nature red in tooth and claw' is an aspect of this (*cf.* Is. 11:6–9), or earthquakes, epidemics, parasites, poisonous insects and reptiles, in addition to the aspect God specified, namely the hard labour of getting a living from the land (Gn. 3:17–19), are questions easier to ask than to answer. But we should take seriously Paul's personification of the created world as 'groaning' in the futility of its present disorder as it 'waits with eager longing for the revealing of the sons of God'.

But a day will come when without warning the entire cosmic order will disintegrate and be reconstructed. 'The day of the Lord will come like a thief, and then the heavens will pass away with a loud noise, and the elements will be dissolved with fire, and the earth and the works that are upon it will be burned up' (2 Pet. 3:10). Peter makes it sound like a nuclear explosion; perhaps it will be; but all we can be sure of is that it will be sudden and catastrophic, as every familiar thing vanishes and each individual is conscious only of being set before the Lord Jesus Christ for judgment. Out of that unimaginable happening, however, says Peter, 'according to his promise we wait for new heavens and a new earth [*i.e.,* a renewed creation] in which righteousness dwells' (verse 13). And then all the chaos will be a thing of the past; full perfection will have come, both for God's people and for the world of nature. Unimaginable? Yes; but certain, none the less.

Peter continues: 'Therefore, beloved, since you wait for these [*i.e.,* new heavens and earth], be zealous to be found by him without spot or blemish, and at peace... beware lest you be carried away with the error of lawless men and lose your own stability. But grow in the grace and knowledge of our Lord and Saviour Jesus Christ. To him be the glory both now and to the day of eternity. Amen' (verses 14, 17 f.). Words in season, surely, in a world like ours! The wise man will hear and heed them.

The end of the problem of evil

The wise reader will note too that in the light of this hope for the world the problem of evil, so-called, fades away. This, the most acutely felt difficulty in Christian theism today, is a two-sided perplexity, with both theoretical and practical angles. Theoretically, the problem is: can we believe in a Creator who is *both* good *and* lord of his world, when we face so much evil – *moral* evil, good in human nature gone wrong; *situational* evil, good folk crushed, the corrupt prospering, possibilities of good being wasted; and *personal* evil, physical and mental suffering through disaster, disease, poverty, cruelty, exploitation, disappointment, despair. Were God good but not sovereign, or sovereign but not good, the reality of evil would be understandable, but surely it is incredible (so men argue) that the evil around us should be real and yet God be both genuinely good and genuinely omnipotent and in charge. Practically, the problem is how to handle and overcome the evil, of whatever kind, that oppresses you and me in our daily lives. Taken apart from the hope of a new world-order, anything said about either side of the problem will sound pretty lame. But view the perplexities in the light of this hope, and the case is altered.

On the theoretical front, the promise of new heavens and earth reminds us that God is in truth actively discharging the responsibility which in sovereign goodness he assumed from the outset, of reordering the disorder, spiritual, moral and physical, that sin produced. How Satan could fall (for that was where it all started), and why God permitted the race to be ruined through Satan dragging Adam down, are matters of mystery, but there is no mystery as to what God is doing about it. He is working towards a state of the cosmos in which there will be no evil activities or situations anywhere. He is saving a great church through his Son Jesus Christ to glorify and enjoy him in the renewed cosmos for ever. He has not stood aloof from humanity's distress; the incarnation and earthly life of the Son was God entering the depths of evil in all its worst forms, and Christ's victory over the personal forces of evil at Calvary (*cf*. Jn. 12:31; Col. 2:15) was the divine achievement guaranteeing the final glorious transformation at the end of Christ's present heavenly reign (*cf*. 1 Cor. 15:22–28).

God works to his own timetable, not to ours, and knows what he is doing (*cf*.2 Pet. 3:3–9); and it is wholly reasonable to suppose (though impossible, of course, to prove at present) that what may now look like delay, and even God letting his plan be temporarily thwarted, will in retrospect be seen as having been necessary to bring out of the fallen world situation the greatest good for eternity, before the arrival of the new order in which sin shall be no more. But once you allow that God may be exercising his sovereign goodness precisely in bringing the greatest possible good out of present evil, even though it is beyond you to say exactly how, your theoretical problem about evil has gone.

As for the practical problem of coping with evil and overcoming it, the short answer is that, over and above other forms of help that God gives, the sure and certain hope of being kept by God's power to enjoy his love and fellowship in the glory of the coming new order is a source of unlimited resilience and unquenchable moral strength. Those who with Paul believe that 'this slight momentary affliction is preparing for us an eternal weight of glory beyond all comparison' (2 Cor. 4:17) find in themselves strength to resist and overcome present pressures of evil in all their many forms. Paul voices something of this on behalf of all Christian people in Romans 8:35–39, with which this study may well conclude.

'Who shall separate us from the love of Christ? Shall tribulation, or distress, or persecution, or famine, or nakedness, or peril, or sword? As it is written, "For thy sake we are being killed all the day long; we are regarded as sheep to be slaughtered." No, in all these things we are more than conquerors through him who loved us. For I am sure that neither death, nor life, nor angels, nor principalities, nor things present, nor things to come, nor powers, nor height, nor depth, nor anything else in all creation, will be able to separate us from the love of God in Christ Jesus our Lord.'

5

SIN

The subject of sin is vital knowledge. To say that our first need in life is to learn about sin may sound strange, but in the sense intended it is profoundly true. If you have not learned about sin, you cannot understand yourself, or your fellow-men, or the world you live in, or the Christian faith. And you will not be able to make head or tail of the Bible. For the Bible is an exposition of God's answer to the problem of human sin, and unless you have that problem clearly before you, you will keep missing the point of what it says. Apart from the first two chapters of Genesis, which set the stage, the real subject of every chapter of the Bible is what God does about our sins. Lose sight of this theme, and you lose your way in the Bible at once. With that, the love of God, the meaning of salvation, and the message of the gospel, will all become closed books to you; you may still talk of these things, but you will no longer know what you are talking about. It is clear, therefore, that we need to fix in our minds what our ancestors would have called 'clear views of sin'.

But this is not easy, for at least three reasons.

In the first place, the biblical doctrine of sin is uncomplimentary to us; and we naturally jib at any view of ourselves which is uncomplimentary. The self-excusing instinct, itself a product of sin (see Gn. 3:12 f.), is very strong. Hence comes the temptation to water down the doctrine of sin. Good men have been yielding to this temptation since the church began. It needs grace and spiritual enlightenment to believe that our sin is as serious a thing in God's sight as the Bible says it is. We need to pray that God will make us humble and teachable when we come to study this theme.

In the second place, the biblical doctrine of sin emerges

from the biblical knowledge of God's holiness, knowledge which is in short supply these days. Sin is properly understood only from the inside, as we find it in ourselves, and like Isaiah in the temple we start seeing sin in ourselves only when consciously facing a holy God (*cf.* Is. 6:3–5). But in modern Christianity, though thoughts of God's goodwill and compassion mean much, his holiness and purity mean little: the liberal Christian leaven in our heritage, plus the moral indifferentism of our culture, plus our desensitizing apathy and lukewarmness in spiritual things, combine to stifle the notion. The really authoritative writers about sin – Isaiah himself, Amos, Hosea, Jeremiah, Ezekiel, Paul, John, Augustine, Luther, John Calvin, John Owen, Thomas Goodwin, Jonathan Edwards – communicate a sense of God's holy presence so strong as to be almost tangible; because they felt it, they were able to share it. Most of us today, however, lack their knowledge of sin because we lack their awareness of God.

In the third place, the biblical doctrine of sin has been secularized in modern times. People today still talk of sin, but no longer think of it theologically. The word has ceased to convey the thought of an offence against God, and now signifies only a breach of accepted standards of decency, particularly in sexual matters. But when the Bible speaks of sin, it means precisely an offence against God. Though sin is committed by man, and often against society, it cannot properly be defined in terms of either man or society. We shall never know what sin really is till we learn to think of it in terms of our relationship with God.

The nature of sin
The words which our Bibles translate as 'sin', in both Old and New Testaments, mean either failing to hit a target or reach a standard, or failing to obey authority. And the standard unreached, the target missed, the path abandoned, the law transgressed, the authority defied, are in each case God's. God, and his will, are the measure of sin. Sin is turning out of the way he has commanded (Ex. 32:8) into a forbidden way of our own (Is. 53:6). Sin is going contrary to

God, retreating from God, turning one's back on God, defying God, ignoring God.

What, in positive terms, is the essence of sin? *Playing God*; and, as a means to this, refusing to allow the Creator to be God so far as you are concerned. Living, not for him, but for yourself; loving and serving and pleasing yourself without reference to the Creator; trying to be as far as possible independent of him, taking yourself out of his hands, holding him at arm's length, keeping the reins of life in your own hands; acting as if you, and your pleasure, were the end to which all things else, God included, must be made to function as a means – that is the attitude in which sin essentially consists. Sin is exalting oneself against the Creator, withholding the homage due to him, and putting oneself in his place as the ultimate standard of reference in all life's decisions. Augustine analysed sin as pride (*superbia*), the mad passion to be superior even to God, and as a state of being bent away from God into an attitude of self-absorption (*homo incurvatus in se*). Sin is thus the devil's image, for self-exalting pride was his sin before it was ours (1 Tim. 3:6). All this was contained in embryo in the first human sin, which was a yielding to the temptation to be 'like God' (Gn. 3:5). Paul tells us that sin began when men who 'knew God . . . did not honour him as God, or give thanks to him' (Rom. 1:21), and he gives us the most exact analysis of the spirit of sin that the Bible contains when he declares that 'the mind of the flesh [the mind and heart of the unregenerate sinner] is *enmity against God*' (Rom. 8:7, RV) – disaffection to his rule, resentment of his claims, and hostility to his word, all expressed in a fixed and unalterable determination to pursue one's own independence in defiance of the Creator. The abstract noun, 'enmity', intensifies the thought, as if Paul had said 'essence of enmity' or 'pure enmity'; 'hostile' (RSV, NIV) is far too weak a translation.

From this self-deifying attitude spring acts of self-assertion against both God and one's fellows: acts of irreligion in the one case and of inhumanity in the other. A being who has shrugged off the first great commandment – love God with all your powers – can hardly be expected to show greater respect for the second – love your neighbour as yourself. Hence the spirit of sin, which disrupts relations between man and his Maker, also disrupts human society. Paul gives three sad catalogues of characteristic forms that this disruptive action takes (Rom. 1:26–31; Gal. 5:19–21; 2 Tim. 3:2–4).

The state of sin

The Bible is emphatic that the state of sin is absolutely universal. It is natural and inevitable for every man to sin. 'There is no man who does not sin' (1 Ki. 8:46). 'Both Jews and Greeks are under the power of sin.... None is righteous, no, not one.... All have turned aside...; no one does good, not even one.... All have sinned and fall short of the glory of God' (Rom. 3:9–12, 23). 'If we say we have no sin, we deceive ourselves' (1 Jn. 1:8). The Bible explains this universal sinfulness in terms of the solidarity of mankind in Adam (*cf.* 1 Cor. 15:22; Rom. 5:12 ff.). Adam, by sinning, became a sinner by nature; Adam's descendants are born sinners, and so sin by nature. The traditional name for the inborn disposition of antipathy to God and his law which we inherit from Adam is *original sin*: a name which, though not found in Scripture, is appropriate enough, whether one takes it as signifying that this disposition comes to us from the original man, or that it is in us from the moment of our own origin, or that all our acts of sin originate from it. The Bible calls this disposition 'the flesh' (often mistranslated in RSV as 'the lower nature') or 'the mind of the flesh' (Rom. 8:7, RV) or, simply, 'sin which dwells within me' (Rom. 7:29; study verses 8–13). This attitude controls and determines the conduct of every man who is not in Christ. Where Christ does not rule, sin does.

The biblical description of the state of sin includes the following points:

1. It is a state of *condemnation*. This shows us the sinner's relation to God as Judge, and to the penal requirement of his law, which declares: 'the soul that sins shall die' (Ezk. 18:20). 'There is...no condemnation for those who are in Christ Jesus' (Rom. 8:1), but apart from Christ Jesus all

men stand under sentence of death, both for their own personal delinquencies (*cf.* Rom. 1:32; 2:8 f.) and by reason of their solidarity with Adam. Just as believers are justified for Christ's sake, through the imputation to them of his righteousness, so Christless men are condemned for Adam's sake, through the imputation to them of his transgression. This does not mean that they are held to have committed Adam's sin personally, but that Adam sinned representatively, in (so to speak) his public capacity as head of the race, and that the rest of men are bound up in the penal consequences of his action. The penal liability which is ours by virtue of our link with Adam is often called *original guilt*, and included in the definition of original sin. Paul works out the thought of original guilt – the thought, that is, that when one sinned, 'all sinned' and by reason of his act 'became sinners' – in Romans 5:12, 15–19.

2. It is a state of *defilement*. This shows us the sinner's relation to God as the Holy One. In Old Testament times, God took pains, by means of various taboos and purity rituals in matters of food and hygiene, to teach the lesson that there are some things that make men unfit for fellowship with him, because they make men unclean – dirty, as it were, and therefore offensive and unacceptable – in his sight. Our Lord set aside and cancelled these typical enactments, declaring emphatically that what defiles a man is not food at all, but sin. 'Perceive ye not, that whatsoever from without goeth into the man, it cannot defile him . . . ? This he said, making all meats clean. And he said, That which proceedeth out of the man, that defileth the man . . . evil thoughts . . . fornications, thefts, murders, adulteries, covetings, wickednesses, deceit, lasciviousness, an evil eye, railing, pride, foolishness . . .' (Mk. 7:18 ff., RV). Isaiah had learned this long before. When he heard the seraphs proclaim the holiness of God in the temple, he was forced to cry 'Woe is me! . . . for I am a man of unclean lips', and to own himself unfit for God's fellowship and, indeed, 'lost' – doomed – because of the adverse reaction to his uncleanness that a holy God must show (Is. 6:3-5).

3. It is a state of *depravity*. This shows us the relation

between the sinner's present state and the image of God in which he was made. That image was, essentially, uprightness (*cf*. Ec. 7:29): man as God made him had a mind to know God's will and a heart to take pleasure in it, love it and do it. It was man's nature then to be holy, as God is holy. But it is not so now. Man's mind is darkened to spiritual things, his will is alienated from God's will, his conscience is insensitive to God's voice (*cf*. Eph. 4:18 f.). He has become, not merely weak, but bad in God's sight; he is positively perverse and ungodly (Rom. 5:6). Morally and spiritually, his character bears Satan's image, not God's; which is what Scripture means when it speaks of fallen men as the devil's children (Jn. 8:44; Mt. 13:38; Acts 13:10; 1 Jn. 3:8).

This depravity, or perversion of God's image, is commonly, and rightly, said to be *total*: not in the sense that everything in man is as bad as it could be, but that nothing in man is as good as it should be. Nothing that man does, no exercise of any faculty, is good without qualification in God's sight. Even when moral men 'do by nature what the law requires' (as they not infrequently do: Rom. 2:14; *cf*. Mt. 7:11), their hearts are wrong; each action is viciously self-regarding in some way, for the sinner's motive is always something more (and therefore something less) than pure love to God, a pure regard for his will and a pure desire for his glory. There is always corruption somewhere in every human action. God, who reads the heart, sees it, even if man does not. 'In me (that is, in my flesh,) dwelleth no good thing' (Rom. 7:18, RV).

4. It is a state of *inability*. This shows us the sinner's relation to God as Lawgiver, and to the precepts of his law. God has not changed his holy law since the fall (how could he?). He still demands of us perfect love to himself and to our neighbour. His right to command, and the rightness of what he commands, is not affected by the depraving of our nature. What is affected is our ability to obey his commands. Adam, before he fell, had it in him to obey God, but we have not. How can we love God while our deepest inner impulse is one of enmity towards him? We cannot. 'The mind of the flesh is enmity against God; for it is not subject to

the law of God, neither indeed can it be: and they that are in the flesh cannot please God' (Rom. 8:7 f., RV). And when God commands those who are in the flesh to repent (Acts 17:31) and believe on his Son (Jn. 6:28 f.) they cannot do it till their hearts are made new (*cf.* Jn. 3:5; 6:44; 1 Cor. 2:14).

Are our wills free, then? The simplest answer is that our wills are free, but we men are not. Our wills are free in the sense that we have power to do what we will in the realm of moral action, but we ourselves, as heirs of Adam, are slaves of sin (Jn. 8:34; Rom. 3:9; 6:16–23); which really means that we shall never in fact will with all our hearts to do the will of God. Therefore man in the state of sin can never please God. His tragedy lies precisely in the fact that his will is free, and that he has power to do what he wants and chooses to do; for what he wants and chooses is always in some form self-glorifying, and so sinful and ungodly, and hence all that he does increases his condemnation.

5. It is a state of *wrath*. This word sets before us the sinner's relation to God as King, and as such Judge (for in Bible times kings were judges, just as before the monarchy Israel's judges were in effect kings). In the Old Testament, the divine King is a warrior, doing battle against his enemies, active in wrath to bring disaster on them. In the New Testament, sinners are his enemies (Rom. 5:10) and stand under his wrath (Rom. 1:18 ff.). The Lord of all things, who is the Judge of all the earth (Gn. 18:25), is against them now, and if he is against them, then all things are against them. He rules his world, but not for their good (see Rom. 1:18 – 2:16; 1 Thes. 2:14-16; Rev. 6:15–17).

6. It is a state of *death*. Life and death, in Scripture, are not primarily physiological concepts, but spiritual and theological ideas. Life means fellowship with God in the knowledge of his love; death means being without this. Sinners are in a state of death (Eph. 2:1) and have no prospect save more of the same (Rom. 6:23).

The knowledge of sin
The deepest division between men in this world may be put as follows: some have knowledge of sin, and some do not.

This division is not only between the church and the world; it exists in the church too. By knowledge of sin I do not mean discernment of others' sins, with virtuous indignation against them. We all sometimes have that, as did the Pharisee in Christ's story who thanked God that he was not like other men such as the tax-collector (Lk. 18:11 f.). But by knowledge of sin I mean rather an awareness of one's own guilt, perversity, uncleanness and lack of moral and spiritual power as seen by God. Whether such knowledge is ours or not does not depend on whether we live morally or immorally by conventional standards, or whether our chosen lifestyle is orderly and controlled as opposed to wild and random. All that can be said about lifestyle is that if you are *not* one of those who squeeze their living into a mould of conventional respectability so that men will think well of them, you may perhaps be more in touch with yourself and better able to see that the biblical diagnosis of sin is a cap that fits you. In Jesus' day this was true of tax-collectors and other disreputables ('sinners') as against the Pharisees, and the pattern has often repeated itself since. The late great Peter Sellers, that marvellous character actor who gave the world Grytpype-Thynne, Henry Crun, Major Bloodnok, Bluebottle, Fred Kite, Inspector Clouseau, the President of the United States, Dr Strangelove, the dreaded Fu Manchu and many many more, said frankly that he did not know who or what he was apart from the roles he played, and writers about him have spoken of the mask behind the mask. In similar fashion religion can be a role-play producing the state of mind which Psalm 36:2 ascribes to the wicked: 'in his own eyes he flatters himself too much to detect or hate his sin' (NIV).

What does it mean to know sin in yourself? It is more than knowing that sometimes you are not quite perfect – though some find it hard to get that far. It means noticing the self-regarding motives – self-asserting, self-advancing, self-justifying, self-gratifying – that fuel your everyday actions. It means seeing that these motives disclose your real self, for they come from your 'heart' – not of course the blood pump, but the real though largely hidden core of our personhood, out of which, as Jesus said, come 'evil thoughts, sexual immorality, theft, murder, adultery, greed, malice, deceit, lewdness, envy, slander, arrogance and folly' (Mk. 7:21 f., NIV). 'The heart is deceitful above all things, and desperately corrupt,' declared God through Jeremiah (17:9 f.); 'who can understand it? I the Lord search the mind and try the heart....' Knowledge of sin means facing the fact that in our fallenness we cannot put our heart into the self-denial, self-humbling, cross-bearing and laying down our life for others which God requires. Some, to be sure, can enjoy going through religious motions – East and West are full of folk for whom this is a fulfilling ego-trip – but no fallen man naturally enjoys the hardships and deprivations of self-abandonment to the living God to whom Teresa of Avila was once bold to say: 'Lord, if this is how you treat your friends, I do not wonder that you have so few.' Finally, knowledge of sin means knowing that you need forgiveness, and that without it you have no hope of fellowship with God.

How does knowledge of sin come? Through God's law, says Paul – the law which reflects God's character and expresses his will for our living, and of which elements are written in every man's conscience (*cf.* Rom. 2:14 f.); the law which was given at Sinai and spelt out by prophets, apostles and Jesus himself. 'Whatever the law says, it says to those who are under the law, so that every mouth may be silenced and the whole world held accountable to God... through the law we become conscious of sin' (Rom. 3:19 f., NIV). Evidently when Paul says 'law' he means standards of living to God in worship as well as living for men by service; standards of required good as well as specifics of forbidden evil; the demand for constant perfection (*cf.* Jas. 2:10) which goes beyond occasional spasmodic effort; and the declaration of retributive judgment on law-breakers. Now in making us conscious of sin, so Paul tells us, the law functions thus:

1. It *identifies* sin, defining and picturing it.
2. It *stirs up* disobedience. Sin is a kind of allergy in the moral and spiritual system of fallen man, an anomalous

reaction to God's law; it breaks out irrationally in an uprush of desire contrary to the divine command. 'I should not have known what it is to covet if the law had not said, "You shall not covet." But sin, finding opportunity in the commandment, wrought in me all kinds of covetousness' (Rom. 7:7 f.). Anyone who ever tries to keep any of God's laws at motivational level, schooling himself to desire only what God wants, has a similar experience. Thus each of us may verify our own total depravity, if hitherto we have doubted it.

3. The law *condemns* the disobedience it foments, so making us see ourselves as we really are – that is, guilty before God, doomed to death. 'When the commandment came, sin revived and I died…for sin, finding opportunity in the commandment, deceived me [by breaking through my defences at one point while I was busy repelling it at another] and by it killed me [*i.e.,* brought me into the living death of knowing every moment that I was lost]' (Rom. 7:9, 11).

Thus, by inducing self-despair, the law teaches us to look away from ourselves and our fancied moral achievement and to come as sinners to Jesus Christ to be forgiven. That this should happen is part of God's plan of mercy. As Luther once explained it, 'As long as sins are unknown, there is no room for a cure, and no hope of one; for sins that think they betoken health and need no physician will not endure the healer's hand. The law is therefore necessary to give knowledge of sin, so that proud man, who thought he was whole, may be humbled by the discovery of his own great wickedness, and sigh and pant after the grace that is set forth in Christ' (*The Bondage of the Will,* tr. J. I. Packer and O. R. Johnston, p.288). In Paul's own words, 'The law was our custodian [*paidagōgos,* the slave put in charge of the child's education] until Christ came, that we might be justified by faith' (Gal. 3:24).

It should be added that Jesus Christ, God's incarnate Son, can truly be described not only as grace incarnate but also as law incarnate. His life and teaching set holiness before us in a way that both instructs and condemns us, and for many Christians meditating on Jesus' words and ways has done more to arouse and deepen a sense of sin than anything else. Nor can we ever think of sin more profoundly than as everything we are, morally and spiritually, that Jesus was not. We said earlier that knowledge of sin comes through knowledge of God; now we should add, through knowledge of God incarnate most of all.

The deceitfulness of sin

We live in an age when all too little stress is laid on the standards of God's law, and the moral example of Christ. It would be good for us to hear more of these matters. Yet more is needed to produce a sense of sin than just highlighting standards. For sin itself, which as we saw Paul personalizes as deceiving and killing people, has at its command what can only be called a kind of anti-rational intelligence that works within us, using fantasies, illusions, unrealities of all sorts, wishful thinking, rationalization, distraction and a hundred and one anaesthetics for the mind. Sin's goal is twofold: to remove barriers to self-destroying ungodliness, and to set up barriers against repentance (not just sorrow at wrong done, but actual turning from it for the future). Sin allures us into both wrongdoing and the comforting conclusion that one is spiritually all right as one is. Sin's method is *deceit*. Paul speaks of '*deceitful* lusts' that have to be renounced (Eph. 4:22); he is reminding his readers that our sinful desires present themselves to us whitewashed, or disguised as the right thing to do, assuring us that we may freely indulge and all will be well. Hebrews 3:13 warns against being 'hardened by the *deceitfulness* of sin' as it tries to fog our minds on the issues of eternity – particularly, in context, on the need for persistence in faith as the way to final glory, which the hard-pressed and bemused Hebrew Christians were being tempted to forget.

Sin's technique of deception is multiform. Temptation exploits both our temperamental weaknesses and our temperamental strengths (so 'let any one who thinks that he stands take heed lest he fall,' 1 Cor. 10:12). Sin can entangle our minds in a devilish sort of situation ethics whereby we conclude that, whatever might be proper to other situations or for other people, circumstances make what I want to do now all right for me this time. Also, sin can paralyse our minds, so mesmerizing us by the dazzling prospect of what it is open to us to do that reason and conscience cannot get a word in edgeways. (Afterwards we shall say, 'I didn't think,' and how right we shall be.) Sins of exploiting people, manipulating systems, ducking responsibilities, withholding goodwill and working out resentments regularly issue from minds that are entangled; sins of sex, greed and violence regularly reflect a mind temporarily switched off, a state of affairs to which alcohol, drugs and exhaustion can contribute disastrously. James' diagnosis covers all cases: 'each person is tempted when he is lured and enticed by his own desire. Then desire when it has conceived gives birth to sin; and sin when it is full-grown brings forth death' (Jas. 1:14 f.).

Hardening (Heb. 3:13; *cf.* Eph. 4:18 f.; 1 Tim. 4:2) is the process whereby one ceases to have a conscience about evil that one is doing, or attitudes of pride, godlessness, love-lessness, brutality, hatred, contempt or whatever that one is indulging. Habit produces hardening, and hardening, insofar as it destroys the sense of sin, rules out the possibility of repentance.

We need to realize that sin works restlessly within us to produce its horrific effects all the time, and that only divine grace can overcome it. The psalmists prayed for knowledge of their sin through grace so that they might forsake it through grace. 'Search me, O God, and know my heart! Try me and know my thoughts! And see if there be any wicked way in me, and lead me in the way everlasting!' (Ps. 139:23 f.; *cf.* Pss. 19:12–14; 119:29). We shall do well to make these prayers our own.

6
THE DEVIL

For over a century now, belief in the devil has seemed to be on the way out. The toothy red imp with the tail and the trident has become a secular figure of fun, while Protestant theologians generally have banished the personal devil of the Bible to the lumber-room reserved for broken-down myths. No doubt this state of affairs is just what the devil has been working for, since it allows him to operate now on the grandest scale without being either detected or opposed. Nor has he wasted his chances. During the past hundred years, he has engineered a world-wide collapse of evangelicalism in all the older Protestant denominations. The present spineless, powerless, unevangelical state of these churches, as compared with what they were a century ago, gives heart-breaking proof of the skill and thoroughness with which he has done his job. The Bible is no longer fully believed, the gospel is no longer thoroughly preached, and post-Christian paganism sweeps through the world like wildfire. Not for centuries has Satan won such a victory.

Was it rational and enlightened, as liberal theologians thought, to give up belief in the devil? Not particularly. The natural response to denials of Satan's existence is to ask, who then runs his business? – for temptations which look and feel like expressions of cunning destructive malice remain facts of daily life. So does hell in the sense defined by the novelist John Updike – 'a profound and desolating absence' (of God, and good, and community and communication); and 'the realisation that life is flawed' (Updike goes on) 'admits the possibility of a Fall, of a cause behind the Fall, of Satan.' Belief in Satan is not illogical, for it fits the facts. Inept to the point of idiocy, however, is disbelief in Satan, in a world like ours; which makes Satan's success in producing such disbelief all the more impressive, as well as all the sadder.

In recent years something of an antidote to the habit of denying Satan has been administered by the charismatic movement's heavy stress on spiritual warfare against the demons and the devil, their general. It was right to take seriously this aspect of New Testament Christianity, but wisdom has not always marked the emphasis. Firstly, demon-possession of unbelievers and demonic attacks on Christians have not been sufficiently distinguished from such forms of mental illness and collapse as yield to rest and drugs. In the gospels, demon-possession is known not just by disintegration of personhood, but also by recognition of Jesus' identity and authority as Son of God, and hostility towards him. Only when this factor appears can demon-possession ever be diagnosed with confidence. Secondly, the assumption that demon-possession today might be as common a problem as in Jesus' day is doubtful. From Acts and the epistles it does not look as if it was a common problem even in the apostolic age. The natural way to read the evidence is to suppose that the coming to earth of the Son of God stirred up a great deal of demonic activity which subsided after his ascension. It is to be feared that the preoccupation of some with finding demons everywhere is really an obsessional ego-trip, which Satan can use as a smoke-screen for his real work of spiritual corruption no less effectively than he can use disbelief in his existence to that end.

From all this it is surely clear that Satan is a person whom churches and Christians ignore at their peril. The New Testament repeatedly cautions us against ignoring him. Paul never fell into this trap: he took the measure of the devil, and could say with truth, 'we are not ignorant of his designs' – 'I am up to his tricks', as a modern scholar puts it (2 Cor. 2:11). It is vitally important that we today should be able to say the same. Like it or not, each of us is personally at war with the devil, for the devil has personally declared war upon each of us. Face this, Paul urges, and learn how to fight him, 'that you may be able to stand against the wiles of the devil. For we wrestle...against principalities, against the powers.... Therefore take the whole armour of God, that you may be able to withstand in the evil day' (Eph. 6:11 ff.). The Christian's life is not a bed of roses; it is a battlefield, on which he has constantly to fight for his life. The first rule of success in war is – *know your enemy*. The purpose of this present study is to enable us to know and to assess Satan, in order that we may fight him effectively.

Difficulties of demonology
It is hard to have right thoughts about the devil; for, in the first place, that branch of demonology which deals with him is entirely a matter of revelation, and, in the second place, our demonology cannot be any more true or adequate than our doctrine of God is. We can see the truth about the devil only in the light of the truth about God. Demonology concerns one aspect – the basic aspect – of the mystery of evil. Evil has to be understood as a lack, or perversion, of good, and we know what good is only when we know what God is. Only through appreciating God's goodness can we form any idea of the devil's badness.

A pitfall, then, confronts us at once: if our thoughts of God are false, our thoughts of the devil will be false too. For instance: if, with many, we should imagine God as every man's heavenly uncle, a person whose job (not always too well done) is to help us achieve our selfish desires for irresponsible fun and carefree comfort, we shall think of Satan as merely a cosmic sour-puss whose sole aim is to thwart our plans and spoil our pleasures. But this is really no nearer to the truth about Satan than the celestial Santa Claus idea is to the truth about God.

The knife-edge
Moreover, when we study demonology we walk on a knife-edge; at our feet all the time are two yawning chasms of error, into which we can all too easily topple. On the one hand, we can take Satan too seriously, as some in the early church and the Middle Ages did. This will cause us to fall out of the peace of God into morbid fears and fancies: the

devil will become the main theme of our theology, and we shall take up a negative view of the Christian life as primarily a course of devil-dodging exercises and anti-Satanic manoeuvres. This was the mistake that led men to become monks and hermits in the early church: they withdrew from ordinary life in order to fight the devil full-time and without distraction, believing that they could not otherwise keep clear of his clutches. The root of their mistake was unbelief: they would not trust God to keep them safe if they stayed in the world (see Jn. 17:15). They were vividly aware that the devil is an adversary of terrible malice and great power, but they failed to realize that by virtue of Christ's cross he is now a defeated foe. The biblical answer to their fears was given by the Reformers and Puritans, who, without minimizing in the least the devil's ferocity against the people of God, offered a worthy exposition of the triumph of Calvary, the scope of Christ's promises, and the reality of his keeping power.

On the other hand, we can also err by not taking the devil seriously enough. This, as has been said, is the characteristic mistake of modern times. The denial that Satan is a personal agent is an extreme form of it. Unwillingness to take the devil seriously has two bad effects: it fools men, by keeping from them the knowledge of their danger as objects of the devil's attacks, and it dishonours Christ by robbing the cross of its significance as a conquest of Satan and his hosts (*cf.* Col. 2:15).

The only way to avoid these mistakes (both of which, we may be sure, please Satan enormously) is to stick close to Scripture. To Scripture, therefore, we now turn.

Portrait of Satan
Peter speaks of 'your adversary the devil' (1 Pet 5:8). 'Adversary' is what the Hebrew word 'Satan' means; 'devil' (Greek *diabolos*) means 'slanderer'. Both terms point to the same basic truth – that it is Satan's nature to think, speak and act in constant malicious opposition to God the Creator, and therefore to God's people also. The devil is '*your* adversary' just because he is *God's* adversary. Man is

God's creature, made in God's image to enjoy God's glory; Satan's ambition ever since man was made has been to deface that image and thwart God's will for our life and destiny.

Satan is an angel, one of the 'sons of God' (Jb. 1:6; 2:1) – but a fallen one. He is one of 'the angels that sinned' (2 Pet. 2:4, AV), 'that did not keep their own position but left their proper dwelling' (Jude 6). He is now 'the commander of the spiritual powers of the air' (Eph. 2:2, NEB), leading 'the superhuman forces of evil in the heavens' (Eph. 6:12, NEB). In order to tempt, he can become 'an angel of light' (2 Cor. 11:14), but his rule is more properly described as 'the power of darkness'. This is darkness in the broadest sense – intellectual, moral and spiritual (Col. 1:13; *cf.* Lk. 22:53). Scripture pictures the devil as a serpent (Gn. 3:1; Rev. 20:2), a dragon (Rev. 12; 20:2), and a roaring lion (1 Pet. 5:8). This indicates his cunning, hatred, ferocity and cruelty against the people of God. Scripture also calls him the tempter (Mt. 4:3; 1 Thes. 3:5), the evil one (Jn. 17:15, RV), a liar and a murderer (Jn. 8:44). These words indicate the character and aim of the strategy with which he assaults us.

Satan was the original sinner. 'The devil has sinned from the beginning' (1 Jn. 3:8). We are told no more about the premundane revolt of the fallen angels than that it took place. The Bible is a practical book, and never spends time on things that have no direct bearing on our lives. Some have thought that the terms in which the proud kings of Tyre and Babylon are described in Ezekiel 28:11–19 and Isaiah 14:12–14 respectively owe their origin to traditional accounts of the fall of Satan, whose image these arrogant monarchs strikingly bore, but the matter is incapable of proof. What is clear, however, is that from the very moment of the creation of this world Satan was on the scene, a rebel against God, seeking by deceit (the first lie, Gn. 3:4 f.; *cf.* 2 Cor. 11:3) to involve Adam and Eve in a similar rebellion.

His mentality
The mentality of Satan is a mystery whose depths we can never fully plumb: not just because Satan is an angel, while

we are men, but also because Satan is purely evil, and we cannot conceive what pure evil is like. No man is so far gone in sin that no vestige of goodness or truth remains in him; no man is wholly motivated by hatred of others; no man has literally no aim in life save to wreck and destroy the creative achievements of another; no man ever says to himself in literally every situation and every sphere of value, 'evil, be thou my good'; no man's character is integrated solely by the power of hate towards God. Though in fallen man God's image is spoiled at every point, so that nothing man does is ever entirely right and as it should be, none of us is purely evil, and we simply cannot imagine a being who is purely evil. We can never, therefore, form a really adequate idea of what Satan is like. Not even Milton could imagine Satan as entirely lacking in nobility; nor is C. S. Lewis's Screwtape entirely without good humour. But Scripture clearly means us to believe in a Satan, and a host of Satanic myrmidons, who are of quite unimaginable badness – more cruel, more malicious, more proud, more scornful, more perverted, more destructive, more disgusting, more filthy, more despicable, than anything our minds can conceive.

One certainty is that, like other professional liars, Satan has at one point at least lost his grip on reality. There is a maggot in his mind, a softening of his brain we might say, which compels him to deny that he is a captive and beaten foe and to believe that if he fights hard enough against God and God's true children he will overthrow them in the end. Like Hitler in his bunker, Satan cannot bring himself to believe that he has lost the war, and cannot now win. In Revelation 12:12 a voice from heaven warns the earth that 'the devil has come down to you in great wrath, because he knows that his time is short!'. Evidently this knowledge takes the form of a furious denial and a vigorous attempt to prove that it is not so, just as fallen man's natural knowledge of God regularly takes the form of a willed, defiant non-acknowledgment of him. But the intense energy of denial proves that the knowledge is there.

There is not much in the Old Testament about Satan, though when he does appear it is always as the adversary of

God's people, trying to exclude them from God's favour either by leading them into irreligious attitudes and actions (disobedience, Gn. 3; presumption, 1 Ch. 21:1; blasphemy and despair, Jb. 1:6 – 2:10) or by slandering them to God's face (Jb. 1:9 ff.; 2:3 ff.; Zc. 3:1 f.; *cf.* the description of satan as 'the accuser of our brethren...who accuses them day and night before our God', Rev. 12:10).

In the New Testament, however, the revelation of Satan is much fuller. It there becomes clear that his power is exceedingly great. He can manipulate physical events (2 Thes. 2:9; *cf.* Jb. 1:2) and suggest to the mind wrong thoughts (Mt. 4:3 ff.). Not only that; he can also inflict disease (Lk. 13:16) and even death (Heb. 2:14). Worse still, he actually holds mankind prisoner behind the locked doors of spiritual darkness and unbelief. He 'is now at work in the sons of disobedience' (Eph. 2:2) to make and keep them blind to God's truth (2 Cor. 4:4) and out of line with God's will, until the time comes to end their lives and so fix their eternal state as one of pain, grief and loss. In this way the devil acts as, first, the gaoler, and ultimately the executioner, of the entire human race. 'The whole world is in the power of the evil one' (1 Jn. 5:19). From Christ's standpoint, the world which he came to save was enemy-occupied territory, Satan being its 'prince' (Greek *archōn*, ruler: Jn. 12:31; 14:30; 16:11) – indeed, its 'god' (2 Cor. 4:4).

His captivity

Not that Satan holds any power independently of God. Satan (though doubtless he has never admitted it, nor will ever believe it) is God's tool. In allowing Satan as much power as he does, God is using him to execute divine judgment on a rebel world. Just as a man can make use of a savage dog which hates him, to drive trespassers off his estate, so God makes use of Satan to punish those who have sinned. Satan and the demons are themselves in a prison-state, and have been since their fall: they are 'kept in everlasting bonds under darkness unto the judgement of the great day' (Jude 6, RV; see Mt. 25:41; Rev. 20:10). They are all in chains. They never have any more freedom of movement than God allows them; and in all that they do, as Calvin said, they drag their chains with them. Satan likes to think, and likes others to think, that he is this world's real ruler (*cf*. Lk. 4:6). The truth is that he cannot exert any power beyond the limits that God sets him (*cf*. Jb. 1:12; 2:6). God keeps him on a chain: it may be a long chain, but it is a real one.

When the Son of God came into the world 'to destroy the works of the devil' (1 Jn. 3:8), Satan used every means to thwart him – and failed. In everything Christ conquered. Not only at the start of his ministry (Mt. 4:1 ff.), but consistently throughout it (Lk. 4:13; 22:28), Satan tempted him to swerve in one way or another from the Father's will (*cf*. Mt. 16:22 f.). But Jesus never fell into Satan's traps; not once did he sin (Heb. 4:15; 1 Pet. 2:22); he repelled all his adversary's attacks, and went on triumphantly to rob Satan of a great part of the dominion that he had hitherto enjoyed. Jesus did this, first by his healings and exorcisms (Lk. 11:17–22; 13:16), and finally by his prayers (Lk. 22:31 f.; Jn. 17:15) and his atoning death. This made certain the salvation of all that great company whom he came to redeem (Jn. 12:31 f.). Calvary was thus a decisive victory over Satan and Satan's hosts (Col. 2:15), which made certain the subsequent dethroning of the devil from life after life. The cross ensured that countless numbers would be 'delivered ... from the dominion of darkness and transferred ... to the kingdom of his beloved Son, in whom we have redemption, the forgiveness of sins' (Col. 1:13 f.). This comes to pass through the preaching of the gospel which summons men to turn from Satan to God (Acts 26:18), and the concurrent work of Christ from heaven who moves men to the response of faith and repentance (Acts 5:31). Satan resists every time and every step of the way, but he cannot stop it happening. He is a decisively beaten foe.

The holy war
A man who is not a Christian is Satan's prisoner: Satan has him where he wants him. If, however, he becomes a Christian, Satan views him as an escaped prisoner, and goes to

war against him to try to recapture him. He tempts (*i.e.* tests) the Christian with malicious intent, hoping to find a weakness and betray him into a course of action that will ultimately lead him back into the prison out of which Christ brought him. Satan seeks to 'enter into' the Christian, as he entered into Judas (Lk. 22:3; Jn. 13:27), *i.e.* to recover control of him and so make him a 'son of the devil' once more (Acts 13:10; 1 Jn. 3:10). All Satan's temptations have this ultimately in view: they are so many 'welcome' notices set up along the broad road that leads to destruction.

His tools

How does Satan tempt? By 'wiles', *i.e.* deceit (Eph. 6:11; *cf.* 2 Cor. 11:3). Normally he keeps out of sight, manipulating 'the world' (external stimuli) and 'the flesh' (inordinate desire within us) as his tools of seduction. Sometimes he works through seemingly innocent wishes and wants (*cf.* Gn. 3:6; Lk. 4:2 f.), or well-meant advice from our friends (*cf.* Mt. 16:22 f.). There is no limit to his subtlety. He has his own servants even in the church (Mt. 13:38), playing the part of pastors and theologians (2 Cor. 11:13–15); they do not, of course, suspect that their teaching and leadership represent Satanic perversions of Christianity, but they do, and Satan makes full use of them accordingly. 'When Satan gets into the pulpit, or the theological chair, and pretends to teach Christianity, when in reality he is corrupting it... pretends to be teaching Biblical Introduction, when in reality he is making the Bible out to be a book that is not worthy of being introduced – then look out for him; he is at his most dangerous work' (R. A. Torrey, *What the Bible Teaches,* p.517). Wrong beliefs about God (*e.g.* resentment and despair, *cf.* 2 Cor. 12:7), wrong conduct in the sight of God (*cf.* 1 Cor. 7:5) – these are the tactical ends for which Satan works, and he has a hundred and one ways of beguiling us into them.

Let us be clear on this. Satan has no constructive purpose of his own; his tactics are simply to thwart God and destroy men. As David Livingstone's motto was 'anywhere, provided it be forward', so Satan's is, in effect, 'anything, provided it be against God'. He is always seeking to produce unbelief, pride, unreality, false hopes, confusion of mind and disobedience, as he did in Eden; if he cannot do this directly, then he labours to do it indirectly, by fostering unbalance and one-sidedness. Living the Christian life is like playing a piece of music on the piano: if you get the notes wrong, you fail; if you get the notes right but the tempo, rhythm, volume or expression wrong you still fail; only when both notes and style are right does the performance succeed. Satan tries both to trap us into doing what is formally wrong and also to distort enough of what is formally right in our habits and actions to make it wrong in its effect. Thought without action, love without wisdom, love of truth without love of people or vice versa, zeal with error, orthodoxy with unrighteousness, conscientiousness with morbidity and despair, selectiveness in one's concern for what is true and right, are samples of this kind of distortion. If we watch against Satan at one point on the battlements of our living, he will try to break in at another, waiting for a moment when we feel secure and happy, and our defences are likely to be down. So it goes on, all day and every day.

Our weapons

What security have we against his attacks? How can we avoid falling victim to them? The only security, as Paul forcefully tells us, is to take to ourselves 'the whole armour of God' – the girdle of truth (the biblical gospel); the breastplate of righteousness (the integrity of an honest conscience); the firmness of stance provided by the gospel of peace (assurance of being reconciled to God); the shield of faith (active trust in Christ and his promises); the helmet of salvation (confidence in Christ's keeping power, now and for ever); and 'the sword of the Spirit, which is the word of God', the weapon with which our Lord routed Satan in the wilderness. Take these weapons, says Paul, 'pray at all times in the Spirit, with all prayer and supplication', and you need not fear Satan's attacks; you will recognize them and be able to resist them (Eph. 6:11–18).

We need not fear the outcome of this fight. For, in the first place, *God is always overruling when Satan tempts.* He will not allow us to be tempted beyond our strength (1 Cor. 10:13); indeed, he exposes us to temptation only in order to make us stronger (1 Pet. 5:6–10), and he has promised to crush Satan in due course under his servants' feet (Rom. 16:20).

And then, in the second place, *Satan always flees when we resist.* 'Resist the devil and he will flee from you' (Jas. 4:7). Pray, and fight; ask Christ to stand by you, and tell the devil to get away from you; and for the moment, at any rate, he has to withdraw. It is remarkable that Paul's inventory of the Christian armour includes nothing to protect the back! We are given no promise of protection if we run away, but we are promised victory every time we stand and give battle. Satan is a defeated and doomed foe; therefore *'Resist him, firm in your faith. . . . And . . . the God of all grace, who has called you to his eternal glory in Christ, will himself restore, establish, and strengthen you. To him be the dominion for ever and ever. Amen'* (1 Pet. 5:9–11).

7
GRACE

In the New Testament, 'grace' is a word of central importance – the keyword, in fact, of Christianity. Grace is what the New Testament is about. Its God is 'the God of all grace' (1 Pet. 5:10); its Holy Spirit is 'the Spirit of grace' (Heb. 10:29); and all the hopes that it sets forth rest upon 'the grace of the Lord Jesus' (Acts 15:11), the Lord who upheld Paul with the assurance, 'my grace is sufficient for you' (2 Cor. 12:9). 'Grace', says John, 'came by Jesus Christ' (Jn. 1:17); and the news about Jesus is accordingly 'the gospel of the grace of God' (Acts 20:24). The apostles' belief in the reality and centrality of grace was so strong that it led them to invent a new style of letter-writing. Instead of the conventional 'hail', the opening greeting of all Paul's thirteen letters takes the form of a prayer for 'grace and peace', or 'grace, mercy, and peace', from God the Father and the Lord Jesus Christ, to be upon his readers; and in place of the usual 'farewell', each letter ends with a further prayer that 'the grace of the Lord Jesus Christ', or 'grace' simply, may be with them. Both Peter's Epistles, and that of Jude, and the Revelation, have similar salutations (*cf.* 2 Jn. 3), and Hebrews and Revelation have similar forms of closure, while 2 Peter ends with the plea, 'grow in the grace...of our Lord Jesus Christ' (3:18). And everything that comes between the salutation and the benediction of these letters illustrates the truth that grace was to the apostles the fundamental fact of Christian life.

It is often said, and truly, that the theme of the New Testament is salvation. But the New Testament salvation is of grace from first to last (Eph. 2:5, 8); it is the grace of God that brings it (Tit. 2:11), and the praise of the glory of God's grace that is the end of it (Eph. 1:6). It thus appears that, rightly understood, this one word 'grace' contains within itself the whole of New Testament theology. The New Testament message is just the announcement that grace has come to men in and through Jesus Christ, plus a summons from God to receive this grace (Rom. 5:17; 2 Cor. 6:1), and to know it (Col. 1:6), and not to frustrate it (Gal. 2:21), but to continue in it (Acts 13:43), since 'the word of his grace... is able to build you up, and to give you the inheritance among all those who are sanctified' (Acts 20:32). Grace is the sum and substance of New Testament faith.

The thought of grace, then, is the key that unlocks the New Testament; and it is the only key that does so. However well we may know the wording of the New Testament, we cannot get inside its meaning till we know something of what grace is. This is why so many people find the New Testament bewildering and baffling (especially the letters of that great champion of grace, Paul), and why they so easily misunderstand it. Persons, even religious persons, ignorant of grace who try to read the New Testament as a book of moral maxims, or mystical aspirations, cannot make head or tail of it. Every book of the New Testament is part of a great organic analysis, historical and theological, of the fact of grace, and must be read as such. We cannot make sense of the New Testament in any other terms.

Unhappily, however, the meaning of grace is not well appreciated today. For the past century and more, this topic has been so neglected by some, and mishandled by others, that the clear and profound understanding of it which the Reformers and Puritans and eighteenth-century Evangelicals bequeathed to their posterity has almost vanished from the British religious scene. The word 'grace' remains as part of our religious vocabulary, and we regularly hear it used in public prayer ('grant us the help of thy grace...', 'give us grace that we may...'). But to many it suggests only vague notions of a celestial battery-charge administered through the sacraments, while to more (one fears) it signifies nothing whatsoever. And meantime many practise in the name of Christianity forms of religion which frustrate and deny the grace of God completely. Both the

95

legalism of the Roman Catholic doctrine of depending for salvation on loyalty to an ecclesiastical system, and the moralism of the liberal Protestant doctrine that all will be saved who try, even a little, to be good, spring from the same root cause – failure to grasp the meaning of grace. No need in Christendom is more urgent than the need for a renewed awareness of what the grace of God really is. Christians long to see reformation and revival in the churches; today as yesterday, it is only from a rediscovery of grace that these blessings will flow.

The nature of grace

Grace is God's undeserved favour, his unmerited love. The word translated 'grace' in the New Testament (*charis*) is used in the Greek Old Testament to render the Hebrew *chen*, also translated 'grace' in AV, which signifies the 'favour' that a suppliant 'finds' in the eyes of a superior person from whom he cannot claim favourable treatment as of right. (For examples of this on the human level, see Gn. 33:8, 15; 34:11; 47:25; Ru. 2:2, 10, 13.) *Chen*, writes Dr Norman Snaith, 'means kindness and graciousness in general – that is, where there is no particular tie or relationship between the parties concerned' (*A Theological Word Book of the Bible*, ed. A. Richardson, *s.v.* 'Grace', p.100). As Dr Snaith observes elsewhere, just because there is no antecedent bond between the parties, 'there is not the slightest breath of censure possible if such good favour is not granted' (*Distinctive Ideas of the Old Testament*, p.130). *Chen* – grace – is thus *free*, in the sense that the person who shows it is in no way obliged to show it. When the Old Testament speaks of individuals, or nations, finding grace in God's sight, or of God being gracious towards them, the stress is always on the fact that God is blessing where he was not bound to (see, *e.g.*, Gn. 6:8; Ex. 33:12 f., 16 f.; Am. 5:15; Jon. 4:2; *etc.*). Of Paul's choice of *charis* as his regular word for God's love, Dr Snaith rightly comments: 'Nothing impressed Paul more than the fact that God's love for men was a free gift from God, entirely undeserved on men's part, depending only upon God's own will' (*op. cit.*, p.176).

Nor is this the whole background of *charis* in the New Testament. It covers the meaning of two more key Old Testament terms. The first is God's *'ahabah,* from the verb *'aheb,* meaning 'love' – election love, as Dr Snaith calls it. This is the love whereby God chose Israel to be his people – spontaneous, selective, unconditional, unevoked, undeserved love (*cf.* Dt. 7:7 f.; 9:4 f.; Ho. 11:1–11). To render this, the Greek Old Testament coined the noun *agapē* which became the regular New Testament word for God's love. But 'love' and 'grace' in the New Testament are virtual synonyms, and *charis* includes all that *'ahabah* means.

The other term involved is God's *chesed.* This is usually rendered as 'mercy', 'pity' in the Septuagint (*eleos, eleemosunē*), and, following this, as 'mercy' or 'loving-kindness' in the AV; but the RSV rendering, 'steadfast love', is better, for the basic thought behind the word is of God's resolute loyalty to the people to whom he has pledged himself. Snaith calls it his covenant-love; it is essentially a matter of faithfulness to the covenant promise whereby he bound himself to be Israel's God and to use all the resources of deity to bless them. The Old Testament prophets constantly stress the fact that God's *chesed* stands firm even when Israel brings herself under temporary judgment by unfaithfulness to her own covenant obligation to serve God. They insist that, after chastening and purging visitations, God's purpose to deliver his people from evil and bring them into perfect fellowship with himself will ultimately triumph. God's *chesed* is as sovereign and efficacious as his *'ahabah* is unconditional and free.

The word 'grace' thus comes to express the thought of God acting in spontaneous goodness to save sinners: God loving the unlovely, making covenant with them, pardoning their sins, accepting their persons, revealing himself to them, moving them to response, leading them ultimately into full knowledge and enjoyment of himself, and overcoming all obstacles to the fulfilment of this purpose that at each stage arise. Grace is election-love plus covenant-love, a free choice issuing in a sovereign work. Grace saves from sin and all evil; grace brings ungodly men to true happiness in the knowledge of their Maker. This is the concept of grace with which the New Testament writers work.

Our word 'grace' is at best somewhat colourless, and often, as we saw, grace is irreligiously imagined to be an impersonal force canalized in some way through the ministrations of the church. Clearly, however, this travesties the biblical teaching. Nowhere does Scripture depict grace in this fashion. When the New Testament uses the word 'grace' for a particular divine gift (a status of acceptance, Rom. 5:1 f.; an ability for service, Rom. 12:6; Eph. 4:7; a Christian virtue, *e.g.* generosity, 2 Cor. 8:1, 4, 6 f.; a Christian privilege, *e.g.* preaching and teaching the gospel, Eph. 3:2, 7 f.; a part of salvation, *e.g.* final glory, 1 Pet. 1:13; *cf.* 3:7), or more generally for the outworking of God's favour in the transformation of men's lives (1 Cor. 15:10; 2 Cor. 4:15; 9:8, 14; 12:9; Jas. 4:6; 1 Pet. 5:5), the thought is always of the gift as God's personal bestowal, given as a proof of his affection towards the individual recipient. And this use of 'grace' for God's love-gifts is in any case secondary and derivative; the primary and fundamental reference of the word is to the love that gives them. (Compare, in English, 'favour' and 'favours'.)

Grace in the New Testament is not, then, an impersonal energy automatically switched on by prayer and sacraments, but the heart and hand of the living almighty God. Grace is certainly found in the church, for it is grace that creates the church, but grace is in no sense subject to the church's control. God's love is free, and it is God himself who chooses whom he will save. Sermons and sacraments proclaim the reality of grace, and the church's prayers invoke it, but it is God alone who exercises it and leads men into the benefits of it.

To the New Testament writers, grace is a wonder. Their sense of man's corruption and demerit before God, and of the reality and justice of his wrath against sin, is so strong that they find it simply staggering that there should be such a thing as grace at all – let alone grace that was so costly to God as the grace of Calvary. The hymn-writers catch this sense of wonder with their use of 'amazed' and 'amazing' in such lines as '*Amazing* love! how can it be That thou, my God, shouldst die for me?'; 'Love so *amazing,* so divine, Demands my soul, my life, my all'; 'I stand all *amazed* at the love Jesus offers me'; '*Amazing* grace!' The world is full of wonders – wonders of nature, wonders of science, wonders of craftsmanship – but they pale into insignificance beside the wonder of the grace of God. Nothing we say can do it justice: all words fall short of it: it is in truth, as Paul says, an 'inexpressible gift' (2 Cor. 9:15).

The riches of grace

The New Testament always connects grace with the Person and work of the Mediator, the God-Man Jesus Christ. 'Grace...came through *Jesus Christ*' (Jn. 1:17; *cf.* 1 Pet. 1:10). 'Be strong in the grace *that is in Christ Jesus*' (2 Tim. 2:1). 'Grace abounded...so that, as sin reigned in death, grace also might reign through righteousness [Jesus' obedience to death] to eternal life *through Jesus Christ our Lord*' (Rom. 5:20 f.). It is in union with the Person of Jesus, crucified and risen, and by virtue of his atonement, that men know grace, and it is faith in Christ – belief of the 'word of the cross' (1 Cor. 1:18), and trust in the risen Saviour – that is the means by which they enter into it. (This does not mean that there was no such thing as grace in Old Testament days; but it does mean that what grace there was – the covenant relationship, the pardon of sins, the joy of God's fellowship, the hope of reward – had reference to the coming Mediator, and the work that he was to do; also, that the faith which appropriated grace 'BC' was a faith that looked forward, however obscurely, to the promised Saviour. See Mk. 14:24; Rom. 3:24 f.; 1 Cor. 10:1–4; Gal. 3:6–14, 15 ff.; Heb. 9:15; 11:24 ff.; 1 Pet. 1:10.)

In the New Testament, the supreme expositor of grace is Paul, and his crowning expositions of grace are Romans 3 – 11, Galatians 2 – 5, Colossians 1 – 3, and Ephesians 1 – 3. In the latter passage, dwelling on God's 'great love with which he loved us' (Eph. 2:4), Paul several times uses the metaphor of *wealth,* speaking of God as 'rich in mercy' (*ibid.*; *cf.* Rom. 10:12), and of 'the riches of his grace' (1:7; 2:7), and of 'the riches of his glory' (3:16; *cf.* 1:18; Rom. 9:23), and of 'the unsearchable riches of Christ' (3:8).

What is this 'wealth' of benefit which comes to men by the grace of God in Christ? There are four focal points in Paul's analysis of it: redemption, regeneration, election and preservation.

Redemption is through Christ, by his death. In Christ, says Paul, 'we have redemption through his blood, the forgiveness of our trespasses according to the riches of his grace' (Eph. 1:7). Redemption means a costly rescue from jeopardy; here, Paul pin-points the jeopardy of guilt before God as that from which we are redeemed. In the same connection, he says elsewhere that we are justified by grace 'through the redemption which is in Christ Jesus' (Rom. 3:24; *cf.* Tit. 3:7). Paul points us to the cross of Christ as both proof of the reality of God's grace and as the final measure of it: 'God shows his love for us in that while we were yet sinners Christ died for us' (Rom. 5:8; *cf.* 1 Jn. 4:8–10).

Regeneration is in Christ, by union with him in his resurrection. Paul expounds it as a co-quickening with Christ (Eph. 2:1, 5 f.; Rom 6:4 ff.; Col. 2:12; 3:1 ff.), and stresses that it springs from the mercy and grace of God alone (Eph. 2:4; Tit. 3:5). Regeneration is the necessary complement of redemption, for without it there is no faith in the Redeemer, and therefore no benefit from his death. Part of the meaning of the spiritual 'death' which is our natural state (Eph. 2:1, 5; Col. 2:13) is that we are impotent to turn to Christ in repentance and faith; part of the effect of regeneration, however, is that faith dawns in our hearts. So Paul writes: 'by grace you have been saved through faith; and this is not your own doing, it is the gift of God' (Eph. 2:8). Whether 'this' refers to faith simply, or to salvation-through-faith as a whole, is not quite certain, but on either view Paul is saying that faith springs from spiritual co-resurrection, with Christ (see the context), and that this co-resurrection, to which we ourselves contribute nothing, derives from God's initiative – it is a fruit of grace. Thus it appears that, as Luke says, men believe 'through grace' (Acts 18:27) as God calls them through his grace (Gal. 1:15).

Election in the New Testament is God's eternal, unconditional choice of guilty offenders to be redeemed and regenerated (called and justified, Rom. 8:30), and so brought to glory (Eph. 1:3–12). It is a choice made in Christ (Eph. 1:4), in the sense that it is a choice both of sinners to be saved in union with God's Son and of him to become man and be their Saviour (*cf.* 1 Pet. 1:20). Paul speaks of this choice as 'the election of grace' (Rom. 11:5), God's 'purpose and grace, which was given us in Christ Jesus before the world began' (2 Tim. 1:9). From the election of sinners flow their redemption, regeneration, faith, and final glory (2 Thes. 2:13 f.). From the appointment of the Son as Saviour flow his incarnation (Jn. 6:38), the cross and resurrection (Jn. 10:15–18), and the calling, drawing and keeping of those whom he was sent to save until the final resurrection (Jn. 6:39 f.; 10:27 ff.; 12:32; 17:2). Paul stresses that election, the source of salvation, is entirely of grace, and not of works, *i.e.* it is not God's response to any foreseen effort or merit on man's part (Rom. 11:6; 2 Tim. 1:19).

Preservation is God keeping in Christ those whom he has united to Christ by faith through the Spirit. Paul shares with Christians his confidence that 'he who began a good work in you will bring it to completion at the day of Jesus Christ' (Phil. 1:6), grounding this certainty on God's faithfulness to his plan, his promise and his people (2 Thes. 3:3; *cf.* 1 Cor. 1:8 f.). In Romans 8:30 he spells out the plan: 'those whom he predestined he also called; and those whom he called he also justified; and those whom he justified he also glorified.' The past tense of 'glorified' argues that because it is fixed in the plan it is as good as done already; thus it is in effect a promise that it will certainly be done in due course. So Paul can say he is sure that God 'is able to guard what I have entrusted to him for that day', and exultantly declares: 'The Lord will rescue me from every evil attack and will bring me safely to his heavenly kingdom' (2 Tim. 1:12; 4:18, NIV; *cf.* 4:8). Christ's own promise undergirds this confidence: 'My sheep hear my voice, and I know them, and they follow me; and I give them eternal life, and they shall never perish, and no one shall snatch them out of my hand' (Jn. 10:27 f.; *cf.* the statement of divine purpose, Jn. 6:38–40, and the Saviour's prayer, Jn. 17:11–24).

The assurance that this line of teaching brings to the regenerate, who want to live as Christ's faithful disciples, whatever the cost, but are haunted by the fear of falling from grace through the failing of their faith, was classically focused by Toplady:

> *The work which his goodness began*
> *The arm of his strength will complete;*
> *His promise is Yea and Amen,*
> *And never was forfeited yet.*
> *Things future, nor things that are now,*
> *Not all things below nor above,*
> *Can make him his purpose forgo,*
> *Or sever my soul from his love.*
>
> *My name from the palms of his hands*
> *Eternity will not erase;*
> *Impressed on his heart it remains*
> *In marks of indelible grace;*
> *Yes, I to the end shall endure,*
> *As sure as the earnest is given;*
> *More happy, but not more secure,*
> *The glorified spirits in heaven!*

To those whose lives mark them out as unregenerate, whatever their claim to the contrary, no such assurance is given, but to Jesus' true disciples it comes as a birthright, and a source of supreme joy.

Such, in outline, is the wealth of grace to which God's people are heirs: election-love and covenant-love, redeeming love and quickening love, a love that saves and a love that keeps. Grace fulfils in the lives of all whom God has chosen the promise of the new covenant – 'I will put my laws into their minds, and write them on their hearts, and I will be their God, and they shall be my people. And...all shall know me, from the least of them to the greatest. For I will be merciful toward their iniquities, and I will remember their sins no more' (Heb. 8:10 ff., citing Je. 31:31 f.). And this purpose is invincible, for where grace exists it *reigns* (Rom. 5:21): it is the dominant factor in the situation, and nothing can thwart its eventual triumph in the life of each of God's elect. No wonder that Article 17 of the Church of England declares: 'the godly consideration of...our Election in Christ is full of sweet, pleasant, and unspeakable comfort to...such as feel in themselves the working of the Spirit of Christ, mortifying the works of the flesh and drawing up their mind to high and heavenly things, as well because it doth greatly establish and confirm their faith of eternal salvation to be enjoyed through Christ, as because it does fervently kindle their love towards God.' No wonder that Paul, surveying God's grace as an 'insider', one who knew himself to be involved with grace both as its herald and as its object, felt constrained to cry out, 'Thanks be to God for his inexpressible gift!' (2 Cor. 9:15).

Grace and law

'The law was given through Moses,' writes John; 'grace... came through Jesus Christ' (Jn. 1:17). In God's economy, law was expounded first, grace afterwards: the Old Testament is as dominated by the reality of God's law as the New Testament is by that of grace. But how is the grace that came afterwards to be related to the law that was there before? The New Testament knows two views which go wrong at this point: legalism and antinomianism.

Legalism (dealt with in Rom. 4 and 9 – 11, Gal. 2 – 5 and Col. 2) frustrates grace by seeking righteousness through works of law and religion, viewing these as part of the ground of our acceptance with God alongside the merits of Christ. But against this Paul insists that faith in Christ for salvation is an exclusive trust, so that a professed trust in him which does not exclude self-reliance entirely is not real faith in God's sight. Hence Paul's warning to the Judaizing Galatians, who thought they needed to supplement their faith in Christ by being circumcised: 'you are severed from Christ, you who would be justified by the law; you have *fallen away from grace*' (Gal. 5:4). Law-keeping plays no part in justification; justification is by faith alone, because it is in and through Christ alone, and thus it is by grace alone. To trust one's own works alongside the work of Christ dishonours him, frustrates grace, and cuts one off from life (*cf.* Gal. 2:21; 5:2).

At the other extreme, *antinomianism* (dealt with in Rom. 6, 2 Pet. 2, Jude and 1 Jn.) errs by turning 'the grace of our God into licentiousness' (Jude 4). Whereas the legalist so magnifies the law as to crowd out grace, the antinomian is so mesmerized by grace as to lose sight of the law as a rule of life. He argues that since Christians are 'discharged from the law' (Rom. 7:6), 'not under law but under grace' (Rom. 6:15), with eternal forgiveness already in their possession, it no longer matters what kind of lives they live. Though antinomianism and legalism are, from one standpoint, opposite poles of error, there is theologically, and often in experience, a link between them: for both proceed on the same false assumption, that the one and only purpose of law-keeping is to gain righteousness with God. Thus the legalist goes about to establish his own righteousness, while the antinomian, rejoicing in the free gift of righteousness by faith, sees no reason to keep the law any more. Many of the antinomians of history have come out of legalism by reaction.

But both errors are answered as soon as we see that the moral law expresses the will of God for man as man. It was never meant as a method of salvation (and it is in any case useless for this purpose); it was given to guide men in the life of godliness. And grace, while it condemns self-righteousness, establishes the law as a rule of conduct. 'The grace of God has appeared for the salvation of all men,' writes Paul, 'training us to renounce irreligion and worldly passions, and to live sober, upright, and godly lives in this world' (Tit. 2:11 f.). So far from giving us liberty to break the law, grace sets us free from the dominion of sin that we might keep the law (Rom. 6:11–23). This is the final answer to antinomianism: grace establishes the law.

A variant of the antinomian recoil from the law is the claim that Christians have no need, nor any duty, to regulate their lives by law, since their resources in Christ suffice to guide them. Thus, Luther held that the Christian's faith naturally produces good works (*i.e.* love and service) by spontaneous impulse; J. A. T. Robinson said that the Christian's love has a built-in moral compass, so that it need not rely on biblical rules, nor need necessarily be led by them; and many have talked as if the prompting of the Spirit in a Christian's conscience supersedes the instruction of the law entirely.

Those who take this line rightly stress the inward spontaneity of genuine Christian living and the ethical creativity of love. But they put asunder what God has joined, namely the Spirit's work of teaching and the word through which he does it. The Spirit continues writing God's law on our hearts all our lives, as he instructs us from Scripture in God's standards and makes us judge how far we yet fall short of the moral and spiritual perfection which they embody. In his letters Paul not only teaches Christians about Christ and the Spirit, but in the second half he regularly drills them in ethics – that is, in the law as it applies to believers (*cf.* Rom. 12 – 15; Gal. 5 – 6; Eph. 4:17 – 6:9; Col. 3:1 – 4:6). It would be hazardous to try to be wiser than Paul in our way of teaching the Christian life. If we remember that as Christians we serve God not for life but from life, as his already justified and adopted sons and daughters, we shall not fall into the legalism which these teachers fear; rather, we shall see God's law as the family code, and it will be our joy to try to live up to it and so please our heavenly Father who loved and saved us.

'By grace you have been saved through faith,' writes Paul; 'and this is not your own doing, it is the gift of God – not because of works, lest any man should boast. For we are his workmanship, created in Christ Jesus for good works, which God prepared beforehand, that we should walk in them' (Eph. 2:8–10). Paul's doctrine of free and sovereign grace both humbles the pride of the self-righteous legalist and condemns the lazy and irresponsible laxity of the antinomian. Rightly understood, this teaching is the parent of joyful assurance and tireless energy in the service of one's Saviour. It has been well said that, in the New Testament, doctrine is grace and ethics is gratitude (see Rom. 12:1); and our Lord has taught that the one who loves most will be the person who is most conscious of the love shown to him (Lk. 7:40 ff.). The world would see a great deal more practical godliness than it does if Christians today knew more about God's grace.

Under grace

To live 'not under law but under grace' (Rom. 6:14 f.), in the sense of having one's whole relationship with God determined by his electing, redeeming, converting and protecting love, is the Christian's supreme privilege. We may well close our study by noting some lines of thought which show how great this privilege is.

The life of grace is a life of *freedom,* in three basic ways.

1. As we saw, the Christian under grace is freed from the hopeless necessity of trying to commend himself to God by perfect law-keeping. Now he lives by being forgiven, and so is free at every point in his life to fail (as inevitably he does in fact, again and again) – and, having failed, to pick himself up where he fell, to seek and find God's pardon, and to start again. Pride, our natural disposition, which is self-protective, self-righteous and vainglorious, will either refuse to admit failure at all or refuse to try again, lest the trauma of failing be repeated; but the humility of the man who lives by being forgiven knows no such inhibitions. The Christian's experience of daily failures, along with his inside knowledge of his own false motives and his tally of shameful memories, make him constantly want to claim for himself Paul's end-of-life self-description, 'the foremost of sinners' (1 Tim. 1:15); daily, however, his shortcomings are forgiven and his joy restored. One reason why, as Jesus taught, we must be ready to forgive our fellow-Christians countless times is that our own life with God is a matter of being forgiven countless times, too.

2. Moreover, the Christian under grace is free from sin's dominion (Rom. 6:14). By virtue of his union with Christ, dead and risen, and the power of the Holy Spirit who

indwells him, the Christian is able to oppose and resist the urgings to sin that infect his moral and spiritual system, and 'by the Spirit...put to death the deeds of the body [the phrase means bad habits, whether of commission or omission]' (Rom. 8:13), and so to advance in Christlikeness (cf. 2 Cor. 3:18) and please God. Paul succinctly spells this out in Romans 6:1 – 8:14, arranging his thoughts as an answer to the question, 'why should not those who are justified by faith cause grace to abound (pardoning grace, that is) by going on sinning as before?' Paul's reply, in brief, is: not only is righteousness (law-keeping) both possible and prescribed for Christians, but it is also a fact that no Christian can go on sinning as before, for union with Christ has changed his nature so that now his heart (his inner man) desires righteousness as before it desired sin, and only obedience to God can satisfy his deepest inner craving. He hates the sin that he finds in himself, and gets no pleasure from lapsing into it. Such is the state of mind of the man who is freed from sin's dominion; he loves holiness because he loves his Saviour-God, and would not contemplate reverting to the days when, as sin's slave, he loved neither. He knows that his freedom has ennobled him and brought him both the desire and the strength for right living, and for this he is endlessly thankful.

3. Finally, the Christian under grace is free from bondage to fear (Rom. 8:15 ff.; cf. 1 Jn. 4:17 f.) – fear, that is, of the unknown future, or of meeting God (as one day we all must do), or of being destroyed by hostile forces or horrific experiences of one sort or another. He knows himself to be God's child, adopted, beloved, secure, with his inheritance awaiting him and eternal joy guaranteed. He knows that nothing can separate him from the love of God in Christ, nor dash him from his Saviour's hand, and that nothing can happen to him which is not for his long-term good, making him more like Jesus and bringing him ultimately closer to his God. So when fears flood his soul, as they do the soul of every normal person from time to time, he drives them back by reminding himself of these things, moving to and fro within the sequence of thoughts which the honest,

homespun Christian verse of John Newton put thus (this is Newton's original):

> Amazing grace (how sweet the sound)
>   That saved a wretch like me!
> I once was lost, but now am found;
>   Was blind, but now I see.
>
> 'Twas grace that taught my heart to fear,
>   And grace my fears relieved;
> How precious did that grace appear
>   The hour I first believed!
>
> Through many danger, toils and snares
>   I have already come;
> 'Tis grace has brought me safe thus far,
>   And grace will lead me home.
>
> The Lord has promised good to me,
>   His Word my hope secures;
> He will my shield and portion be
>   As long as life endures.
>
> Yes, when this flesh and heart shall fail
>   And mortal life shall cease,
> I shall possess within the veil
>   A life of joy and peace.
>
> The earth shall soon dissolve like snow,
>   The sun forbear to shine;
> But God, who called me here below,
>   Will be for ever mine.

And how can fear stand in face of that?

8

THE MEDIATOR

The mediator is a familiar figure in modern industrial and international negotiations. The pattern of events that calls for his services is depressingly common. Things get tense; both sides feel there is no comon ground for continuing the discussion; then one walks out – and at once a mediator has to be found to go to and fro between the estranged negotiators trying to bring them together again. The mediator is thus, as his name suggests (and as the Greek word for mediator, *mesitēs*, literally means) the man in the middle. He has links with both sides; he sympathizes with both, and both trust him. He serves the cause of justice, peace and good-will. His job is to represent each side to the other and find a basis for restoring their friendship.

The New Testament uses the word 'mediator' once of Moses (Gal. 3:19, AV, NIV) and four times of the Lord Jesus Christ. In 1 Timothy 2: 5, Paul says: 'there is one mediator between God and men, the man Christ Jesus.' In Hebrews 8:6; 9:15 and 12:24 we learn that Jesus is the mediator of a new and better covenant. It is not too much to describe these passages as the key, not merely to the New Testament, but to the whole Bible; for they crystallize into a phrase the sum and substance of its message. It is a commonplace of modern theology that the Bible is a book of witness to Christ, prophetic witness in anticipation in the Old Testament, apostolic witness in retrospect in the New. This is right; but to give the thought its proper precision and guard it against misunderstanding, we need to say that the Bible is a book of witness to Christ, not as teacher or example merely, nor even primarily, but *as mediator*. The mediation of Jesus between God and men, whereby the new and everlasting covenant has been established, is the Bible's main theme.

A mediator needed

God and man are estranged. Communication and friendship between them have broken down. Due to sin, mutual hostility now prevails. 'The sinful mind [the mind and heart of man in his natural state] is hostile to God. It does not submit to God's law, nor can it do so' (Rom. 8:7, NIV). And God, for his part, now fights against man, in the sense that 'the wrath of God is revealed from heaven against all ungodliness and wickedness of men, who by their wickedness suppress (NEB 'are stifling') the truth' (Rom. 1:18; *cf.* 5:10). The whole world stands guilty before God the Lawgiver and Judge (Rom. 3:29). 'All have sinned and fall short of the glory of God' (verse 23; whether God's glory is here viewed as a standard, an achievement, or a hope – see the commentaries – the point is for our purposes the same). As Isaiah says, 'all we like sheep have gone astray' from the path which God the Shepherd meant us to follow (53:6). To go some way of our own rather than God's way is as natural to us as breathing: we are not ordinarily aware of doing either till someone makes us conscious of it, yet we are actually doing both all the time. Thus, men are 'without God in the world', 'alienated from the life of God because of the ignorance that is in them, due to their hardness of heart' (Eph. 2:12; 4:18). This is the basic trouble with our human situation.

The imaginative writing of the modern West (poems, plays, novels) might lead us to think that our deepest problem at present is estrangement from our fellow-men and our own true self. It has been well said that most serious novels today are concerned with the problems of integrity (the curse of Adam), loss of identity (the curse of Cain), and loss of communication (the curse of Babel). At bottom, however, these are problems, not in man's relation with himself and his fellows, but in his relation with God – for the curse in each case is the outworking of God's wrath. And the tortured writing of today which holds these problems up to view, for all its acute observation and analysis, is at this point shallow rather than profound, for it catalogues the symptoms without insight into the disease.

The root reason why men feel alone and lost, caught in a nihilistic vortex, once the props of convention and cultural stability are kicked away, is that they are estranged from God. As Baxter sang three centuries ago, 'he wants not friends that hath thy love' – but the man estranged from God loses friendship with his fellows and even with himself. This is the predicament which current literature depicts, though without awareness of the meaning of its own subject-matter. What the prose and poetry of our twentieth-century 'waste land' is really telling us is the same thing that the Bible tells us – namely, that we need a mediator to bring us to God.

In Old Testament days, God prepared Israel for the coming of Christ. How did he do this? By bringing home to Israel the need for a mediator. This was the central lesson of the Old Testament economy. It was a lesson which God taught, paradoxically, by actually instituting in Israel two classes of mediators. He sent prophets to represent him to his people, and priests to represent his people to him. The prophets spoke to Israel in God's name, so maintaining communication between him and them; the priests offered sacrifice to God in Israel's name, so maintaining fellowship between them and him.

But the prophetic messages were fragmentary and often enigmatic ('by divers portions and in divers manners', Heb. 1:1, RV), and the priestly sacrifices never brought sustained peace of conscience and boldness of access into God's presence (for 'it is impossible that the blood of bulls and goats should take away sins', Heb. 10:4; see 9:8 f.; 10:1–22). Revelation and forgiveness under the Old Covenant were real, but limited and incomplete, and perfect communion with God was never attained. Thus the very inadequacy of Old Testament mediation was designed to make men see the need for a mediatorial ministry of greater efficacy. To have a broken-down old car to drive is much better than nothing, and one may be thankful for it, yet the frustrations of driving it make you long for a good one; and similarly, the experience of living under the Old Covenant could not but arouse longings for something better – a better covenant, founded on better promises, holding out a better hope, and resting on the efficacy of better sacrifices. The Epistle to the Hebrews is devoted to showing how the mediation of Christ supplies all that before was lacking (see 7:19, 22; 8:6; 9:23; 11:40), since 'by a single offering he has perfected for all time those who are sanctified' (10:14) – perfected them, that is, so far as their relationship to God is concerned.

Also, the Old Testament dispensation, as Paul explains in Galatians 3:19–25, was overshadowed by the law, which God 'added' through Moses 'because of transgressions' (verse 19) – that is, to make the Israelites see sin as something that impedes fellowship with God, and so to bring home to them their need of a Saviour from its guilt and power. (Whether the precise meaning of 'because of transgressions' is 'to make wrongdoing a legal offence' [so NEB], or 'to make transgressions abound' [cf. Rom. 5:20; 7:7 ff.] does not affect the point of the phrase.) The law could not give life (verse 21), for it conferred no ability to conform with its demands, but it could and did make men realize that they were helpless slaves of sin (see Rom. 7:7–13), and so prepare them to welcome Christ and trust him. So Paul writes: 'Scripture has declared the whole world to be prisoners in subjection to sin...we were close prisoners in the custody of law, pending the revelation of faith. Thus the law was a kind of tutor in charge of us until Christ should come' (Rom. 7:22–24, NEB). The Epistle to the Galatians shows in detail how the mediation of Christ, through which the twin gifts of justification and the Spirit are bestowed (cf. 3:1–14), brings men out of bondage to sin and the law into the glorious liberty of the sons of God.

A Mediator provided

The one Mediator between God and men is the man Christ Jesus, the man who is the Word made flesh, God the Son incarnate. All previous mediation in Israel was typical and anticipatory of his, and its efficacy, such as it was, was due to his pre-incarnate activity in and through it. Thus, it was the Spirit of Christ who spoke by the prophets (1 Pet. 1:10), and there was a real partaking of Christ by the Israelites in the wilderness under Moses (1 Cor. 10:1–4). Sins committed by God's people before the incarnation were (so to speak) put on Christ's account, to be atoned for in due course at Calvary (Heb. 9:15); that is how it was that God could actually remit them, so that Abraham, David and many more Old Testament saints knew already, before Christ came, the joy of justification and assurance of pardon (see Rom. 4:1–8, citing Gn. 15:6; Ps. 32:1 f.). Hence Paul's comment that one reason why God set forth Christ to be 'a propitiation... by his blood' was 'to show his righteousness, because of the passing over of the sins done aforetime, in the forbearance of God' (Rom. 3:25, RV): the fact that God had forgiven sins under the Old Covenant, although no adequate reparation had been made, had looked like unrighteousness on the part of the divine Judge.

Concerning the man Christ Jesus, the one and only Mediator, two questions may be asked.

First, why did the Mediator come?
He came into the world because, as he tells us some thirty times in John's gospel, he was *sent.* He had been destined for his mission from all eternity (1 Pet. 1:20). 'The Father sent his Son as the Saviour of the world' (1 Jn. 4:14). His Father had 'chosen... in him', *i.e.* chosen to be saved by his work, through union with his Person, a great company of sinful mankind (Eph. 1:4); these were 'given' him, that he should do everything necessary to bring them to God and to glory (Jn. 6:37, 39; 17:2, 6, 9, 24; *cf.* Heb. 2:13; Jn. 10:14–16, 27–29; 11:52). Thus, in another sense, he was 'given' for them: 'God so loved the world, that he gave his only Son, that whoever believes in him should... have everlasting life' (Jn. 3:16). 'The saying is sure... that Christ Jesus came into the world to save sinners' (1 Tim. 1:15).

What was it that he, as the Mediator, came to do, and that only he, as the God-man, could do?

1. He came to *reveal God to men.* Before we can know and love God, we must be shown what he is like. In Old Testament times, God's words, in conjunction with his ordering of events, had indicated something of his nature

and character, but no disclosure of this kind could be final and definitive. To bring men to the point where they know that the whole truth about God's outlook and attitudes has been set before them, a different sort of revelation was needed. Therefore God sent his Son, who perfectly bears his image (Heb. 1:3; Col. 1:15; 2:9; 2 Cor. 4:4; Phil. 2:6), and who is perfectly identified with his Father's purposes of love, to live as a man among men, and so make God perfectly known. 'No man hath seen God at any time; the only begotten Son...he hath declared him' (made him known, RSV; literally, *expounded* him, Jn. 1:18, RV). Jesus could say: 'He who has seen me has seen the Father' (Jn. 14:9), for Father and Son were 'in' each other in a complete union of essence, power, character and purpose (14:10; 10:38; 17:21; *cf.* 10:30; 17:11).

2. He came to *redeem men from sin*. Scripture knows nothing of the speculation, popular in some places, that the Son of God was made flesh in order to perfect creation. Its uniform witness is rather that he became man in order to redeem. As he said himself, 'the Son of man...came...to give his life as a ransom for many' (Mk. 10:45). Isaiah 53 had foretold that the iniquities of erring men should be put away by the death of a righteous servant of God in their stead. The background here was the Hebrew sacrificial system, instituted by God centuries before to teach the principle that atonement for sin is made by the death of a perfect substitute for the sinner. God's righteous servant, said Isaiah, would be made 'an offering for sin' (verses 10 ff.). But where could a perfect, sinless, wholly righteous servant of God be found? None qualified except the incarnate Son of God, who because he was man could be tempted, but because he was God could not and did not sin. Christ affirmed his own sinlessness (Jn. 8:46; 14:30), and the New Testament writers often call attention to it when proclaiming the efficacy of his atoning work (2 Cor. 5:21; 1 Pet. 2:22; 3:18; 1 Jn. 2:1).

3. He came to *restore man to God*. God the Son was always 'in the bosom of the Father' (Jn. 1:18), enjoying the full riches of his Father's fellowship, love, and glory (see

Jn. 10:15; 17:5, 23–26). But the sons of Adam were lost, banished from God's presence by reason of sin. The Son of God came into the world in order that sinners might come to share his experience of God's fellowship, love, and glory. He came to seek us where we are in order that he might bring us to be with him where he is. He came to take us as his own brothers and make us his Father's adopted sons, that we might see and share the Son's glory and bear the Son's own image, the family likeness (see Jn. 12:26; 14:3; 17:24; 20:17; Rom. 8:14–17, 29; 1 Cor. 15:45–49; 2 Cor. 3:18; Phil. 3:21; Col. 3:4; Heb. 2:11 f.; 1 Jn. 1:3; 3:1 f.). When, as the second God-appointed head of our race, the 'last Adam' (1 Cor. 14:45, 47), Christ receives those who by faith receive him, he introduces them at once into a relationship in which the Father's view of them corresponds to the Father's view of him; for Christ's sake, and in Christ, the Father, reckons righteousness to them (because Christ is righteous) and accounts them his sons by adoption (because Christ is his Son by nature) (Jn. 1:12; Rom. 4; 5:15–19). Following upon this, Christ works in them by his Spirit to transform them into his own likeness and root sin out of them (Col. 3:10), and some day, this task completed, he will bring them to 'the holy city, new Jerusalem' (Rev. 21:2), where nothing unclean may come (Rev. 21:27), there to enjoy the vision of God and the bliss of knowing him as their own God and Father (Rev. 21:3, 7; 22:4) for evermore. This consummation cannot fail; it is guaranteed by his own promise (Jn. 6:39 f.; 10:27–29) and prayer (Jn. 17:11, 15, 24). Well did Isaac Watts sing of the Mediator:

> *In him the tribes of Adam boast*
> *More blessings than their father lost.*

Second, how is the Mediator's work done?
Protestant theology is accustomed to say that the Mediator has fulfilled his mission by taking on the threefold office of prophet, priest and king. This view of Christ's ministry derives directly from the Epistle to the Hebrews, the fullest analysis of his mediation that the New Testament contains.

It is worth tracing out these three themes.

1. Jesus' primary office is that of *king*. It is to this that his title, 'Christ', always points in the New Testament. 'Christ' is not just a label, like an English surname, but a title of royalty: 'Jesus *Christ*' corresponds to '*Prince* Philip', not 'Philip *Mountbatten*'. The title marks Jesus out as God's Messiah, the anointed son of David of Old Testament prophecy (Is. 9:6 f.; 11:1 ff.; Je. 23:5 f.; Ezk. 37:24 ff.; Am. 9:11 f.; *etc.*). The basic affirmation of the New Testament is Peter's on the day of Pentecost: 'God has made him both Lord and Christ, this Jesus whom you crucified' (Acts 2:36). Accordingly, the Jesus of Hebrews, as of the rest of the New Testament, is an *enthroned* Jesus, who sits as king 'at the right hand of the Majesty on high' (1:3; *cf.* verses 8, 13; 8:1; 10:12 f.). The Christhood of Jesus, thus understood, is the presupposition of everything else that the New Testament has to say about him.

The New Testament declares Christ's kingdom to be universal and all-embracing. Jesus is God's vice-gerent throughout the universe. '*All* authority in heaven and on earth has been given to me' (Mt. 28:18); God has 'put *all* things under his feet' (Eph. 1:22; *cf.* Heb. 2:8 f.; Phil. 2:9 ff.). The goal of the kingdom is the actual eliminating of all active opposition to God's will, and all disharmony caused by sin, as well as the salvation of God's people (1 Cor. 15:24 ff.; Eph. 1:10–12). Towards this goal, really, if not always in appearance, all things move continually under Christ's dominion.

As God's Saviour-king, Jesus has absolute control over all creatures, and an absolute claim upon men. No man has a right not to be his disciple; and equally, no man need fear once he has become his disciple. For the Christ who rules us rules all things for us. To the question, 'How doth Christ execute the office of a king?' the Westminster Shorter Catechism replies: 'Christ executeth the office of a king, in subduing us to himself, in ruling and defending us, and in restraining and conquering all his and our enemies' (answer 26). His dominion is thus our security as he leads us home to God along the path of cross-bearing discipleship. So

Watts' words will find an echo in every true Christian heart:

> My dear Almighty Lord,
>   My Conqueror and my King,
> Thy sceptre, and thy sword,
>   Thy reigning grace I sing.
> Thine is the power; behold, I sit
> In willing bonds before thy feet.
>
> Should all the hosts of death,
>   And powers of hell unknown,
> Put their most dreadful forms
>   Of rage and mischief on;
> I shall be safe, for Christ displays
> Superior power, and guardian grace.

This is the significance of Jesus' mediatorial kingdom for the Christian believer.

2. But Jesus the king is also *priest*. He is a royal high priest for ever 'after the order of Melchizedek' (Heb. 5:6; 6:20, citing Ps. 110:4). Hebrews 7 – 10 expounds the perfection and finality of Jesus' perpetual priesthood, showing how it supersedes and abolishes the priesthood of the Old Covenant, making the very idea of human priestly mediation from henceforth superfluous, even blasphemous. The Shorter Catechism analyses the work of Jesus' priesthood thus: 'Christ executeth the office of a priest, in his once offering up of himself a sacrifice to satisfy divine justice, and reconcile us to God, and in making continual intercession for us' (answer 25).

(i) With regard to the once-for-all *sacrifice* of Christ, his finished work of making reconciliation for sins, we can only refer here to Hebrews 9:1 – 10:18, a passage from which we learn that when Jesus 'tasted death' (2:9) on the cross, shedding his life-blood in physical death and consciously enduring the sinner's destiny of God-forsakenness, which is spiritual death (see Mk. 15:34), he thereby made purification for all sins for ever (9:23; 10:12, 14, 17) in God's immediate presence, the 'holy place' which the tabernacle typified (9:12, 24 f.). Thus he ensured that when believers approach God now, access will not be barred to them (10:19–22), nor sin's penalty inflicted on them.

(ii) With regard to Jesus' constant *intercession* for his people, 'those who draw near to God through him' (Heb. 7:25; *cf.* Rom. 8:34), the New Testament verb signifies both more and less than our English 'intercede' would suggest. More, because it primarily means, not making requests alone, but actively intervening in a situation on someone's behalf to do whatever is necessary to secure their welfare. Less, because it carries no suggestion of the 'pleading' of conscious impotence. No doubt the God-man still expresses to the Father his desire for the fulfilment of what he knows to be the Father's own will for those 'given' him, just as he did when he was on earth (see the 'high-priestly prayer' of Jn. 17; *cf.* 14:16). But this is not all that his intercession involves. Christ's priestly intercession is a royal intervention from the throne, an intervention rooted in the fact that he, the king, is present with God (Heb. 9:24) as the advocate of his people, the eternally effective propitiation for their sins in virtue of his once-for-all sacrifice (1 Jn. 2:1 f.). We should therefore define Christ's intercession as that heavenly activity, of whatever kind, whereby he makes sure that all who come to God through him, pleading his name, trusting him for forgiveness, access, grace to help in time of need, and ultimate glory, will not be disappointed. The New Testament does not encourage us to speculate as to the exact nature of this activity, but rather to rejoice in the knowledge that, whatever precise form it takes, it is certainly and infallibly efficacious.

3. Finally, the royal priest is also *prophet*. God spoke by him, and preached the gospel through his lips (Heb. 1:2; 2:3). The apostles' ministry was, so to speak, an extension of his prophetic office; they preached in his name, with his inspiration (*cf.* 1 Cor. 2:13), and in their preaching he preached, so that through their words many who never met him in the flesh nevertheless heard his voice (see Lk. 10:16; Jn. 10:16; Eph. 2:17). And the same thing happens when the apostolic gospel is preached today: as the Spirit of Christ works with the Word, men still hear the voice of

Jesus. Still 'Christ executeth the office of a prophet, in revealing to us, by his word and Spirit, the will of God for our salvation' (Shorter Catechism, answer 24). Thus every Christian in every age can say:

> *I heard the voice of Jesus say,*
> *"Come unto me and rest…".*

Such is our Mediator: God incarnate, man divine; prophet, priest, and king. 'Hallelujah! What a Saviour!'

A Mediator proclaimed

Now at last we can appreciate the four gospels! That may sound strange, but it is no more than the truth. Many who rightly regard them as the most wonderful books in the world, because of the skill with which they present the most wonderful person of all time, quite fail to understand them. They read them with an opposition in their minds between the gospels (stories and practicality) and the epistles (theology and theory). They read them as if they were biographies, focusing on Jesus from a human-interest standpoint as a fascinating person who had an intriguing career. Some, missing altogether the evident signs of careful crafting, have spoken of them as 'artless memoirs'.

But in fact these four books are precisely, as the title of each says, 'the gospel' – that is, a proclamation of facts about Jesus which add up to the view of him as Mediator which we saw in the epistles: prophet, king and sacrifice for sins (to use the evangelists' categories), and as such bringer of salvation – new life and hope through a new relationship to God. The truth is that the gospels were written by men whose theology was that of the epistles, to edify others who shared, or at least were learning to share, the same beliefs. Gospels and epistles thus belong together. And the evangelists' focus is not so much on Jesus as a human being (though his real humanity is foundational to their viewpoint) as on his being the divine Mediator, God bringing God to men in grace and power in order thereby to bring men to God in faith and repentance.

Everything in the gospels is so angled as to highlight this mediation theme: the view of Jesus' life (birth – baptism – public ministry – passion – resurrection – ascension); the healing and feeding miracles, which picture the grace that heals and feeds our souls; the teaching (invitations to faith, and guidance for disciples); the quoted fulfilments of Scripture (Mt. 1:22 f.; 4:14 f.; 8:17; 12:17 ff.; Lk. 22:37; 24:25 ff., 44 ff.; *etc., etc.*); and in John's case the author's explanatory comments (1:1–18; 2:11, 21 f.; 3:31–36; 7:39; 8:20; 11:51 f.; 12:37–43; 13:1; 18:32; 20:31).

As I said earlier, I believe that some who love the gospels and read them much do in fact misread them. Overlooking what is central and concentrating on what is away from the centre, they end up knowing something about the person of Jesus but almost nothing about his mediation. I also believe that some who love theology and are at home in the epistles do not read the gospels anything like enough, so that they know the doctrine of mediation but are hardly acquainted with the man Christ Jesus. To both sorts I make this plea: appreciate the gospels! They really are the most enriching books in the world, once you see what, or rather whom, you are looking at – namely, Jesus the Mediator, whose saving ministry is set forth in theological terms in the epistles. The Christ of the epistles is the Jesus of the gospels. Many gains accrue to us from climbing those theological Himalayan peaks, Paul's great letters and Hebrews; one is, that hereby we are prepared to read the gospels with understanding, so that what we find in them will lead us at every turn to say from our hearts

> *Jesus, my Shepherd, Husband, Friend,*
> *My Prophet, Priest and King;*
> *My Lord, my Life, my Way, my End,*
> *Accept the praise I bring.*

Are you there yet?

9

RECONCILIATION

The verb 'reconcile' (two related verbs in the Greek) and
the noun 'reconciliation' are not common words in the New
Testament. Only Paul uses them in connection with the
relations of God and men, and he does so in only five places
(Rom. 5:10–11; 11:15; 2 Cor. 5:18–20; Eph. 2:14–17; Col.
1:19–22). And yet these are keywords in biblical theology.
For it is not too much to say that to Paul reconciliation was
the sum and substance of the gospel. In his hands, reconciliation became in effect a theological technical term, describing
and interpreting the central fact of the Christian message –
the saving work which God wrought through the cross of
the Lord Jesus Christ. Thus, he refers to the gospel as 'the
word of reconciliation' and to the preaching of it as 'the
ministry of reconciliation'. He sums up its content in the
great affirmation: 'God was in Christ, reconciling the world
to himself'. He formulates its application as an appeal to
sinners to be 'reconciled to God'. And he describes the
response of faith for which the gospel calls as 'receiving our
reconciliation' (see 2 Cor. 5:18 ff.; Rom 5:11). Plainly,
reconciliation is the heart of the gospel according to Paul.
And of all the great words that the New Testament uses to
explain the saving work of Christ – redemption, justification,
and the rest – reconciliation is perhaps the most full and
expressive.

The meaning of reconciliation
What is reconciliation? The general idea conveyed by the
Greek root from which the relevant terms are formed is
that of *change* or *exchange,* and the regular meaning which
these terms bear both in secular Greek and in the Bible is
that of a change of relations, an exchange of antagonism for

amity, a turning of enmity into friendship. To reconcile means to bring together again persons who had previously fallen out; to replace alienation, hostility and opposition by a new relationship of favour, goodwill and peace; and so to transform the attitude of the persons reconciled towards each other and to set their subsequent mutual dealings on a wholly new footing.

The initiative in reconciliation may be taken either by a third party who stands outside the dispute, or by one or other of the disaffected parties themselves, either the one who gave offence or the one who took it. In two places in the New Testament we read of reconciliation on the human level, and in each case it is the person who caused the breach (the brother who wronged his fellow-Christian in Matthew 5:24, the woman who left her husband in 1 Corinthians 7:11) who is envisaged as making the move to end it. Both times the verb is in the passive, and the person seeking to 'make it up' is said to 'be reconciled' to the other – presumably because in these circumstances the decision which actually effects the reconciliation is that of the injured party. 'Be reconciled to me,' writes a scapegrace son to his mother in a first-century Egyptian papyrus: he is asking her to forgive him and accept him back. In such a case the offender can only confess his fault, offer reparation and request pardon; he must then submit to the injured party's decision, yea or nay. Only when the latter grants pardon and shows himself willing to let bygones be bygones can we say that the offender 'is reconciled' to the one whom he wronged.

But this is not what happens in the reconciliation of God and men; for here it is God, the injured party, who takes the initiative. 'God was in Christ, reconciling the world to himself' (2 Cor. 5:19). The healing of the breach which man's sin had made is God's own work. We never read of man reconciling God, or of God being reconciled; God is the Reconciler himself. So that when in 2 Corinthians 5:20 Paul exhorts his readers: 'be reconciled to God', his meaning is not that they should try to make amends for their sins in hope of thereby inducing God to be favourable to them, but that they should humbly and thankfully accept by faith the reconciliation which God has already achieved for them in Christ.

Enmity and wrath

Reconciliation presupposes estrangement on at least one side, and in the case of God and sinners it seems clear that the estrangement was mutual. On the one hand, those whom God is said to have reconciled to himself were before 'estranged and hostile in [their] mind, doing evil deeds' (Col. 1:21). This, according to the Bible, is the natural state of every child of Adam. 'The mind that is set on the flesh is hostile to God' (see Rom. 8:7). Sinful man is opposed to God and to everything that is of God; it is his nature to disobey God's law, to disbelieve his gospel, to grudge him service and to chafe under his restraint. If sinners could dethrone God, repeal his laws and cancel his judgment, they would. Men are born rebels against their Maker. Man in sin is at inveterate enmity with God.

On the other hand, God is equally at enmity with sinners. This has been often denied, but the Bible is in no doubt about it. We were reconciled to God through the death of Christ 'while we were *enemies'*, says Paul in Romans 5:10, and commentators of all schools agree that this term here signifies as part, if not all, of its meaning 'objects of divine hostility', which the context certainly seems to demand. 'The word *enemies* is applied to men not only as descriptive of their moral character, but also of the relation in which they stand to God as the objects of his displeasure. There is not only a wicked opposition of the sinner to God, but a holy opposition of God to the sinner' (C. Hodge, *Romans*, p.136). Again, says Paul, we were all 'by nature *children of wrath*' (Eph. 2:3), heirs of the vengeance which God has proclaimed against those who transgress his laws.

The biblical idea of the wrath of God is well defined by James Orr: it is 'an energy of the divine nature called forth by the presence of daring or presumptuous transgression, and expressing the reaction of the divine holiness against it in the punishment or destruction of the transgressor. It is the "zeal" of God for the maintenance of His holiness and honour, and of the ends of His righteousness and love, when these are threatened by the ingratitude, rebellion and wilful disobedience or temerity of the creature' (Hastings' *Dictionary of the Bible*, 1, pp.77 f.). God's wrath against sin is not a fitful flicker, but a steady blaze; not a mark of uncertain temper, but an aspect of the consistent righteousness of the just Judge of all the earth. To this hostile reaction of God, Paul tells us, all sinners, as such, are exposed. The first truth expounded in Romans is that 'the wrath of God is revealed from heaven against all ungodliness and wickedness of men' (Rom. 1:18). The background of the good news of grace is the bad news of judgment; the context within which the New Testament announces God's reconciling mercy is the declaration of his active wrath. Men are opposed to God in their sin, and God is opposed to men in his holiness. Those who are under the rule of sin are also under the wrath of God. It is against the dark backcloth of this view of the natural relations of man and his Maker that the gospel of reconciliation is expounded.

The making of reconciliation

Reconciliation means peace-making: and Christ made peace, we are told, 'by the blood of his cross' (Col. 1:20). 'We were reconciled to God by the death of his Son' (Rom. 5:10). How are we to understand this? We cannot here go fully into Paul's view of the atonement, but we may make three points which spring directly from the texts which we are studying.

1. Reconciliation was made, we are told, through the *blood* of Christ (Col. 1:20). This points to the thought of *sacrifice,* according to the Old Testament pattern which required the shedding of blood for the remission of guilt.

2. Paul's analysis of the meaning of reconciliation is that through the blood-shedding of Christ peace was made between God and men (Col. 1:20), the enmity between them was destroyed (Rom. 5:10; Eph. 2:16), and the divine wrath was turned away from them for ever (Rom. 5:9–10). This points to the thought of *propitiation;* indeed, 'propitiation' is defined as the turning away of God's wrath, and is

no more than a technical name for the reconciling, pacificatory effects of the cross as described above.

3. God reconciled the world to himself, says Paul, by means of a judicial exchange: 'him who knew no sin he made to be sin on our behalf; that we might become the righteousness of God in him' (2 Cor. 5:21, RV). Paul has just affirmed that reconciliation means the non-imputation of their trespasses to the trespassers; here he shows that the ground of this non-imputation is the imputing of their trespasses to Christ, and his bearing God's holy reaction to them. As Paul says in Galatians 3:13 (NIV), 'Christ redeemed us from the curse of the law by becoming a curse for us.' The reason why we do not have to bear our own sins is that Christ bore them in our place. This points to the thought of *substitution*.

It was, then, by a substitutionary, propitiatory sacrifice on the part of the sinless Son of God that our reconciliation was achieved. So much did salvation cost; and it was for God's enemies that this price was paid. 'Christ died for the ungodly . . . God shows his love for us in that while we were yet sinners Christ died for us' (Rom. 5:6, 8). God quenched and put away his own just wrath against us by sending his own Son to atone for our sins in the darkness of Calvary. It is this that teaches us the measure of the mercy of God; this that shows us the meaning of 'God is love' (see 1 Jn. 4:8–10).

The receiving of reconciliation
Reconciliation was made by Christ's death, but it is not possessed till it is received. And it is received by faith; not by working and earning it, but by believing and taking it; not by resting in a theory of atonement, but by receiving a living Saviour. 'God was in Christ, reconciling the world to himself,' announces Paul; therefore 'be reconciled to God' (2 Cor. 5:19–20). 'Be reconciled to God' means 'receive your reconciliation' (*cf.* Rom. 5:11); and that means 'receive the Reconciler, who brings the reconciliation with him'. Christ's gifts and Christ himself cannot be separated. 'It is the living Christ, with the virtue of His reconciling death in

Him, who is the burden of the apostolic message,' wrote James Denney. And he continued: 'If a man with the sense of his sin on him sees what Christ on His cross means, there is only one thing for him to do – ...to abandon himself to the sin-bearing love which appeals to him in Christ, and to do so unreservedly, unconditionally, and for ever. That is what the New Testament means by faith' (*The Christian Doctrine of Reconciliation*, pp.287, 289). Faith both takes and gives: it takes God's promises, God's Son, and God's salvation, and it gives itself up to God's service. It takes the Lord as Saviour, and gives itself to the Saviour as Lord. So the reconciliation is received, and guilty sinners find peace with God.

This, then, is the conclusion of the matter. Reconciliation means the ending of enmity and the making of peace and friendship between persons previously opposed. God and men were at enmity with each other by reason of men's sins; but God has acted in Christ to reconcile sinners to himself through the cross. The achieving of reconciliation was a task which Christ completed at Calvary. In virtue of Christ's finished work of atonement, God now invites sinners everywhere to receive the reconciliation and thus be reconciled to himself. Believers enjoy through Christ an actual reconcilement with God which is perfect and final. Nothing can be added to it, because nothing is lacking in it. And as it is perfect, so it is everlasting. The new life that it brings, in which you know God as your Father, Jesus Christ the Reconciler as your friend, and yourself as fully and freely forgiven, is both joyous and endless. Reconciliation is the very heart of the gospel, and must for ever be the crowning theme of Christian praise.

> *O Christ, what burdens bowed thy head!*
> *Our load was laid on thee;*
> *Thou stoodest in the sinner's stead,*
> *Didst bear all ill for me.*
> *A victim led, thy blood was shed,*
> *Now there's no load for me.*

Death and the curse were in our cup:
  O Christ, 'twas full for thee!
But thou hast drained the last dark drop,
  'Tis empty now for me:
That bitter cup, love drank it up;
  Now blessing's draught for me.

Jehovah lifted up his rod;
  O Christ, it fell on thee!
Thou wast sore stricken of thy God;
  There's not one stroke for me.
Thy tears, thy blood beneath it flowed;
  Thy bruising healeth me.

For me, Lord Jesus, thou hast died,
  And I have died in thee:
Thou'rt risen – my bands are all untied,
  And now thou liv'st in me:
When purified, made white and tried,
  Thy glory then for me!

God draws us into fellowship with himself by different routes; it is a mistake to expect one man's journey into faith to be a carbon copy of another's. The demand that conversion experiences correspond only stirs up misplaced and distracting anxieties. We are all different people with different starting-points, and God deals with us as we are where he finds us. Richard Baxter said, 'God breaketh not all men's hearts alike.' But at one point all the roads to Christ converge: at the point of realizing that one is out of step and out of fellowship with God, and has no hope but in the reconciliation that Christ himself brings. Different people express this in different terms, not all biblically adequate, but what is expressed – the sense of need for a new relationship with God, the exclusive trust in Christ to bring it about, the resting of all hope henceforth on him, the risen Lord – is the same thing everywhere. Real Christianity – the life of knowing God, as distinct from the life of being prepared for knowing God – starts here, in what Paul calls the receiving of reconciliation; here, and nowhere else.

10
FAITH

Faith has been a controversial subject ever since the church began. In apostolic days, Paul argued that one of the basic differences between Christianity and Judaism was that the former was a religion of justification by faith – faith alone, without works – while the latter was not. 'We hold', wrote Paul, 'that a man is justified by faith apart from works *of law*' (Rom. 3:28). Two of his greatest epistles were given up to the development and defence of this position – Romans and Galatians, the most majestic exposition and the most passionate polemic respectively that the New Testament contains.

Fifteen centuries later, Luther fastened on to this same point – indeed, this same text – as expressing the sum of the Christian gospel, and of the entire controversy between the Reformers and Rome. Article 11 of the Church of England gives quiet but decided approval to Luther's claim: 'That we are justified by Faith only is a most wholesome Doctrine, and very full of comfort . . .' *Sola fide* – by faith alone – was a great Reformation slogan, and it is not too much to describe the word 'alone' as the rock on which the Western church split apart in those tempestuous days. Evangelicals have ever since maintained this emphasis on justification by faith *alone*, and insisted, often in warlike tones, that without this adjective the gospel would be lost.

But modern Christians do not always see why this stress was made, and why controversy on this point should have seemed so important. What need was there, they ask, to disrupt the church over the word 'alone'? Was anything vital at stake in these arguments? Was not this, perhaps, just one more case of furious theologians losing their sense of proportion? Is there anything here that matters to us, as

Christ's servants and witnesses today?

A review of what the Bible says about faith will help to answer these questions.

The nature of faith

First of all, what is faith? Let us clear some ground. The *popular* idea of faith is of a certain obstinate optimism: the hope, tenaciously held in face of trouble, that the universe is fundamentally friendly and things may get better. 'You've got to have faith,' Mrs A. urges Mrs B.; all she means is, 'keep your pecker up'. But this is only the form of faith, without its proper content. An attitude of trust divorced from any corresponding object of trust is not faith in the Bible sense of the word.

By contrast, the historic *Roman Catholic* idea of faith has been of mere credence and docility. Faith, to Rome, is just belief of what the Roman church teaches. Indeed, Rome actually distinguishes between 'explicit' faith (belief of something understood) and 'implicit' faith (uncomprehending assent to whatever it may be that the Roman church holds), and says that only the latter – which in reality is just a vote of confidence in the teaching church, and may go along with total ignorance of Christianity – is required of laymen for salvation! It is evident that faith, as Rome thinks of it, is at best only the content of faith without its proper form. For knowledge, much or little, divorced from any corresponding exercise of trust, is not faith in the full Bible sense, and it is precisely the due exercise of trust that is missing from the Roman Catholic analysis. Faith, according to Rome, is just trusting the church as a teacher; but according to the Bible, faith means trusting Christ as a Saviour, and this is a different thing.

In the Bible, faith, or believing (noun, *pistis;* verb, *pisteuō*), involves both credence and commitment. Its object is variously described as God (Rom. 4:24; 1 Pet. 1:21), Christ (Rom. 3:22, 26), God's promise (Rom. 4:20), Jesus' Messiahship and Saviourhood (1 Jn. 5:1), the reality of the resurrection (Rom. 10:9), the gospel (Mk. 1:15), the apostolic witness (2 Thes. 1:10).

Its nature, however, is always the same. It is a *responsive* apprehension of God and his saving truth; a recognition in the facts put forward of God's answer to one's own otherwise hopeless need; a realization that the word of the gospel is God's personal address, and Christ's personal invitation, to oneself, the hearer; a reliant outgoing of the soul in trust and confidence towards the living God and his living Son. This is made clear by the commonest New Testament construction with the verb *pisteuō – eis,* or occasionally *epi,* with the accusative, meaning 'to believe *into*' or '*upon*'. This construction scarcely appears in the Greek Old Testament and is not found at all in classical Greek; it is a new linguistic idiom, developed in the New Testament to express the idea of a movement of trust going out to, and laying hold of, and resting upon, the object of its confidence.

Such is the Christian concept of faith. The Reformers made this point by insisting that faith is not just *fides* (credence) but, rather, *fiducia* (confident trust). There is a Sunday School acrostic which expresses it perfectly: *F-A-I-T-H* – 'Forsaking *All, I T*ake *H*im'. In the words of Bishop J. C. Ryle:

'Saving faith is the *hand* of the soul. The sinner is like a drowning man at the point of sinking. He sees the Lord Jesus Christ holding out help to him. He *grasps* it and is saved. This is faith. (Hebrews 6:18.)

'Saving faith is the *eye* of the soul. The sinner is like the Israelite bitten by the fiery serpent in the wilderness, and at the point of death. The Lord Jesus Christ is offered to him as the brazen serpent, set up for his cure. He *looks* and is healed. This is faith. (John 3:14 f.)

'Saving faith is the *mouth* of the soul. The sinner is starving for want of food, and sick of a sore disease. The Lord Jesus is set before him as the bread of life, and the universal medicine. He *receives* it, and is made well and strong. This is faith. (John 6:35.)

'Saving faith is the *foot* of the soul. The sinner is pursued by a deadly enemy, and is in fear of being overtaken. The Lord Jesus Christ is put before him as a strong tower, a hiding place, and a refuge. He *runs* into it and is safe. This is faith. (Proverbs 18:10.)' (*Old Paths*, pp.228 f.)

Such indeed is the regular idea of faith throughout the New Testament. The only exceptions are these:

1. Sometimes 'the faith' is used for the body of truths believed (Jude 3; 1 Tim. 4:1, 6, *etc.*).

2. Sometimes 'faith' means a narrower exercise of trust which works miracles (Mt. 17:20 f.; 1 Cor. 13:2). Even in New Testament times, however, saving faith was not always accompanied by 'miracle-faith' (*cf.* 1 Cor. 12:9); nor vice versa (*cf.* Mt. 7:22 f.).

3. Once, in James 2:14–26, 'faith' and 'believe' denote bare intellectual assent to truth, without the answering response of a life of trustful obedience. But it looks as if James here is simply mimicking the usage of those whom he seeks to correct (*cf.* verse 14), and we need not suppose that he would normally use the word in so limited a sense (his reference to faith in verse 15, for instance, clearly carries a much fuller meaning).

The source of faith

The Bible treats faith's convictions as certainties, and equates them with knowledge. The voice of faith is: 'We *know....*' Upon what, now, is the certainty of faith grounded? Not on demonstration by argument, nor yet on experimental proof. Articles of faith cannot be proved by reason, nor verified by controlled experiments; man is in no position to make an independent check on what he is told about his God. Nor, again, is faith's certainty grounded, as Roman Catholics would suggest, upon confidence in an infallible teaching church; for the church on earth is not infallible, and has taught error often. Nor is this certainty based on some esoteric mystical experience, or private revelation. No, the certainty of faith springs directly from the consciousness of resting on the word of a God who 'cannot lie' (Tit. 1:2), and is therefore utterly trustworthy in all that he says. Faith echoes David's acknowledgment: 'And now, O Lord God, thou art God, and thy words are true' (2 Sa. 7:28).

But where are God's words found? In Holy Scripture,

the written witness of prophets and apostles to the Father and the Son. The words of Christ, and of those who wrote the Bible, were God-inspired in such a sense as to constitute them God's Word, God's own witness to himself. To receive Christ's witness was, and is, to certify that *God* is true (Jn. 3:33). To reject the apostolic gospel was, and is, to make *God* a liar (1 Jn. 5:10). For the words of the Saviour and his apostles were, and remain, God's words. 'And we also thank God constantly for this,' wrote Paul to the Thessalonians, 'that when you received the word of God which you heard from us, you accepted it *not as the word of men but as what it really is, the word of God*' (1 Thes. 2:13). This is where faith starts: where the apostolic gospel, the central biblical message, is heard or read, and the realization dawns that this is the very truth of God.

However, sin and Satan have so blinded fallen man that he cannot discern that the witness of Christ and the apostles is God's truth, nor 'see' and grasp the realities of which it speaks (*cf.* Jn. 3:3; 1 Cor. 2:14), nor 'come' in self-renouncing trust and poverty of spirit to Christ (Jn. 6:44, 65), till the Holy Spirit has enlightened and renewed him (2 Cor. 4:4–6; Jn. 3:3–8). Only those who are divinely 'taught' and 'drawn' come to Christ and abide in Him (Jn. 6:44 f.). Saving faith is thus God's gift (*cf.* Eph. 2:8; Phil. 1:29). If we ourselves have faith, that is only because God in his mercy opened our eyes; and if we desire that others should come to faith, we need to pray that God will open their eyes also; for they will never believe otherwise, any more than we ourselves would have done.

Faith and salvation
Now that we know what faith is, we can see why our evangelical ancestors insisted so strongly that salvation was by faith *alone*. They had two reasons for doing this, and both still apply.

1. This emphasis is needed *to safeguard the glory of Christ as Saviour.*

Faith is coming to Christ; faith means letting oneself fall into his open arms. Faith thus links a man to Christ, so that he becomes a man in Christ. And in Christ, through Christ, because of all that Christ is and all that Christ did, believers have a perfect salvation. In the eighth chapter of the epistle to the Romans, Paul passes in review the blessings that belong to 'those who are in Christ Jesus' (verse 1). No condemnation, and no separation (verses 1, 35 ff.); sonship and heirship (verses 14 ff.); a sure hope of resurrection and glory (verses 11, 23, 30); the strength and comfort of the Holy Spirit (verses 15 ff., 23, 26 ff.); eternal security and assured triumph through God's almighty love (verses 28–39). Nobody can need more than is freely given in Christ, and faith, by uniting us to Christ, makes it all ours. So, to deny the adequacy of faith alone for salvation is to deny that Christ is an adequate Saviour. And the way to highlight the absolute sufficiency of Christ is to emphasize the absolute sufficiency of faith. 'What must I do to be saved?' was the Philippian gaoler's question. 'Believe in the Lord Jesus, and you will be saved,' was the apostle Paul's answer. For the honour of Christ, it needs to be stressed that this was, and still is, a complete answer to the question asked.

2. This emphasis is needed *to safeguard the genuineness of faith itself.*

True faith is an exclusive, whole-hearted trust, a complete going out of oneself to put one's entire confidence in God's mercy. True faith springs from real self-despair, and involves a complete abandoning of trust in one's own morality or religion or character to commend one to God. 'To one who does not work but trusts him who justifies the ungodly,' wrote Paul, 'his faith is reckoned as righteousness' (Rom. 4:5). To him – but not to anyone else. And if one insists on adding one's own works to faith – that is, to Christ – as a contribution to one's acceptance with God, or treating Christ's merits as no more than a makeweight to supplement one's own, that is not true faith, and it will not secure the acceptance that is desired. 'Christ will either be a whole Saviour or none at all,' wrote John Berridge bluntly. 'And if you think you have any good Service of your own to recommend you unto God, you are certainly without any interest in Christ: Be you ever so sober, serious, just and devout, you are still under the Curse of God…provided you have any allowed Reliance on your own Works, and think they are to do something for you, and Christ to do the rest' (*Works*, p.355). In the quaint words of the hymn, then, 'cast thy deadly doing down'; stop trusting to your religion, your prayers, your Bible-reading, all your little pieties; they will not save you, and until you cease to trust them Christ will not save you either, for you do not yet truly believe upon him.

> Nothing *in my hands I bring,*
> *Simply to thy cross I cling;*
> Naked, *come to thee for dress,*
> Helpless, *look to thee for grace.*

This is how true faith speaks. Faith abandons hope in man's own accomplishments, leaves all works behind, and comes to Christ alone and empty-handed, to cast itself on his mercy. Such is the faith that saves.

Faith and works

But does this mean that saving faith throws a halo over idleness, and that the gospel of justification by faith only is really hostile to moral endeavour? Indeed not. 'Faith is a lively thing,' wrote Luther, 'mighty in working, valiant and strong, ever doing, ever fruitful; so that it is impossible that he who is endued therewith should not work always good works without ceasing…for such is his nature.' What saves is faith alone, but the faith that saves is never alone; it is always 'working through love' (Gal. 5:6), becoming a moral dynamic of unparalleled power in the believer's life. The proof that a man's faith is real is precisely this – that it makes him work. How does it do this? By making him feel the constraint of Christ's love for him, and the greatness of the debt of gratitude which he owes to his God. As we said once before, Christian doctrine is grace, and Christian conduct is gratitude. The believer does not do what he does as a means to being justified, but there are no limits to what he will do for his Lord out of gratitude for the justification that he has received.

The paradoxical truth is that there is no 'holiness teaching' in the Bible that will so completely and powerfully transform a man's life as the gospel of justification by faith alone. In a day of feeble churches and Christians, this is a truth worth pondering.

The life of faith

The history of theology inclines us to think of faith only in connection with justification, and this connection is basic. But Scripture ranges more widely, seeing faith as the controlling principle of the entire Christian life. How do you think of the Christian life? The New Testament pictures it as a *walk* (Eph. 4:1, 17; 5:2, 15, AV and RV; 'live', the RSV and NIV paraphrase, loses the picture) that is also a *fight*, since world, flesh and devil constantly oppose us and have to be beaten back. In this fight it is for faith, the responsive exercise of the renewed heart in thought, desire and resolve, to discern and resist the enemy, drawing strength from God by prayer for faithful obedience through thick and thin and energetic refusal to be crushed by strain, perplexity or discouragement. The life of faith is lived not on beds of ease but on battlefields.

The epistle to the Hebrews is the classic New Testament treatment of faith as a principle of persistence against pressures in the power of a hope that begets what the world calls heroism – brave acceptance of the unacceptable for a noble end. The theme is unforgettably illustrated in Hebrews 11, the Old Testament heroes' gallery, and applied to the author's hard-pressed readers with shattering power in Hebrews 12. (It is no wonder that A. W. Pink devoted a third of his 1300-page exposition of Hebrews to these two chapters!) What Hebrews says about faith may be summed up thus:

1. Faith is 'being sure of what we hope for and certain of what we do not see' (11:1, NIV) – the emphasis being, as always in Scripture, on the reality of faith's objects rather than the degree of confidence we feel about them.

2. Specifically, faith honours and pleases God by taking his word about things (creation, 11:3; rewards, 11:6; God's

faithfulness to his promises, 11:11; this life as a journey home, 11:13–16; the fact that obedience always makes sense, even when it looks like nonsense, 11:17–19; *etc.*).

3. Faith approaches God boldly through Christ (4:16; 10:19–22) to find help and strength for the winning of moral, spiritual and circumstantial victories (11:32–38; 4:16) and for the enduring of hostility both from within and from outside oneself (sin within, 12:1–4; ill-treatment from without, 10:32–34; 12:3).

4. Faith interprets trouble as God's discipline of his child (12:5–11) and, so far from being daunted, rejoices to think of it as proving one's sonship to God and preparing one for peace and pleasure to come.

5. Faith takes courage from examples of living by faith which the 'great cloud of witnesses' have left us (12:1; 13:7), from thoughts of their present happiness (12:23), and from knowing that when we come to God here on earth we plug into the present worship and fellowship of the heaven that will be our own home one day (12:22–24). In other words, faith appreciates the communion of saints.

6. Faith battles against temptations to unbelief, apathy and disobedience, sustaining against them the quality sometimes called 'stickability' (Canadians say, 'stick-to-it-iveness'), and referred to in the letter as *patience* and *endurance* (Greek, *hypomonē*) (6:11 f.; 10:36; 12:1). Faith in God produces faithfulness to God.

Taking our cue from Hebrews 11, we should read all Bible biography as object-lessons about faith and unbelief, and the way that both express themselves, the one in faithfulness and obedience, the other in unfaithfulness and disobedience, and the reaction of God in each case. There is a lifetime of study here, but we cannot explore it further now.

'Sometimes', said a student, 'I feel my faith is like tissue paper; I could put my hand right through it.' That put vividly what many feel. How can weak faith be made strong, and little faith become great? Not by looking within, to examine your faith; you cannot strengthen faith by intro-spection, any more than you can promote growth in a plant by pulling it up to inspect its roots. You strengthen your faith, rather, by looking hard at its objects – the promises of God in Scripture; the unseen realities of God and your life with him and your hope of glory; the living Christ himself, once on the cross, now on the throne. 'Inwardly we are being renewed day by day...we fix our eyes not on what is seen, but on what is unseen. For what is seen is temporary, but what is unseen is eternal' (2 Cor. 4:16, 18, NIV).

Recalling times when God's help was experienced in the past can also increase strength for the life of faith in the present. 'Recall the former days,' says the writer to the Hebrews (10:32). 'My soul refuses to be comforted...I will call to mind the deeds of the Lord; yea, I will remember...' (Ps. 77:2, 11). 'My soul is cast down within me, *therefore* I remember thee...' (Ps. 42:6). 'The Lord stood by me...So I was rescued...The Lord will rescue me...and save me' (2 Tim. 4:17 f.). Sang John Newton:

> *His love in time past*
> *Forbids me to think*
> *He'll leave me at last*
> *In trouble to sink;*
> *Each sweet Ebenezer*
> *I have in review*
> *Confirms his good pleasure*
> *To help me quite through.*

But perhaps the best prescription of all for invigorating feeble faith is that given in Hebrews 12:

'...*lay aside* every weight, and sin which clings so closely, and...*run* with perseverance the race that is set before us, *looking to Jesus* the pioneer and perfecter of our faith [*i.e.*, the one who enables us to live a life of faith modelled on his], who for the joy that was set before him endured the cross, despising the shame, and is seated at the right hand of the throne of God. *Consider him* ...

'...*lift* your drooping hands and *strengthen* your weak knees...

'See that you *do not refuse* him who is speaking' (12:1–3, 12, 25).

Take these thoughts as medicine. *Dose* your heart with them as many times a day as you need – there is no such thing as an overdose – and the benefit is guaranteed. Also, *take* the verbs in italics as an exercise plan. Before me lies a copy of the famous *Royal Canadian Air Force Exercise Plans for Physical Fitness* (12 minutes daily for women, 11 for men). A similar length of time spent daily in checking that one is taking to heart the things that this passage tells Christians to do can work wonders for the fitness and vigour of one's faith. *Try* it and see.

11
JUSTIFICATION

Of the thirty-nine occurrences of the verb 'justify' in the New Testament, twenty-nine come in the epistles or recorded words of Paul. The noun 'justification' occurs only twice (that need not surprise us; Greek always prefers verbs to nouns); and on both occasions it is Paul who uses it (Rom. 4:25; 5:18). These figures suggest straight away that the doctrine of justification is a special concern of Paul's, and so it proves to be. It is his way of formulating the essential gospel message – that through Christ's death guilty sinners, once justly under wrath, come into a new relationship with God as his beloved sons, under grace. The New Testament has many ways of expressing this, but the most full, explicit and precise is Paul's doctrine of justification. Justification means to Paul *God's act of remitting the sins of, and reckoning righteousness to, ungodly sinners freely, by his grace, through faith in Christ, on the ground, not of their own works, but of the representative righteousness and redemptive, propitiatory, substitutionary blood-shedding of Jesus Christ on their behalf.* (For the parts of this definition, see Rom. 3:23-26; 4:5–8; 5:18–19.) This, to Paul, is the heart of Christianity.

Luther called justification 'the article of a standing or falling church', and Paul would fully have endorsed the description. Justification is indeed a foundational subject. The aim of this study is to bring out the chief points in Paul's exposition of it.

The meaning of justification
To 'justify' in the Bible means to 'declare righteous': to declare, that is, of a man on trial, that he is not liable to any penalty, but is entitled to all the privileges due to those who

139

have kept the law. Justifying is the act of a judge pronouncing the opposite sentence to condemnation – that of acquittal and legal immunity. It is an act of administering the law which settles a person's relation to the law. This is so whether the judge in the case is human (*cf.* Dt. 25:1; Pr. 17:15) or, as here, divine (*cf.* Rom. 8:33). The Church of Rome has always maintained that God's act of justifying is primarily, if not wholly, one of *making* righteous, by inner spiritual renewal, but there is no biblical or linguistic ground for this view, though it goes back at least as far as Augustine. Paul's synonyms for 'justify' are 'reckon (impute) righteousness', 'forgive (more correctly, *remit*) sins', 'not reckon sin' (see Rom. 4:5–8) – all phrases which express the idea, not of inner transformation, but of conferring a legal status and cancelling a legal liability. Justification is a judgment passed on man, not a work wrought within man: God's gift of a status and a relationship to himself, not of a new heart. Certainly, God does regenerate those whom he justifies, but the two things are not the same.

Justification is God's fundamental act of blessing, for it saves from the past and secures for the future. It consists, on the one hand, of the pardon of sin, and the ending of our exposure to God's enmity and wrath through our reconciliation to him (Acts 13:39; Rom. 4:6 f.; 5:9 ff.); on the other hand, it includes the bestowal of a righteous man's status and a title to all the blessings which God promises to the just, a thought which Paul amplifies by linking justification with the adoption of believers as God's sons and heirs (Gal. 4:4 ff.; Rom. 8:14 ff.). Both aspects of justification appear in Romans 5:1–2, where Paul says that justification brings peace with God (because sin is pardoned) and also hope of the glory of God (because the rights of the righteous are bestowed on the believer). This hope is a certainty, for the justifying sentence is the judgment of the last day brought forward into the present: it is a final verdict, which will never be reversed. 'Those whom he justified he also glorified' (Rom. 8:30). Note that Paul puts 'glorified' in the past tense: what God has resolved to do is as good as done! The justified man can accordingly be sure that nothing will ever separate him from the love of his Saviour and his God (Rom. 8:35 ff.). The coming inquisition before Christ's judgment-seat (see Rom. 14:10–12; 2 Cor. 5:10) may deprive him of rewards which greater faithfulness would have brought him (1 Cor. 3:15), but never of his justified status. He is eternally secure.

The ground of justification

The doctrine of justification as presented by Paul sounds paradoxical, almost shocking; for it tells us that God, the holy Lawgiver and just Judge, who reveals inflexible righteous wrath against 'all ungodliness and wickedness of men' (Rom. 1:18), now reckons righteousness to the unrighteous and justifies the ungodly (Rom. 3:23–24; 4:5). This is welcome news, no doubt; but is it for the perfect Judge to do such a thing? Paul answers this question explicitly by affirming that God justifies sinners in a manner designed 'to shew his righteousness, because of the passing over of the sins done aforetime, in the forbearance of God; for the shewing, I say, of his righteousness at this present season: that he might himself be just, and the justifier of him that hath faith in Jesus' (Rom. 3:25–26, RV). The statement is emphatic, for the point is as crucial as it is unexpected. What Paul is saying is that the gospel which proclaims God's apparent violation of his justice is really a revelation of his justice. So far from creating a problem about the justice of God's dealings, it actually solves one; for it makes clear, as the Old Testament never did, the just grounds of God's pardon and acceptance of believers both before and since Christ's coming. The gospel shows how a just God can justly justify believing sinners.

Justification explained

How is this possible? Through the full discharge of the claims which God's law makes upon them – in other words, on the grounds of real and actual righteousness; for compliance with the claims of God's law is the first and basic thing that righteousness means. The only way in which justification can be just is for the law to be satisfied so far as the justified are concerned. But the law makes a double demand on sinners: it requires both their full obedience to its precepts, as God's creatures, and their full endurance of its penalty, as transgressors. How could they conceivably meet this double demand? The answer is that it has been met already by the Lord Jesus Christ, acting in their name. The eternal Son of God was 'born under the law' (Gal. 4:4) in order that he might yield double submission to the law in his people's stead. Both aspects of his submission are indicated in Paul's words: 'he . . . became *obedient* – unto *death*' (Phil. 2:8). His life of righteousness culminated in his dying the death of the unrighteous according to the will of God: he bore the penal curse of the law in man's place (Gal. 3:13) to make propitiation for man's sins (Rom. 3:25).

And thus, 'through one act of righteousness' – the life and death of the sinless Christ – 'the free gift came unto all men to justification of life' (Rom. 5:18, RV). In virtue of Christ's righteousness, wrought out by him as man's God-appointed representative, 'the righteousness of God' (*i.e.* righteousness *from* God: see Phil. 3:9) is bestowed on believers as a free gift (Rom 1:17; 3:21–22; 5:17; *cf.* 9:30; 10:3–11): that is to say, they receive from God the right to be treated, and the promise that they shall be treated, no longer as sinners, but as righteous. Thus they become 'the righteousness of God' in and through him who 'knew no sin' personally, but was representatively 'made sin' (treated as a sinner, and punished) in their place (2 Cor. 5:21).

This is the thought expressed by the traditional phrase 'the imputation of Christ's righteousness' – namely, that believers are righteous (Rom. 5:19) and have righteousness (Phil. 3:9) in God's sight (Rom. 4:11), not because they are righteous in themselves, but because Christ their Head was righteous before God and they are one with him, sharers of his status and acceptance. His righteousness becomes theirs in the sense that they are accepted and rewarded as his righteousness, his full obedience to the Father, deserves to be. The imputing of his righteousness to them in this sense is not an arbitrary legal fiction, as is sometimes alleged, for it is grounded on a real union between themselves and him.

They are justified 'in Christ' (Gal. 2:17); and God reckons them righteous and declares them so, not because he accounts them to have kept his law personally (which would be a false judgment), but because he accounts them to be united by faith to the One who kept it representatively (and that is a true judgment). Sinners, then, are justly justified on account of the obedient law-keeping and blood-shedding of Jesus Christ; and it is on this that their assurance of present and future salvation must rest.

> *My hope is built on nothing less*
> *Than Jesus' blood and righteousness.*

> *Jesu, thy blood and righteousness*
> *My beauty are, my glorious dress;*
> *Midst flaming worlds, in these arrayed,*
> *With joy shall I lift up my head.*

The means of justification
Faith in Christ, says Paul, is the means whereby righteousness is received and justification bestowed; sinners are justified 'by' or 'through' faith (Greek, *dia* and *ek pisteōs* or *pistei*). Faith is not the ground of justification; if it were, faith would become a meritorious work and Paul would not be able to describe the believer as 'one who does not work'(Rom. 4:5). Faith is rather the outstretched empty hand which receives righteousness by receiving Christ.

Paul quotes the case of Abraham ('Abraham believed God, and it was reckoned to him as righteousness') to prove that it is when a man rests his soul on God's gracious promise that he is justified (Gal. 3:6; Rom. 4:3 ff., quoting Gn. 15:6). The context and scope of the argument in Romans 4 shows that when Paul cites this verse as teaching that Abraham's faith was 'reckoned as righteousness' (Rom. 4:5, 9, 22), what he means us to understand is that faith – whole-hearted reliance on the divine promise (verses 18 ff.) – was the occasion and means of righteousness being imputed to him. Paul is not suggesting that faith, regarded either as righteousness or as a substitute for righteousness, is the *ground* of justification; the discussion throughout

Romans 4 is not concerned with the ground of justification at all, only with the means of securing it. We have already quoted texts from Romans 3 and 5, where the ground of justification is discussed, to show that according to Paul it is not our faith, but Christ's righteousness, on which our justification is founded.

A comment, as brief as I can make it, on Paul's way with words, may help to clarify what goes on in Romans 4. Paul's letters reveal him as a man with a strong clear head who knows what he wants to say and has the communicator's instinct for orderly, persuasive presentation; but who, because he is not interested in language and verbal skills as such (*cf.* 1 Cor. 2:1–4; 2 Cor. 10:10), and because he wants to address ordinary folk man to man, uses language in a somewhat loose way, with few definitions, no technical terms, no quest for elegance, and a habit (perhaps unrealized; we all do this more than we realize) of repeating words that mean a lot to him and using them in slightly different senses.

(Example: in the phrase *firstborn of all creation* in Colossians 1:15, *firstborn* is used exclusively to mean 'existing prior to', but in *firstborn from the dead* in verse 18 it is used inclusively to mean that Jesus was the first of the dead to be raised. Jehovah's Witnesses, who are Arians, hold that *firstborn* must bear the same sense both times and signify in verse 15 that the Son was the first creature to be made. Paul's explanation of *firstborn* in verse 16 – '*for* in him *all* things were created' – rules that out, and was doubtless meant to, for Paul would have realized the ambiguity; but we have to admit that it is his shifting use of the word that made the misunderstanding possible.)

Also, Paul is a very compressed writer, the most concentrated in the New Testament, and he often gives only the barest outline of an analytical argument, leaving the reader to draw out corollaries and implications for himself. Yet he always says enough to make things clear, and those whose eye is on the logical flow will not misunderstand his occasional oddities and ambiguities of language.

Now in Romans Paul runs true to type: everything is

terse, and key words are used in distinct though connected senses. Within seven verses, for instance, *law* is used to mean (i) God's command (7:22, 25; 8:3); (ii) sustained energy, both of sin (7:23, 25; 8:2) and of firm intention, however ineffective ('the law of my mind', 7:23) and of the Spirit (8:2; unless 'law of the Spirit' means, as some think, the message of the gospel); and (iii) a recurring process (7:21). *Righteousness* is another word whose meaning shifts. It is used to mean (i) that quality which God shows when judging sin retributively (3:25; *cf.* 2:5; 3:5 f.), and also when justifying the unjust justly (3:26); (ii) God's gift of acceptance, freely bestowed on believers for Jesus' sake (5:17), so that now despite their sins they are 'in the right' with God; (iii) man's due obedience to God (6:13, 16, 18, 20; 14:17).

When in Romans 4 Paul speaks of God 'reckoning righteousness' to men, he appears to be using the word in sense (ii), of the accepted status which Abraham 'had' and we may have through faith (verses 11, 23–25). The phrase thus means the same as 'justify', Paul's verb used four times between 3:24 and 3:31. The rendering which declares Abraham's faith to have been 'reckoned' or 'counted *as* righteousness' (verses 3, 5, 9, 22), though found in RSV, NIV, NEB and most modern versions, is not good; 'as' suggests equivalence or identity, as if 'righteousness' was being used here in sense (iii). 'As' represents the Greek preposition *eis,* meaning 'towards' or 'with a view to' in a wide range of contexts, and '*for* righteousness' (AV, RV) was a much better way to translate it, although 'reckon' and 'count' are no doubt improvements on the older word 'impute'. Paul is not saying here that faith is our righteousness, but that we are justified through believing. Certainly, faith is the occasion and means of our justification, but Christ's obedience (5:19), his righteousness in sense (iii) (verse 18), his propitiation for our sins (3:25; again, follow AV and RV against the moderns), is its ground.

Paul and James

It is sometimes thought that James 2:21–25 contradicts Paul

by teaching that God accepts men on the double ground of faith and works. A study of these verses in their context, however, shows that this is not James' meaning. It must be remembered that Paul is the only New Testament writer to use 'justify' regularly for God's act of accepting man. When James speaks of 'being justified', he is using the word in the more general sense of being vindicated, or proved right, in regard to claims made on one's behalf. (There is a rather similar use of it in Matthew 11:19.) To be justified in this sense means, not to be accepted by God as righteous, but to be shown to be a genuine believer; a man is justified in James' sense when his life gives evidence that he has the kind of living, working faith which secures acceptance with God. James himself quotes Genesis 15:6 for the same purpose as Paul does – to show that it was faith which secured Abraham's acceptance as righteous (2:23). But now, he says, this Scripture statement was 'fulfilled' (confirmed and proved true by later events) some thirty years after, when Abraham was 'justified by works, when he offered his son Isaac' (2:21). Abraham's act on that occasion proved the reality of his faith, and so of his acceptance with God. James' point throughout the whole section (2:14–26) is that a bare profession of faith, unaccompanied by the good works which true faith would produce, provides no sufficient grounds for inferring that a man is saved – a point with which Paul would heartily have agreed.

The centrality of justification

The reason why the doctrine of justification is central to the gospel is that God's basic relationship to us as his rational creatures is that of Lawgiver and Judge, so that our standing before him is always determined by his holy law. The sinner's first problem, therefore, is to get right with God's law, for until he is right with the law he cannot be right with the God whose law it is. As long as the law condemns him, true worship and fellowship with God are impossible for him. The gospel of justification, however, solves his problem by showing him how, through faith in Christ, the condemning voice of the law against him may be silenced for ever. Now he may draw near, unafraid, to worship his Maker.

> *A debtor to mercy alone,*
> *Of covenant mercy I sing;*
> *Nor fear, with thy righteousness on,*
> *My person and offering to bring.*
> *The terrors of law and of God*
> *With me can have nothing to do;*
> My Saviour's obedience and blood
> Hide all my transgressions from view.

Thus the knowledge of one's justification is the basis of all true religion. It has always been so; it always will be. The issue is not, can one state the doctrine with full biblical accuracy (that, as we have seen, is a task that demands care), but, does one know its reality in experience? True religion does not begin till the question presses: how may I get rid of my sins? And it exists only in those who know that the answer is: not by seeing what I can do for myself, but by putting my trust in Jesus and in what he did for me.

12

REGENERATION

Regeneration, like so many biblical keywords, is a picture-word – *re*-generation, *second* birth. It denotes a new beginning of life. Various views have been held in Christian history as to what this involves and when and how it comes about, and it is well to begin by glancing at some of them.

Historical survey

In the early days of the church, regeneration was uniformly thought of as the blessing symbolized and conveyed by the rite of baptism. *The Fathers* took it to cover both spiritual quickening and also remission of sins (which is actually an aspect of justification). *The Mediaevals,* on the other hand, defined regeneration more accurately as an infusion of grace, and rightly distinguished it from remission of sins, but then included both under justification, which they mistakenly understood as God's work of *making* men righteous.

The Reformers distinguished justification from regeneration, as deliverance from the guilt and dominion of sin respectively, and insisted that neither blessing was possessed, not even by the baptized, where faith was absent. *Calvin* defined regeneration so broadly as to include all that is involved in God's re-creating of man in the image of Christ here on earth – spiritual quickening, conscious conversion (faith and repentance) and lifelong sanctification, but other Reformers limited the term to God's initial work of raising the spiritually dead.

In the next century, the *Puritan* era, it was usual to treat regeneration and effectual calling as synonymous names for this first work of grace which creates faith, and to equate conversion with both. This is reflected in the way that the Authorized Version of the Bible (1611) substitutes 'be converted' for the grammatically correct 'turn' or 'convert' of the earlier Protestant translation.[1] The AV has decisively moulded English religious usage, and it is still our habit to use 'be converted' and 'be born again' interchangeably. There is perhaps no harm in this, provided we remember that in the New Testament itself the verb rendered as 'be converted' is really always active, and in the texts quoted it signifies man's act of turning to God, not the work of God turning sinners to himself. Theology may justify the explanation of man's turning in terms of his being turned, but even so one can only regret that theology was thought to justify the mistranslation of these verses.

Since the seventeenth century, *Reformed theologians* have tended to distinguish between regeneration and new birth. They defined regeneration as the first act of God instilling spiritual life into dead souls, below the level of consciousness; and they understood the new birth as the first conscious manifestations of that life in new spiritual apprehension, affections and acts – the initial exercises of faith and repentance. On the basis of this narrowed definition, they have insisted strongly that regeneration must be related to faith as cause to effect. Deny this, they say, and you deny faith to be a gift of God's grace; and what you are saying then is that man is his own saviour, inasmuch as his faith is the decisive factor in his salvation and now becomes 'all his own work'.

The biblical conception

We have glanced at some of the ideas about regeneration which Christians have held; now we turn to the Scriptures themselves. How does the Bible present regeneration?

The noun thus translated means rebirth (*palingenesia*): it speaks of a creative renovation wrought by the power of God. It occurs only twice. In Matthew 19:28, it refers to the coming renewal of the cosmos at the end of the age – what Peter terms 'the restoration of all things' (Acts 3:21, RV). In

[1] See Mt. 13:15; 18:3; Mk. 4:12; Acts 3:19. In Lk. 22:32; Jn. 12:40 and Acts 28:27, the earlier English versions had themselves gone against the grammar and used the passive, and the AV here simply follows where they had led.

Titus 3:5, however, where Paul speaks of God as having saved us 'by the washing of regeneration' ('the cleansing power of a new birth', Phillips) 'and renewal of the Holy Spirit', the inner quickening of the believer here and now is clearly meant. This is the reference of the word which concerns us at present.

The context to which the idea of regeneration belongs is the biblical conception of the subjective side of redemption as *renewal*. In the Old Testament, we find God promising to give his people a new heart and to put in them a new spirit (Ezk. 36:26) – to circumcise their hearts by writing his laws upon them, and so to bring them to know, love and obey him. (See Dt. 30:6; Je. 31:31–34; Ezk. 36:25–27.) In the New Testament, this promised renewing becomes a reality through union with Christ; for 'if any one is in Christ, he is a new creation' (2 Cor. 5:17; see also Gal. 6:15).

It is worth pausing for a moment over B. B. Warfield's analysis of the change as 'a radical and complete transformation wrought in the soul (Rom. 12:2; Eph. 4:23) by God the Holy Spirit (Tit. 3:5; Eph. 4:24), by virtue of which we become "new men" (Eph. 4:24; Col. 3:10), no longer conformed to this world (Rom. 12:2; Eph. 4:22; Col. 3:9), but in knowledge and holiness of the truth created after the image of God (Eph. 4:24; Col. 3:10; Rom. 12:2)' (*Biblical and Theological Studies,* p.351). This renewing work goes on throughout the Christian's life (his inner man is 'renewed every day', 2 Cor. 4:16): as a continuing process, it is normally called sanctification. Regeneration is the initial act by which the process is begun.

The chief expositor of regeneration in the New Testament is the apostle John. The word he uses to express the idea is *gennaō,* which can mean both 'beget' and 'give birth to'. Nicodemus understood our Lord to be speaking of a new *birth* (Jn. 3:4); John in his first epistle clearly has in view a new *begetting* (*cf.* 1 Jn. 3:9). Man is begotten, or born 'again', 'anew' – or, more likely, born 'from above' (Jn. 3:3, 7, Moffatt and RV margin) – 'of the Spirit' (Jn. 3:8, *cf.* verse 5), or simply 'of God' (Jn. 1:13, nine times in 1 Jn.). The verb is used each time in the aorist or perfect tense to denote the decisive, completed character of regeneration. *Pace* Calvin, it cannot be regarded as an unfinished process. Like natural birth, if it has happened at all it has happened completely. One is reborn at a certain point of time, and from then on one is spiritually alive.

What, according to John, is this new birth? It is not an alteration of, or addition to, the substance or faculties of the soul; but a drastic change wrought upon fallen human nature which brings a man under the effective dominion of the Holy Spirit and makes him responsive to God, which previously he was not. It is not a change which man does anything to bring about, any more than infants do anything to induce, or contribute to, their own procreation and birth; it is a free act of God, not prompted by any human merit or exertion (*cf.* Jn. 1:12–13; Tit. 3:3–7), but wholly a gift of divine grace.

The need of regeneration

Why does man need regeneration? Because, as our Lord explained to Nicodemus, as long as a man remains 'flesh' (Jn. 3:6) – remains, that is, the sinner that he was born – he is not able to enter God's kingdom. *There are no spiritual activities without regeneration.* One who has not been born from above cannot *see* (*i.e.* understand) God's kingdom (the realm of salvation), nor *enter* it (by faith in the Saviour) (Jn. 3:3, 5). The implication of the fact that some receive Christ is that they have been born of God (Jn. 1:12–13); they would not do so otherwise. Without regeneration, nobody would believe. As Paul puts it, 'the man without the Spirit [*i.e.* the unregenerate] does not accept the things that come from the Spirit of God, for they are foolishness to him and he cannot understand them, because they are spiritually discerned' (1 Cor. 2:14, NIV). Christ's conversation with Nicodemus forms an eloquent commentary on this text. Sinners – even the most cultured and religious – cannot receive the things of the Spirit, which are the truths concerning Christ, till the Spirit himself has made them new creatures. That is why Nicodemus and his Jewish friends needed the new birth. Jesus told him: 'Do not marvel that I said to you, *"You* [plural] *must be born anew"'* (Jn. 3:7).

The fruits of regeneration

In the conversation between Christ and Nicodemus, recorded in John's gospel, the Saviour showed that there are no spiritual activities without regeneration; in his first epistle, John labours the converse truth that *there is no regeneration without spiritual activities.* The fruits of regeneration are repentance, faith and good works. The regenerate believe rightly in Jesus Christ (1 Jn. 5:1). They do righteousness (2:29). They do not live a life of sin (3:9; 5:18: the verbs 'commits sin', 'cannot sin', 'does not sin', express habitual actions, as the present tense regularly does in Greek, and not absolute sinlessness, as 1:8–10 makes clear). They experience faith's victory over the world (5:4). They love their fellow-Christians (4:7). These are the marks by which the regenerate are known; for no man could do any of these things were he not born again. But we have no warrant for regarding anyone as regenerate without these marks. Any who lack them, whatever they may claim, are to be adjudged unregenerate children of the devil (3:6–10). Regeneration is known by its fruits.

Here, incidentally, is a sufficient answer to the question whether spiritual regeneration was a reality in Old Testament times. Fallen human nature was no less incompetent in spiritual things then than it is now. Had there been no regeneration in Old Testament times, there would have been no faith, and Hebrews 11 could never have been written.

Formulating regeneration

It appears that John's idea of the new birth corresponds most nearly with the common Reformed definition of regeneration: it is a secret work of the Spirit upon the sinner, inscrutable as the blowing of the wind, but manifesting itself at once by faith in Christ and a life of obedience and love. The subjects of regeneration (leaving aside the question of infants) are to be sought among those whom

God has brought under the sound of the gospel; faith in the gospel, and in the Christ of the gospel, will be the first indication that regeneration, in John's sense, has taken place. We should note, indeed, that both Peter and James use the new birth image in a broader sense to cover the whole work of effectual calling – the process by which God not only makes men able to receive the gospel, but actually brings them to faith through it and so installs them as members of his family. It is in this broader sense that James writes 'of his own will he brought us forth by the word of truth' (Jas. 1:18) and Peter speaks of Christians as 'born anew…of imperishable (seed), through the…word of God' (1 Pet. 1:23). However, since John gives the classic treatment of the subject, we shall be wise to model our usage on his. So we shall say, with T. C. Hammond, that regeneration is an act of God whereby a soul undergoes 'a spiritual resurrection into a new sphere of life, in which he is alive to God and united to him in Christ. God has implanted in the new-born soul a totally *new principle* of life…Conversion on this interpretation is the natural and inevitable expression…of the new nature communicated by the Spirit of God. "God turns us and we turn."' (*In Understanding Be Men*[6], p. 140)

The signs of life

One of the saddest experiences for a wife or husband is stillbirth, and there is often a tense moment when a baby is delivered as everyone waits for it to squawk and wave its limbs, and then suck, and so show itself to be fully alive. In the same way, not every churned-up soul becomes a live birth spiritually, and signs that new life has really come must be sought from people's actual behaviour. The signs whereby a regenerate person may be known correspond to the natural actions of the newborn child.

First, the baby *cries,* instinctively; and the born-again person instinctively prays, crying to God in dependence, hope and trust as a child to his father. The gospel which he received and to which he responded by embracing Christ as his Saviour and Lord promised him adoption into God's family (Gal. 4:4 f.), and now it is his nature to treat God as his Father, bringing to him all his own felt needs and desires. We (believers, the regenerate ones) 'received the Spirit of sonship. And by him we cry, "*Abba*, Father"' (Rom. 8:15, NIV). The new Christian's prayers are honest and heartfelt, as children's cries for help always are, and though as he matures prayer may become harder (this does happen) it never ceases to be the most natural activity in which he engages. Constantly to look up to God as your Father in heaven and to talk to him in and from your heart is thus a sign of being regenerate.

Second, the baby *sucks,* instinctively; and the born-again person also feels a hunger for spiritual food – first the milk and then the meat of God's revealed word (1 Pet. 2:2; Heb. 5:12–14; 1 Cor. 3:2). He listens to the word preached and taught and discussed; he reads it in his Bible, and in books that throw light on the Bible; he asks questions about it; he meditates on it, memorizes it, chews the cud on it, labours to squeeze all the goodness out of it. 'Oh, how I love thy law! It is my meditation all the day...How sweet are thy words to my taste, sweeter than honey to my mouth!' (Ps. 119:97, 103). Constantly to crave for God's word and to want to go deeper into it is thus a second sign of being regenerate.

Third, the baby *moves,* turning its head, flexing its limbs, later on rolling, crawling, tottering, toddling, exploring; and similarly the born-again person moves in the spiritual realm into which he has now come, sorting out priorities, reshaping his life in the light of his new allegiance, exploring Christian relationships and ways of worship, using enterprise for the Lord in many kinds of work and witness. Constantly to be 'zealous for good deeds' (Tit. 2:14), and to be wanting and trying to do more and more for God's kingdom is thus a third sign of being regenerate.

Fourth, the baby *rests,* relaxing completely and sleeping soundly in adult arms and wherever else feels firm; and in the same way the born-again person rests in the knowledge that God's everlasting arms are underneath him, and is able to spend his days, whatever pressures they bring, without panic and in peace. 'I have calmed and quieted my soul, like a child quieted at its mother's breast' (Ps. 131:2). 'He gives to his beloved sleep' (Ps. 127:2). Constantly to live in quiet contentment, concerned only to be faithful in obedience and leaving it to God to overrule the outcome, is thus a fourth sign of being regenerate.

Childlikeness towards God, said Jesus — meaning simple trust, responsiveness and dependence – is the spirit in which alone we enter the divine kingdom and live its life (Mt. 18:3 f.). It is evident that such childlikeness (not to be confused with childishness, something much less admirable) resolves into the four marks of the regenerate which we have just surveyed. It is evident too that this fourfold disposition is the root out of which grow those fruits of regeneration which John pinpointed – the docility before God which grasps and holds apostolic faith in Christ; the concern to please God which expresses itself in renouncing sin and practising righteousness; and the appreciation of God's saving love which begets self-sacrificing love of fellow-Christians in imitation. Childlikeness before God is what regeneration is really all about, inasmuch as the gospel calls for it and regeneration is no more (and no less!) than the work of God in our hearts which leads to the gospel being whole-heartedly received. If only God would make us all simple enough to see this and, having seen it, never to lose sight of it! Then the Christian world would be a very different place.

13
ELECTION

We have all been caught up in arguments about election, and we know from experience how they go. Texts from Paul are waved like banners; the words 'Calvinist' and 'Arminian' fly like bullets; people blink and go red; everyone ends up flustered and hot under the collar. Sometimes, looking back on these unhappy exchanges, we find ourselves resenting the very existence of the doctrine which occasions such high feelings.

At such times, we see it as a mere useless encumbrance, serving no purpose save to divide Christians who are otherwise united, and to give agnostics ground for criticizing the Christian view of God, and to put distraction and stumbling-blocks in the path of those whom we seek to point to Christ. We could almost reproach God for having put it in the Bible at all, and we feel sure that our wisest course for the future will be to put it out of our minds, and to try to stop others from thinking or talking about it any further. Having reasoned from the fact that our arguments about election are not edifying, to the conclusion that the doctrine itself is not edifying, we feel certain that it is part of our Christian duty to play it down: to insist that it is not a doctrine that matters much, and that we should all be well advised to give our minds to something more profitable.

Can we dismiss it?
No doubt it is easy to get the subject of election out of proportion; no doubt it has often been done. But whether this fact gives us warrant to dismiss the doctrine as really unimportant is another question. It does not look as if Paul would have thought so. If we look again at the texts in which he deals with election, we shall see that his attitude to

the subject is quite different from ours. To start with, he neither makes an issue of it nor gets embarrassed about it. He is neither puzzled by it nor ashamed of it; he simply accepts and expounds it as an integral part of his gospel. And when he introduces it into his teaching, it is for one end only – to help Christians see how great is the grace that has saved them, and to move them to a worthy response in worship and life. (Verify this from Rom. 8:28 – 11:36; Eph. 1:3–14; 1 Cor. 1:26–31; 1 Thes. 2:13–14; 2 Tim. 1:9–10.)

Practical relevance

Sometimes the thought of election leads Paul to issue an invitation to praise: 'Praise be to the God and Father of our Lord Jesus Christ, who... *chose* us in him before the creation of the world to be holy... In love he predestined us to be adopted as his sons... to the praise of his glorious grace...'(Eph. 1:3 ff., NIV). Sometimes, again, Paul invokes election to bring Christians assurance and encouragement ('comfort' in the strong Bible sense of the word): 'Who shall bring any charge against *God's elect*? It is God who justifies; who is to condemn?... Who shall separate us from the love of Christ?' (Rom. 8:33 ff.). Sometimes, too, Paul makes election a basis for ethical appeal: 'Put on therefore, *as God's elect*... a heart of compassion, kindness, humility, meekness, longsuffering...'(Col. 3:12, RV). Such a handling of our theme admonishes us to revise our previous too-hasty judgment: for we can hardly be right in treating the doctrine of election as an unedifying encumbrance when in Paul's hands it becomes a motive and mainspring of worship and assurance and holy living. A doctrine which has this salutary tendency cannot really be either unedifying or unimportant. What our experience (and much church history with it) does show, however, is that election is a truth which is very easily misunderstood and misapplied.

Not for idle curiosity

The fact is that the doctrine of election, dealing as it does with the inmost secrets of God's will, is strong meat: very nourishing to those who can take it, but acutely indigestible to those whose spiritual system is out of order. And the symptoms of indigestion (let it be said) appear not only when the doctrine is rejected, but also when it is misapplied. Biblical teaching on election is meant to make Christians humble, confident, joyful and active, but the doctrine can be held and propagated in a way that makes them instead proud, presumptuous, complacent and lazy; so that this teaching may become a stumbling-block to those who receive it no less than to those who object to it. Both as regards the content and the application of the doctrine, we do well to heed the warning prefixed by Calvin to the chapter of his *Institutes* which bears the awesome title, 'Of eternal election, by which God has predestinated some to salvation and others to destruction':

'The subject of predestination, which in itself is attended by considerable difficulty, is rendered very perplexed, and hence perilous, by human curiosity, which cannot be restrained from wandering into forbidden paths... Those secrets of his will which he has seen fit to manifest are revealed in his word – revealed in so far as he knew to be conducive to our interest and welfare....Let it, therefore, be our first principle that to desire any other knowledge of predestination than that which is expounded by the word of God, is no less infatuated than to walk where there is no path, or to seek light in darkness.... The best rule of sobriety is, not only in learning to follow wherever God leads, but also when he makes an end of teaching to cease from wishing to be wise...' (III. xxi. 1).

Humbly, reverently, and attentively, then, with party pride and prejudice and memories of past arguments as far as possible laid aside, let us turn to the Word of God to see what it does and does not say about our subject. What doctrine of election does the Bible set before us?

1. THE IDEA OF ELECTION

The verb 'elect', or 'choose' (in Hebrew, usually *bachar;* in Greek, both in the Septuagint and the New Testament, usually *eklegomai)*, expresses the idea of picking out, or selecting, something or someone from a number of available alternatives. Thus, in the Old Testament we find David choosing five sling-stones from the brook to fight Goliath with (1 Sa. 17:40), and the runaway slave selecting a dwelling-place 'where it pleases him best' (Dt. 23:16), and Joshua inviting Israel, if they will not serve the Lord, to choose which of the heathen gods they will bow down to (Jos. 24:15). In a similar sense, we read in both Testaments of God choosing out men for himself, to perform certain appointed tasks and to enjoy certain predestined privileges.

Free and unconditional

This divine choice of sinners for a preordained destiny is presented as an act of *grace, i.e.* of undeserved favour and benefit. God's choice is not occasioned by meritorious achievements on the part of those whom he chooses. Election is of grace, and grace excludes merit absolutely The election of grace, declares Paul, 'is...no longer on the basis of works: otherwise grace would no longer be grace' (Rom. 11:5 f.). God's gracious election is thus *free* and *unconditional,* for it does not depend upon, nor is called forth or constrained by, anything whatever in those who are its subjects. It is a spontaneous resolve on God's part, just as were his decisions to create and to redeem. God owes sinners no mercy of any kind, only condemnation; thus it is no injustice if he does not resolve to bless them, but it is a wonder of free grace when he does. So Paul argues: 'Is there injustice on God's part [in choosing to bless one and not another]? By no means! For he says to Moses, "I will have mercy on whom I have mercy, and I will have compassion on whom I have compassion." So it depends not upon man's will or exertion, but upon God's mercy...he has mercy upon whomever he wills...' (Rom. 9:14–18). The fact that God chooses to bless certain guilty sinners cannot be acounted for in any terms other than his own 'good pleasure which he purposed in Christ' (Eph. 1:9, NIV): they are 'predestined according to the plan of him who works out everything in conformity with the purpose of his will' (verse 11). If you, a Christian, should ask, why did God choose me? – 'but, Jesus, why me?' as a modern lyric puts it – the Bible answer is, because in his mercy he was pleased to – and that is the end of the matter. At this point, therefore, you should stop asking questions, and start to worship and give thanks.

The Bible brings out the free and unconstrained character of divine election, not only by such explicit statements as those quoted above, but also by passages which stress, first, that God's choice precedes the existence of the persons chosen (Eph. 1:4, *etc.*), and determines his dealings with them from the moment of their birth (Je. 1:5; Rom. 9:10–13); secondly, that those chosen had nothing in them by nature to commend them to God, being as bad as, if not worse than, the rest of men ('stubborn', AV 'stiff-necked', Dt. 9:4–6; 'foolish...weak...low....despised', 1 Cor. 1:27 f.; 'who did not pursue righteousness', Rom. 9:30, *cf.* verses 23 f.; 'by nature children of wrath, like the rest of mankind' (Eph. 2:3, *cf.* verses 1–10 with 1:3–12); thirdly, that the obedient faith of the elect (*i.e.* everything about them that does in fact please God) flows from their election, and so cannot have been the grounds of it (see Acts 13:48; 2 Thes. 2:13; 1 Pet. 1:2).

Three aspects

The idea of election appears in the Bible in three connections. There is, *first,* in the Old Testament, God's selecting of Abraham and his family, Israel the nation, to be his covenant people (Is. 41:8 f.). There is, *second,* in both Testaments his selecting of particular members of the covenant community for particular pieces of service: Moses (Ps. 106:23), Aaron (Ps. 105:26), the priests (Dt. 18:5), the kings (1 Sa. 10:24; 2 Sa. 6:21), the Messiah ('my chosen', Is. 42:1; *cf.* 49:5), the apostles (Jn. 6:70; 15:16). In both these connections, God's election was to privilege and responsibility, but it did not guarantee the final salvation of those elected. Many Israelites died under judgment (*cf.* 1 Cor. 10:5–10); so did Judas, a chosen apostle. The blessings of election were in these cases forfeited by unbelief and disobedience. But the New Testament speaks of election in a *third* connection, namely, God's selecting of certain individuals to bring them to salvation. Paul says most about this. He presents it as an election from eternity (Eph. 1:4; 2 Thes. 2:13 – 'from the beginning of time,' NEB; 2 Tim. 1:9), which issues in an effective calling of the elect to faith and an equally effective keeping of them in faith till they come to glory (Rom. 8:30; 2 Thes. 2:14). This is election, not to privilege and opportunity merely, but to eternal life itself.

The very idea of election (choosing *out*) implies that some are not elected. God discriminates; he selects some, not all. Out of the nations, he chose only Israel (Am. 3:2; Ps. 147:20). Out of Israel after the flesh, salvation in Christ was enjoyed only by a remnant 'according to the election of grace': 'the election obtained it, and the rest were hardened' (Rom. 11:5, 7, RV). Speaking of his elect at Corinth, whom he purposed to bring to faith through Paul's preaching, Christ told Paul in a vision, 'I have many people in this city' (Acts 18:10), but this did not mean the whole population (*cf.* 1 Cor. 1:26–29). Part of the mystery of election is that God never appears to have chosen all whom he might have chosen. Thus he impresses upon us that his choice is absolutely free, and teaches us to value the grace that has come to us personally.

2. ELECTION AND THE PLAN OF SALVATION

The New Testament (Paul's epistles and John's gospel especially) presents the saving work of God, not as a series of unconnected actions, but as a single complex operation, the carrying through of a unified composite purpose by the three Persons of the Godhead in conjunction. The final issue of this mighty plan is the glorifying of the whole church: this is yet future. The fountain-head from which all this saving activity has flowed, and will flow till the work is finished, is God's purpose of election, dating (if the word may be allowed) from before the foundation of the world. (See Eph. 1:3–4.) In Romans 8:29–30, Paul surveys the whole plan from end to end, speaking of its final step in the past tense to show that, since God is resolved on it, the thing is already as good as done: 'God knew his own before ever they were, and also ordained that they should be shaped to the likeness of his Son, that he might be the eldest of a large family of brothers; and it is these, so fore-ordained, whom he has also called. And those whom he called he has justified, and to those whom he justified he has also given his splendour [glory]' (NEB).

Chosen in Christ

God chose us, says Paul, 'in Christ': that is, to be saved through Christ's mediation and in union with his Person (Eph. 1:4). All the blessings that flow from election are enjoyed in and through him – sonship to God (verse 5), redemption from sin (verse 7), the gift of the indwelling Spirit, who seals us as God's property (verse 13), and the inheritance prepared for us (verse 11). (That inheritance itself is elsewhere defined as a matter of being like Christ and with Christ, bearing his image, sharing his glory, and seeing him as he is: Jn. 17:24; Rom. 8:17; 2 Thes. 2:14; 1 Jn. 3:2.) Accordingly, back in eternity, when God chose us to be saved by Christ (2 Tim. 1:9; 1 Pet. 1:2), he also appointed his Son to become man and be our Saviour (2 Tim. 1:10; 1 Pet. 1:20). And when, in the fullness of time, the Son of God came into the world, by his own testimony he came specifically to fulfil this eternal plan – that is, to die for, and give life to, all whom the Father had 'given' him (Jn. 6:39; 10:29; 17:2, 24), those whose appointed Shepherd he claimed to be and to whom he referred as 'my sheep' (Jn. 10:26–29). 'I lay down my life for the sheep....' 'My sheep hear my voice, and I know them, and they follow me; and I give them eternal life; and they shall never perish....' (verses 15, 27 f.). We speak of the 'work' of Christ, meaning the atonement, but in the perspective set by God's electing purpose Christ's heavenly ministry of drawing sinners to himself (Jn. 12:32), interceding for them (Rom. 8:34; Heb. 7:25), and preserving them for glory (2 Tim. 4:17 f.), is as truly part of Christ's work as was his earthly ministry of suffering and sin-bearing. What Christ did for us on earth, and what he does for us in heaven, are two parts of a single undertaking. It is as much his work to apply redemption as it was to obtain it. To give his sheep eternal life, and to raise them up at the last day (Jn. 6:39), belongs to his appointed ministry no less than his atoning death did. The first part of his work, by which he 'obtained eternal redemption' (Heb. 9:12, RV), was finished at Calvary, but the second part, that of communicating redemption to the redeemed, will continue (in Cowper's words),

> *Till all the ransomed church of God*
> *Be saved, to sin no more.*

Accordingly, in an epistle dominated by the thought of election, Paul writes of the work of Christ as follows: 'Christ *loved the church* and *gave himself up for her,* that he might *sanctify her, having cleansed her* . . . that he might *present the church to himself* [*i.e.,* at his return] in splendour . . . holy and without blemish' (Eph. 5:25–27). Such is the range and scope of the saving work of Christ when viewed in the light of election.

3. ELECTION AND EVANGELISM

But if all this is so, says someone, on what principles should we evangelize? If Christ came to save only the elect, what gospel is there for the rest? And, since we cannot tell elect unbelievers from non-elect unbelievers, what gospel can we preach to anybody? How can we offer Christ to the unconverted, and assure them that if they come to him they will find life, when for all we know we are speaking to people whom he does not intend to save? Indeed, why need we evangelize at all, for surely the elect will be saved anyway?

Why evangelize?
We can sum up the Bible answer to these questions by making three points.

163

First, the texts we have been studying tell us that God has chosen, not only whom he will save, but also the method by which he will save them. They are to be saved through being divinely *called*: that is, they are to be brought to faith by the Spirit through the word of the gospel. '...whom he predestined he also *called*' (Rom. 8:30). 'God chose you from the beginning to be saved *through...belief in the truth.* To this he *called* you through our gospel' (2 Thes. 2:13–14). God saves no adult apart from faith in Christ. Hence his way of bringing about the salvation of his elect is to send someone to tell them the gospel. Thus Christ sent Paul to the Gentiles 'to open their eyes, that they may turn from darkness to light and from the power of Satan to God, that they may receive forgiveness of sins and a place among those who are sanctified by faith in me' (Acts 26:18). And thus he sends us to hold forth the word of life and make disciples in our generation. This is where our evangelism comes in. It is the means by which God brings his elect to faith. It is an essential link in the chain of God's purposes.

Offering Christ
Second, the grounds on which the Bible tells us to offer Christ to the world have nothing to do with election. We are to call on everyone to turn and trust him, for the four reasons following: first, everyone is sinful and guilty, and needs him (Rom. 3:19–26; Acts 4:12); second, he is a perfect and sufficient Saviour for everyone who trusts him (Jn. 3:16; Acts 13:39; Rom. 1:16; Heb. 7:25); third, he graciously invites everyone who needs him to come to him and find peace (Mt. 11:28 f.; Jn. 6:37; Rev. 3:20); fourth, God positively commands that everyone who hears the gospel should repent and believe on Christ's name (Acts 17:30; 1 Jn. 3:23). We are to evangelize in obedience to Christ's command (Mt. 28:19), and under the constraint of his love (2 Cor. 5:14). We are not to speculate as to whether our unconverted friends are elect or not (that is none of our business): we are to look simply to their need of Christ, and to do all we can in honest Christian compassion to meet that need by our witness and our prayers.

It will help here to remind ourselves again that the God of the Bible is the 'blessed and only Sovereign...who ...dwells in unapproachable light, whom no man has ever seen or can see' (1 Tim. 6:15 f.), the great and undomesticated God who, as he made plain to Job, is under no obligation to explain to us all his reasons for doing what he does (*cf*. Jb. 40:1–8; 42:1–6). We need to be very clear that God's revelation of himself in Scripture does not enable us to guess more about what he is up to than he explicity tells us. When you have read a certain amount of a theologian you know roughly how he ticks and what his position will require him to say about this or that, but you cannot take your Maker's measure in that way.

An Einstein using baby talk could make himself known to a two-year-old as a kind and friendly adult, yet the child would have no notion how all his ideas, plans, schemes of value and priority and judgments of possibilities regarding life as a whole fitted together in his mind, partly because he would not have talked to the child about these things and partly because the child could not have understood him if he had. In that sense, therefore, the adult remains unknown to the child even when he has made himself known – really, genuinely known – as the child's kind friend. Now with God we are in the position of the two-year-old. God has talked and talks still to us in the human language of the written Scriptures, and from what he tells us that he said and did we truly know him. Yet we may be sure that most of what God himself knows to be true regarding his own ideas, plans, values, priorities and judgments of possibilities is unknown to us. So when we cannot see how two things God has said about himself mesh together we should be neither surprised nor worried. Such discoveries are only to be expected.

In the present case, some stumble over the question, how can God's offer of Christ to all who hear the gospel be *bona fide*, and how can his command to spread the gospel evince the genuine good-will of which we want to assure all to whom we take it, when he has resolved from eternity whom he will and will not save. The short answer is: we don't know how, but we can see that it is so from the ministry of

Jesus Christ, God the Son incarnate, concerning whom we say: God is Jesuslike (*cf.* Jn. 14:9). It is beyond doubt that Jesus' constant indiscriminate invitations to men to come to him, believe on him, become his disciples and so find life were *bona fide* expressions of good-will: Jesus wept over Jerusalem's unbelief (Lk. 19:41–44), and the look on his face evidently showed both his real concern for the rich young ruler and his real sorrow when the young man went away (*cf.* Mk. 10:21, 23, 27). So from Jesus himself we see that, whatever the truth about election, God takes no pleasure in the death of those who, hearing the gospel, choose to disregard it and die rather than turn and live (*cf.* Ezk. 18:23, 32; 33:11).

The New Testament view of the divine love which it celebrates is that God, having in love gone one mile, as it were, in giving his Son to become the Saviour of all believers, now goes a second mile by bringing all his chosen to faith. The particularity of election and redemption is thus set within the framework of God's general goodwill, not in opposition to such a framework. So we are to invite all to trust Christ, just as Christ himself did (Mt. 11:28 f., *etc.*), because they need him, because he will save them if they come to him, and because God himself is calling them; and, like Christ, we are to look to God to identify his elect by bringing them to faith (*cf.* Jn. 6:35–45). Which brings us to the next point.

No election – no hope
Third, election, so far from undermining evangelism, undergirds it, for it provides the only hope of its succeeding in its aim. The fact that only the elect are saved through the preaching of the gospel does not mean that some are shut out of the kingdom who would otherwise be in it; what it means, rather, is that some do enter the kingdom by faith, whereas otherwise none would. 'An unspiritual person... does not accept anything of the Spirit of God: he sees it all as nonsense; it is beyond his understanding...' (1 Cor. 2:14, JB). The gospel, therefore, will never register with him, and he will never come to faith, unless God 'calls' him.

But the only persons whom God calls, according to Scripture, are the elect: 'those whom he predestined he also called' (Rom. 8:30). Were there no election, there would be no calling, and no conversions, and all evangelistic activity would fail. But as it is, we know, as we spread God's truth, that his word will not return to him void. He has sent it to be the means whereby he calls his elect, and it will prosper in the thing for which he has sent it. (See, again, Acts 18:9–11, with 1 Cor. 1:9.)

4. ELECTION AND THE CHRISTIAN LIFE

Election is the family secret of the sons of God, something about which they have a right to know, and for their own good ought to know. It is not for nothing that Peter exhorts: 'give diligence to make your calling and election sure' (*i.e.*, certain in itself and therefore certain to yourselves: 2 Pet. 1:10, RV).

Election is known by its fruits in a person's life. Paul knew the election of the Thessalonians from their faith, hope, and love, the transformation in their lives which the gospel had brought about (1 Thes. 1:3–6), and the more that the qualities to which Peter exhorts us (virtue, knowledge, temperance, patience, piety, kindness, love) appear in our lives, the more sure of our own election we are entitled to be.

How does this help?
What is the value and effect of the knowledge of our own election? Does it allow us to become complacent, and to conclude that, since we are elect, it does not matter how we live? No; as the passage quoted from 2 Peter itself indicates, only if we are daily 'perfecting holiness in the fear of the Lord', evidencing the genuineness of our faith by our works, have we any right to be sure of our election at all. In fact, the faithful Christian's knowledge of his election has a very different tendency. It awakens awe in him, as it sets before him the greatness of the God in whose hands we all are, and who disposes of us all at his own pleasure. It

humbles him, for it reminds him that his salvation is not in the smallest degree his own achievement: he has nothing that he has not received. But it also thrills him, by assuring him that his salvation is all of God, and that in God's hands he is safe for ever. The reason why he is in Christ now is that God chose him to be in Christ from all eternity; and God's choice guarantees that he will be kept secure in Christ to all eternity. '... Whom he predestined ... called ... justified he also *glorified*.'

Exulting certainty

Thus the knowledge of our election turns our hope of glory from a diffident longing to an exulting certainty, and strengthens us to face the most nightmarish future on earth with triumph in our hearts. It is no accident, but the most cogent spiritual logic, that leads Paul on from a review of God's electing purpose to break out, 'What then shall we say to this? If God is for us, who is against us? ... Who shall bring any charge against God's elect? ... Who shall separate us from the love of Christ? ... we are more than conquerors through him who loved us. For I am sure that neither death, nor life, ... nor things present, nor things to come, ... will be able to separate us from the love of God in Christ Jesus our Lord' (Rom. 8:29–39). And as the Christian surveys this unfathomable, free, almighty, endless love of the Father and the Son that laid hold on him before time began and has ransomed him and quickened him and is pledged to bring him safe through life's battles and storms to the unutterable joys which God has in store for his children, so he finds himself longing more than anything to answer love with love, and the language of his heart is the language of Murray M'Cheyne's hymn:

> *Chosen, not for good in me,*
> *Wakened up from wrath to flee;*
> *Hidden in the Saviour's side,*
> *By the Spirit sanctified –*
> Teach me, Lord, on earth to show,
> By my love, how much I owe.

14

HOLINESS AND SANCTIFICATION

The two English nouns in our title represent a single word-group in both Hebrew and Greek.[1] In English, we have no adjective from the verb 'sanctify', nor any verb from the adjective 'holy'. This, perhaps, is not a very great tragedy; if the words 'sanct' and 'holify' existed, they would sound so ugly that nobody would want to use them: but it does mean that we have to employ two word-groups in English where both biblical languages use only one.

The ideas which these word-families convey are of fundamental importance. This is reflected in the frequency of their occurrence: members of the *q-d-sh* family appear nearly 1,000 times in the Old Testament, and members of the *hag-* family nearly 300 times in the New. The general idea which they invariably express, in some form or other, is that of separation, or being set apart. They are found only in religious contexts, where the relations of God and his creatures are under discussion. In these contexts, they are used in four connections which between them span almost the whole of biblical teaching. They denote (i) the nature of God; (ii) the duty of man; (iii) the work of grace in and upon the Christian and the church; (iv) the state of future glory.

A balanced perspective

The fact that in both Hebrew and Greek a single set of words links these four themes together should warn us against trying to understand any one of them in isolation from the other three. We need this warning particularly,

[1] The Hebrew family is *qadosh* (holy), *qadash* (sanctify), and *qodesh* (holiness); the corresponding Greek family is *hagios* (holy), *hagiazō* (sanctify), and three nouns, *hagiasmos*, *hagiōsynē*, and *hagiotēs* (holiness).

perhaps, in connection with the third theme – holiness, or sanctification, as a work of grace. For here we Evangelicals frequently go astray. Too often we deal with the subject of sanctification in a theological vacuum, in a way that is really dangerous. Our special 'holiness movements', and 'holiness teaching' and 'holiness meetings' direct our attention to this one topic exclusively, and so, by the very fact of their existence, encourage us to approach and study it without even asking ourselves whether the biblical teaching on the holiness of God, and of his law, and of heaven, might not be relevant to it.

We need to realize that this whole approach – the fragmentation-approach, we might call it – is wrong. It puts asunder things that God has joined, and makes it certain that sooner or later we shall run off the track. For the truth is that these other three themes provide the context and fix the perspective in which alone Bible teaching about sanctification can be properly understood. Outside this context, we are bound to fail, more or less, to get the hang of it, just as we are bound to fail, more or less, to appreciate a detail from a great painting if we refuse to view it in its proper place in the painting as a whole.

It is to be feared that our unbalanced preoccupation with this one theme, taken out of context, has tended to produce an unbecoming lop-sidedness of character and outlook. Christian people seeking holiness have become self-centred, small-minded and conceited, through thinking too much about themselves and too little about God. Many have succumbed either to a priggish asceticism which equates holiness with mere abstinence from this and that (sex, alcohol, jeans, jazz, jokes, rock music, long hair and sideburns, live theatre, depilatory treatment, political interest or whatever), or else to the cult of some special experience, identified with holiness ('the second blessing', 'the fullness of the Spirit', 'Spirit-baptism', 'entire sanctification', etc.), which they have pursued sometimes to the neglect of common-or-garden Christian morality. 'When people talk', wrote Bishop Ryle in 1879, 'of having received "such a blessing," and of having found "the higher life," after hearing some earnest advocate of "holiness by faith and self-consecration," while their families and friends see no improvement and no increased sanctity in their daily tempers and behaviour, immense harm is done to the cause of Christ' (*Holiness*, 1879, p.xv). Ryle's words remain uncomfortably relevant today, as does the 1979 comment of the inner-city pastor who, when asked what he thought of the Higher Life, replied: 'It's all right if you've got the money and leisure for it.' It will, however, help us to avoid this kind of self-deception if we relate all our thoughts about sanctification to God's own holy character, which we are called to reflect, and to his holy law, by which we are commanded to live.

We will now try to outline our four themes in their own proper order and connection.

1. THE HOLINESS OF GOD

'Holy' is the word which the Bible uses to express all that is distinctive and transcendent in the revealed nature and character of the Creator, all that brings home to us the infinite distance and difference that there is between him and ourselves. Holiness in this sense means, quite comprehensively, the 'God-ness' of God, everything about him which sets him apart from man.

Most of what the Bible says about God's holiness is said in the Old Testament. There, God is often called 'the Holy One of Israel', or simply 'the Holy One' (*e.g.* Is. 40:25). He swears by his holiness, *i.e.* by himself and all that he is (Am. 4:2). His 'name' – that is, his revealed nature – is regularly spoken of as 'holy' (*e.g.* Is. 57:15). The angels worship him by crying 'Holy, holy, holy, is the Lord of hosts' (Is. 6:3). In the New Testament, references to the divine holiness are less common, but we do on occasion find the word 'holy' applied to all three Persons of the Godhead. Christ prays 'Holy Father' (Jn. 17:11); the devils identify Christ as 'the Holy One of God' (Mk. 1:24); and the Comforter's name is the Holy Spirit (the name occurs, in fact, nearly 100 times).

Infinite superiority

When God is called 'holy', the thought conveyed is that of deity, and more particularly of those qualities of deity which mark out the infinite superiority of the Triune Jehovah over mankind, in respect of both powers and perfections. The word points to God as standing above and apart from men, a different kind of being on a higher plane of existence. It focuses attention on everything in God that makes him a proper object of awe and worship and reverent fear, and that serves to remind his human creatures how ungodlike they really are. Thus it denotes, *first,* God's infinite greatness and power, contrasted with the smallness and weakness of us men and women; *second,* it denotes his perfect purity and uprightness, which stands in glaring contrast with the unrighteousness and uncleanness of sinful humanity, and which call forth from him that inflexible retributive reaction to sin which the Bible calls his 'wrath' and 'judgment'; *third,* it denotes his determination to maintain his own righteous rule, however much it may be resisted and opposed – a resolve which makes it certain that all sin will eventually receive its due reward. The biblical idea of God's holiness involves all this.

Judgment on sin

The connection between holiness and judgment on sin is brought out in a verse like Isaiah 5:16, in which Israel is told: 'the Lord of hosts is exalted in judgment, and God the Holy One is sanctified in righteousness' (RV). When the holy God asserts himself in righteous judgment against evil-doers, then he 'is sanctified', *i.e.* his holiness is revealed and vindicated. The RSV renders, 'the Holy God *shows himself holy* in righteousness.' Such acts of power and justice declare his greatness and manifest his glory before men: by these means, God makes himself known and gets himself honour. The connection between these things is brought out at the close of another prophecy of judgment (Ezk. 38:23, RV): 'And I will *magnify* myself, and *sanctify* myself, and I will *make myself known* in the eyes of many nations; and they shall know that I am the LORD.'

As God sanctifies himself by revealing his holiness in acts of judgment, so in the Old Testament men 'sanctify God' when they honour his revelation by reverent observance of his will (*cf.* Nu. 20:12; 27:14; Is. 8:13). This honouring of God's holiness is the essence of worship. In a parallel sense, Peter exhorts Christians to 'sanctify in your hearts Christ as Lord' (1 Pet. 3:15, RV; RSV has 'reverence'). We 'sanctify' the Lord Jesus Christ by letting him rule over our lives.

2. THE HOLINESS OF MAN

God's holiness, as we have seen, means not only his infinite power, but also what the hymn calls his 'aweful purity'. The holiness to which he calls his people is not an aspiration after the former, but an imitation of the latter. Holiness is the Bible word for man's due response to God as *his* God, within the covenant relationship. God commands those whom he has separated from other peoples to be his people, that they should separate themselves from all that displeases him and is contrary to his will. Holiness of life is what he requires of all those whom he has brought into fellowship with himself.

This demand is the ground-bass of all the Old Testament legislation. 'Ye shall be holy men unto me' (Ex. 22:31, RV). 'You shall be holy; for I the LORD your God am holy' (Lv. 19:2). 'I am the LORD your God; consecrate yourselves therefore, and be holy.... You shall not defile yourselves ...I am the LORD who brought you up out of the land of Egypt, to be your God; you shall therefore be holy, for I am holy' (Lv. 11:44–45). The same demand is made in the New Testament (1 Pet. 1:15–16). The demand is for a family likeness: God's son (the nation in the Old Testament, Ex. 4:22; the individual Christian in the New Testament, Rom. 8:14 ff.) must strive, just because he is God's son, to be like his Father. This is what the call to holiness means; and the noun itself (in the New Testament, *hagiasmos*, sometimes rendered 'sanctification' in the English versions) denotes the state of being dissociated from the practice of sin and devoted to the life of Godlikeness.

Negative

The New Testament enlarges on the negative side of holiness – separation from activities that defile – in 2 Corinthians 6:17 ff.: 'Come out from them, and be separate from them, says the Lord, and touch nothing unclean; then I will welcome you, and I will be a father to you….Since we have these promises, beloved, let us cleanse ourselves from every defilement of body and spirit, and make holiness perfect in the fear of God.' Elsewhere, Paul applies this principle to a specific case – sexual sin. 'This is the will of God, even your sanctification, that ye abstain from fornication; that each one of you know how to possess himself of his own vessel [his body or his wife: expositors differ] in sanctification and honour….For God called us not for uncleanness, but in sanctification' (1 Thes. 4:3–7, RV). The state of holiness and the practice of filthiness are absolutely exclusive of each other.

It may be observed in passing that, though avoidance of sexual sin is not the whole of holiness, all God's people need special warning at this point (which is doubtless why both Testaments deal with it so frankly and fully). The records of 'holiness movements' provide abundant – indeed, shattering – proof of this.

The Old Testament also speaks of moral uncleanness, and of ritual uncleanness as well. Its regulations regarding holiness (*cf.* especially Lv. 11 – 22) make much of the need to avoid, or if one cannot avoid, then to purge away, ritual uncleanness in connection with such things as food, disease, menstruation, and death. It has been argued that these prescribed abstinences and purifications had hygienic value, and perhaps they did; but the New Testament tells us no more about them than that they were typical in their meaning and hence temporary in their application. Christ lays it down that what really defiles is not food, but sin (Mk. 7:18–23); Paul condemns Christian teachers who treat some foods as unclean, arguing that God created all edible things 'to be received with thanksgiving by those who believe and know the truth' (1 Tim. 4:3 ff.). From such passages it becomes clear that the ritual defilement of 'unclean' meats and other 'unclean' created things was merely a type of the true defilement, that of the unclean heart. It would seem that God's reason for putting his Old Testament people under these typical laws was partly to maintain the separateness of Israel's national life and partly to impress upon his people the fact that in his eyes defilement was a real and serious thing, and cleansing from it was all-important.

Positive

The positive side of holiness is the maintaining of loyalty to God and the living of a life which shows forth to others the qualities of faithfulness, gentleness, good-will, kindness, forbearance, and uprightness, on the model of God's own display of these qualities in his gracious dealings with us. The New Testament stresses this aspect of the matter by representing righteousness as the pathway to holiness (Rom. 6:19; *cf.* Eph. 4:24). According to the New Testament, holiness is neither a feeling nor an experience, but a kind of living in which the character of the Father and the Son is mirrored in one's outlook and conduct.

The Christian's holiness, like his Master's, is his living out a relationship to the world of men whereby he is *in* it without being *of* it (see Jn. 17:14–16). This requires both separation and identification, both detachment and involvement.

Being *of* the world means being controlled by what preoccupies the world, the quest for pleasure, profit and position ('the lust of the flesh and the lust of the eyes and the pride of life,' 1 Jn. 2:16). Christians must negate that preoccupation, even though the world will then hate them, as it hated Christ, for exposing its concerns as tawdry and trivial (as indeed they are) and those whom these concerns enslave as degrading their own humanity (which indeed they do). Such ill-will is inevitable and must be taken in one's stride.

A holy person's life will not centre on *things*: instead, a certain frugality will mark it, an eschewing of luxury and display, a sense of stewardship of all possessions, and a readiness to let them go if need be for the Lord's sake. Holy people do not undervalue this world's good things, as if

God did not make or provide them (Manicheism, the belief that material things are bad, is no part of holiness), but they refuse to be enslaved to them. Nor do they squint sideways to compare their material showing with that of others; they know that keeping up with the Joneses is not holiness, even if Jones goes to their church or is in orbit in some Christian celebrity circuit. The holy person lives free from the passion for possessions, just as he does from other forms of self-seeking and self-indulgence. His treasure is with God, and his heart too (*cf.* Mt. 6:19–21). The cheerfulness of his disregard of the world's scale of values, and the straight-forward, single-minded, spontaneous ardour of his love for God may make him somewhat unnerving company, though if so it is because he is so much more honest and human than we who watch him, not because he is odd and we are normal.

But with this separation goes an equally breath-taking identification with others and their needs. The Reformers' claim that you cannot be holy if you leave the world for a monastery or a hermit's hut may have been overstated, but there is deep truth in it. As (to quote John Wesley) there is nothing more unchristian than a solitary Christian, so nothing is more contrary to holiness than losing interest in one's fellow-men. Detachment from the world in the sense of ungodly goals must be balanced by commitment to the world in the sense of needy people.

The outward form of Jesus' own holiness was association with all sorts of folk down to tax-collectors and other disreputables, in whom he took as much interest as he did in any. Indeed, he showed special concern to affirm the poor, the obscure and the underprivileged, whom society treated as ciphers, and was known for his unrabbi-like habit of making friends with them and spending time in their company (*cf.* Mt. 9:9–13; 11:5, 19). This element of Jesus' holiness must be part of the holiness of his disciples also. If separation as described fulfils the first great commandment, identification of this kind is needed to fulfil the second. General Booth once took as a New Year motto for the Salvation Army the one word 'others'; holy folk have that motto in their hearts all the time, and their behaviour at home and outside, in the family and in the wider world, shows it. Thus holy persons are not restful company; they are too much alive for that, as praying and labouring they pour themselves out in love for others. The Christ of the gospels, and the Paul of Acts and the letters, are the models here.

The word 'holiness' suggests to modern man something pale, anaemic, withdrawn, negative and passive. That shows how little modern man knows about it! Scriptural holiness is in fact the most positive, potent and often passionate quality of life that is ever seen.

3. THE GIFT OF HOLINESS

Augustine's famous prayer, 'Give what you command, and command what you will,' expressed a profound insight into biblical theology. God does indeed give what he commands; the holiness which he requires of his people is also his gift to them. God himself sanctifies sinners. In the Old Testament, he declares: 'I, the LORD, sanctify you' (Ex. 31:13; Lv. 20:8; 21:8). The New Testament proclaims 'Christ Jesus, whom God made our.... sanctification' (1 Cor. 1:30); 'Christ... loved the church and gave himself up for her, that he might sanctify her' (Eph. 5:25 f.); 'you were sanctified...in the name of the Lord Jesus Christ and in the Spirit of our God' (1 Cor. 6:11); 'we have been sanctified through the offering of the body of Jesus Christ once for all' (Heb. 10:10). Holiness, or sanctification, is here set forth as the gracious gift of God.

Position
The New Testament makes it clear that this gift has two aspects. The first aspect is *relational* and *positional*. In this sense, God sanctifies sinners once and for ever when he brings them to himself, separating them from the world, delivering them from sin and Satan, and welcoming them into his fellowship. In this sense, therefore, the meaning of sanctification approximates to that of justification, adoption, and new birth. The epistle to the Hebrews always uses the verb 'sanctify' in this way (see Heb. 2:11; 10:10, 14, 29;

13:12). From this standpoint, sanctification is a once-for-all benefit which the Christian begins to enjoy upon his conversion, through faith in Christ (see Acts 26:18), and to which he can look back as a past event. It is in virtue of this event that the New Testament addresses him as a 'saint' (*hagios*) – *i.e.*, because he has been 'sanctified in Christ Jesus' in the sense explained (see 1 Cor. 1:2). The New Testament does not say that Christians must lead holy lives in order to become saints; instead, it tells Christians that, because they are saints, they must henceforth lead holy lives! This, then, is the first and fundamental aspect of God's gift of sanctification.

Progression

The second aspect of the gift is *recreative* and *progressive*. In this sense, sanctification is the gracious work of the Holy Spirit in the believer throughout his earthly life whereby he grows in grace (1 Pet. 2:2; 2 Pet. 3:18; Eph. 4:14 f.) and is changed more and more in mind and heart and life into the image of the Lord Jesus Christ (Rom. 12:2; 2 Cor. 3:18; Eph. 4:23 f.; Col. 3:10). The verb 'sanctify' is clearly used with this application in John 17:17; 1 Thessalonians 5:23; Ephesians 5:26.

In this sanctifying work, God calls for our co-operation, as he 'works in [us] to will and to act according to his good purpose' (Phil. 2:13, NIV). He summons us to 'mortify' our sins (put them to death) through the Spirit (Rom. 8:13; Col. 3:5), and to devote ourselves to the practice of the 'good works' which the ethical parts of the New Testament prescribe in such detail. The hymn that speaks of 'Holiness by faith in Jesus, Not by effort of our own' is drawing a false antithesis. Certainly, holiness is by faith in Jesus – all our strength for holiness must be drawn from him by faith and prayer, for without him we can do nothing (Jn. 15:5 ff.). But equally holiness is by effort; for when we have knelt to acknowledge our weakness and ask for help, we are then to stand on our feet and strive against sin (Heb. 12:4), resist the devil (Jas. 4:7), and fight the good fight of faith (1 Tim. 6:12; *cf.* Eph. 6:10–18). Holiness is no more by faith without effort than it is by effort without faith. It is important to keep the balance here; it has not always been kept.

4. THE HOLINESS OF HEAVEN

Holiness is the end and purpose of our election (Eph. 1:4), our redemption (Eph. 5:25–27), our calling (1 Thes. 4:7; *cf.* 1 Pet. 1:15; 2 Tim. 1:9), and of God's providential disciplining of us (Heb. 12:10); but its full attainment lies beyond this world. Zechariah's vision of a restored Jerusalem in which 'HOLY TO THE LORD will be inscribed on the bells of the horses' and 'every pot in Jerusalem and Judah will be holy to the LORD Almighty' (Zc. 14:20–21, NIV) is a picture, given in typical terms, of the predestined holiness of the Church; but it will not find its ultimate fulfilment until new Jerusalem, 'the holy city', appears as a bride adorned for her husband (Rev. 21:2). Then, when the work of grace is ended, God's people will be separate, not merely from the dominion of sin, but from its very presence. There will be no sin in heaven, for those who are in heaven will not have it in them to sin any more. Glorification means, among other things, the final uprooting of sin from our nature. Holiness will thus be perfect in heaven. To be unable to sin again will be both our freedom and our joy. Meanwhile, with this hope before us, our daily calling is to 'strive... for the holiness without which no one will see the Lord' (Heb. 12:14).

15

MORTIFY

I remember my first evening meal in theological college. We were all strangers to each other, and conversation was exploratory, hearty and random. I told the man opposite me, a grinning little Welshman, that I was a Puritan addict. He asked why. I told him the Puritans had done me good; they went deep, and were magnificent on mortification. 'Mortification!' he said. 'Let's have a talk after the meal.'

That night we walked the river banks of Oxford for about two hours. I told him what John Owen's sixty pages on the mortifying of sin had done for me when a popular brand of holiness teaching was driving me round the bend. He told me of his agonies in an overheated community where perfectionism was professed, moral standards were tumbling and the word mortification was taboo because everyone was supposed to have got beyond that. In such an atmosphere God had taught him that sin is not rooted out of us nor rendered impotent in us at any stage in this life, and that watching, praying, suspecting yourself and often examining your heart and actions are vital disciplines lest you enter into temptation without realizing what you are doing. He had felt bound to leave the community eventually (and was vilified for doing so), but while in it he had known touches of revival, and both then and later he was uncannily sensitive to spiritual realities, as Christians moulded by revival often prove to be. He successfully pastored two awkward parishes over more than twenty years and was used to change many lives for God. He was a gregarious extravert, and one of the most cheerful men I have known. He spoke regularly of mortification to the end of his days, the only evangelical pastor I know to have done so. He thought the subject was important. So do I: hence this study.

The Christian is committed to a lifelong fight against the world, the flesh and the devil. Mortification is his assault on the second. Two texts from Paul show that it is an essential ingredient in Christian living: 'Mortify therefore your members which are upon the earth' (Col. 3:5); 'If by the Spirit ye mortify the deeds of the body, ye shall live' (Rom. 8:13). I cite the RV; modern versions (RSV, NEB, NIV) have 'put to death', which is what both the Greek verbs used literally mean. The verb in the second text is in the present tense, implying that mortification must be continuous ('if ye ... *keep on mortifying* ... ye shall live'). The verb in the first is in the aorist tense, implying that mortification, once commenced, will be successfully accomplished.

The first tells us that Christian privilege makes mortification obligatory. Paul argues thus (Col. 3:1–5): 'As those who now share Christ's risen life, whose citizenship and prospects are in the heavenly realm, who are no more children of wrath but sons of God and heirs of glory, you must behave as befits your status. You must be what you are, and not what you were. Therefore you must mortify sin.' The second tells us that mortification is necessary as a means to an end. It is the way to 'life', spiritual well-being in this world and glory with Christ in the next. It will not earn us life (Christ has done that for us already), but it is part of the 'work of faith' (1 Thes. 1:3) through which we lay hold and keep hold of Christ's free gift (*cf.* 1 Tim. 6:12; Phil. 3:12–14). It is one of the 'works' without which 'faith' (*i.e.* a profession of faith) is 'dead' (Jas. 2:26). Paul's argument may be expanded thus: if you would make your calling and election sure by proving your faith true, if you would so run as to obtain, so travel as to arrive, you must mortify sin. 'He who doth not kill sin in his way,' observed John Owen grimly, 'takes no steps towards his journey's end.'

The evident importance of the subject makes the long-standing neglect of it among Christians appear both sad and odd. Causes of this neglect include, perhaps, evangelical recoil from the externalism of traditional Catholic mortification (hair shirts, standing for hours in cold water and all that), where the object of attack seemed to be the physical body rather than indwelling sin in the soul, and the censure of Colossians 2:23 seemed obviously to apply. But a deeper cause is surely the shallowness of Christian understanding and experience in these days. Since we hardly know God and so hardly know ourselves, and since most of us think of self-examination as old-fashioned and morbid and never try it, we are hardly aware of indwelling sin at all.

There is an old comedy short (maybe one of Mack Sennett's, I can't be sure) in which an escaped lion takes the place of the shaggy dog beside the armchair and the comic affectionately runs his fingers through its mane several times before realizing that, as we say, he has a problem. We act like that with regard to our sinful habits. We treat them as friends rather than killers, and never suspect how indwelling sin when indulged enervates and deadens. This, one fears, is because we are already its victims, never having known what it is to be really alive in our relationship with God, just as children born with crippled legs never know what it is to run around, as distinct from hobbling. Such is the nemesis of our modern neglect of mortification.

So it is a theme on which no contemporary writing of significance seems to be available. For help in understanding the Bible teaching about it, one has to go back to the great Puritans of the seventeenth century ('an age,' wrote Bishop J. C. Ryle, 'when I am obliged to say, experimental religion was more deeply studied, and far better understood, than it is now'). Most useful of all are the relevant writings of the man Spurgeon called 'the prince of divines', John Owen. These are: *The Nature, Power, Deceit, and Prevalency of the Remainders of Indwelling Sin in Believers;* and the section on mortification (Bk. 4, ch. 8) in *A Discourse concerning the Holy Spirit* (*Works*, ed. W. Goold, vols. 6 and 3). The present writer is bound to say that he owes to these fearsome-sounding treatises not merely much material for this study, but almost all the light he has ever had on the themes with which it deals.

Mortification is war; and four steps are involved in effective warfare.

Our enemy

We must know our enemy. The starting-point in mortification is recognizing that we fight, not merely sins, but *sin*. As we saw in earlier studies, the Bible portrays sin as 'a positive and destructive principle endemic in man' (A. M. Hunter): a hereditary impulse, rooted deep in our nature, which drives us continually into a blind opposition towards God. The mind which it masters is, simply, 'enmity against God; for it is not subject to the law of God, neither indeed can it be' (Rom. 8:7, RV). Sin is a lust for self-assertion in defiance of God; the very idea of conscious dependence and grateful worship and obedient fellowship with the Creator is utterly abhorrent to it. It is the root of all actual sins, and so of fallen man's family likeness to the devil (*cf.* Jn. 8:44; 1 Jn. 3:8–12). Christ gives a list of the fruits by which we may know it (Mk. 7:21–22); Paul gives two (Gal. 5:19–21; Col. 3:5,8). Sin is the innate energy which gives birth to these things.

Sin enslaves the unbeliever completely (*cf.* Rom. 6:16–23). He is at peace with it, for it has won his heart. But the convert takes Christ as his master and model, and resolves that he will no longer be the self-asserting, God-resisting person he was. This is his 'change of mind' (which is what *metanoia,* the Greek word for 'repentance', really means). Hereby he puts off 'the old man, which waxes corrupt after the lusts of deceit' and dons the new (Eph. 4:22–24, RV). He renounces sin; he wills its death in him; and thus in intention he has 'crucified the flesh' and its lusts (Gal. 5:24).

But sin does not forthwith die. On the contrary, it takes on a life of its own, and the Christian now finds it active within him as a kind of devilish *alter ego,* a shadow-self, opposing, resisting, and to a greater or less degree thwarting all his attempts to do the will of God. 'Sin', wrote Owen, 'is compared to a person, a living person, called the "old man", with his faculties and properties, his wisdom, craft, subtlety, strength.'

The Christian thus finds himself in conflict with a part of himself: 'the desires of the flesh are against the Spirit, and the desires of the Spirit are against the flesh. . to prevent

183

you from doing what you would' (Gal. 5:17). He wants to be perfect, but he never is, and at every stage of his life he is forced to say with Paul: 'the good which I would I do not; but the evil which I would not, that I practise... it is no more I that do it, but sin which dwelleth in me' (Rom. 7:19-20, RV). Sin is always in rebellion against the law of his mind (Rom. 7:23; *cf.* 25); 'neither is it expressible,' wrote Owen, 'with what vigour and variety sin acts itself in this matter. Sometimes it proposeth diversions, sometimes it causeth weariness, sometimes it finds out difficulties, sometimes it stirs up contrary affections, sometimes it begets prejudices, and one way or another entangles the soul, so that it never suffers grace to have an absolute and complete success in any duty.' Sin is already at war with us (Rom. 7:23; 1 Pet. 2:11), it seeks our ruin; and the only way to preserve ourselves is to fight back. This we do by mortification.

Our objective

We must know our objective. To get this clear is step two. In ignorance of one's enemy, one fights blind; without a clear objective, one fights aimlessly, 'as one that beateth the air.' He who aims at nothing never achieves anything else. We must, then, be clear as to what we are trying to do.

The two words translated 'mortify' in the texts with which we began this study both mean 'put to death'. This is our aim: so to drain the life out of sin that it never moves again. We are not promised that we shall reach our goal in this life, but we are commanded to advance towards it by assaulting those inclinations and habits in which sin's presence is recognized. We are not merely to resist its attacks. We are to take the initiative against it. We must seek, in Owen's phrase, 'not a mere disappointment of sin, that it be not brought forth... but a victory over it, and pursuit of it to a complete conquest'; not merely the *counteraction,* but the *eradication* of it. Killing, so far as we can compass that, is the end in view.

Mortification is *a life's work.* Sin 'will not otherwise die, but by being gradually and constantly weakened,' warns Owen; 'spare it, and it heals its wounds, and recovers strength.' The Bible and church history bear repeated witness to the disastrous consequences of ceasing to mortify before sin is dead. And it never dies in this world, however weak it may grow.

Moreover, mortification is *a painful discipline*. Sinful habits have become so much part of ourselves that to attempt their destruction is like cutting off a hand, or plucking out an eye (*cf.* Mt. 5:29–30). 'Carnal self', which, naturally enough, longs to live, will do all it can to deter us from the task of killing it.

Nonetheless, mortification is *an effective discipline*. It is a part of healthy Christian experience to enjoy a continually increasing degree of deliverance from sins, as by mortification the strength of sin is steadily drained. And few things afford the Christian such relief and encouragement as the memory of sins which once ruled him, but which he has conquered by the power of the Spirit of God.

Our superiority

We must know our superiority. This is step three. Nobody has much heart for a fight he does not think he can win. To expect defeat is thus to ensure it. If I imagine that, try as I might, I am bound to fail, I shall not even try as I might. But the Christian is forbidden such disastrous pessimism. God obliges him to expect success when he meets sin. For Scripture tells him that at conversion the Spirit united him to the living Christ. This was his regeneration. It made him a 'new creation' (2 Cor. 5:17), and ensured his permanent superiority in the conflict with sin. The Bible describes what then occurred in three complementary ways, each of which from a different angle confirms that this is so. We have met these thoughts before, but it will be good for us to review them again.

1. *The Spirit implanted a new life-principle*. As the direct result of union with the risen and living Christ, regeneration is spoken of as being 'quickened' or 'raised' with him (Eph. 2:5; Col. 2:12–13; 3:1). As the beginning of spiritual life in man, it is spoken of as being 'born again' and 'begotten of God' (Jas. 1:18; 1 Pet. 1:3; 1 Jn. 5:18). The dynamic thus

implanted is the 'new heart' and 'new spirit' promised in Ezekiel 36:26, the 'new man' put on at conversion (Eph. 4:24), the 'seed' of God in his children's hearts (1 Jn. 3:9). This new energy finds its characteristic expression in the same attitude and relationship to God as that which marked Christ's human life; a spontaneous affinity to God and love for him and for his word and his people. Godlessness is as distasteful to it as godliness is to sin. Faith, love and opposition to sin are its natural fruits, and sure signs of its presence (Gal. 5:6, 17). It is the Christian's new nature and true self, the 'inner man' which delights in God's laws (Rom. 7:22). It replaces sin as the reigning power in his heart and the dominant impulse in his life. It is no longer his nature to sin. Insofar as he does so, he acts out of character, and his heart is not in it. He can never sin with all his heart again.

2. *The Spirit dealt a death-blow to sin.* This is clear, from what was said above. The end of God's justifying and regenerating us is 'that the body of sin [our sinful character] might be destroyed [brought to nothing], that henceforth we should not serve sin' (Rom. 6:6). By our regenerating union with Christ and the incoming of the new life, sin receives a blow from which it can never recover. Its power is broken, and its ultimate destruction guaranteed. Accordingly, God tells his people that 'sin will have no dominion over you' (Rom. 6:14). Its reign has ended as far as they are concerned. Their part is now by mortification to hasten the demise of their dethroned and doomed enemy. Hereby he assures them that however furious or stubborn sin may prove, however deeply it may have entrenched itself behind bad habits and temperamental weaknesses, sustained pressure cannot fail to uproot and rout it.

3. *The Spirit took up residence in the heart.* The Spirit now indwells the believer (Rom. 8:9–11; 1 Cor. 6:19), to convey life each moment from Christ to him (Col. 2:19) and thus to make the 'seed' in his heart grow and bear the Spirit's fruit (Gal. 5:22). The Spirit is present in person to oppose indwelling sin. He teaches the Christian to understand revealed truth and apply it to himself, stirs him up to obey it and strengthens him as he does so. He 'is at work in

you, both to will and to work for his good pleasure' (Phil. 2:13). Sin can be mortified only 'through the Spirit', for he alone makes men willing and able for the task. But where the indwelling Spirit exerts his sovereign power, failure is impossible.

When the Christian fights sin, therefore, he opposes a dethroned and debilitated foe; he is animated by the energy of what is now the deepest and most powerful instinct in his nature; and he goes in the strength of the Holy Spirit of God. His superiority is assured; he may join battle with confidence; he is going to win.

Our resources

We must know how to use our resources. This is the fourth essential. It is true that we could not mortify sin by our own unaided efforts; but it is no less true that the Spirit will not mortify sin in us without our co-operation. He will prosper our striving, but he will not bless our sloth. We ourselves, then, must attack sin; and the outcome of the conflict will depend on whether we fight wisely and make good use of our available strength. The three prime rules for doing so are these:

1. *Grow.* 'Growing, thriving, and improving in universal holiness,' wrote Owen, 'is the great way of the mortification of sin . . . The more we abound in the fruits of the Spirit, the less shall we be concerned in the works of the flesh . . . This is that which will ruin sin, and without it nothing will contribute anything thereunto.' We must nourish our new nature on God's truth and exercise it constantly in prayer, worship, witness and a consistent, all-round ('universal') obedience. We should plan to practise and develop the qualities most contrary to the sins we have to get rid of – generosity if the problem is greed, a habit of praise if it is self-pity, patience and forbearance if it is bad temper, planned living if it is sloth, or whatever. We must forestall sin's attempts to regain control of our hearts and powers by preoccupying ourselves in the active service of God. Feeble Christians, the careless, the half-hearted and the double-minded, can never mortify sin.

2. *Watch.* It is our responsibility to shun temptation as far as we can. To expect God by his sovereign power to kill lusts in us while we read the books and keep the company and expose ourselves to the influences which we know foment them is presumption, not faith, and is more likely to bring down a curse than a blessing. It has been truly said that though you can't stop birds flying over your head you can stop them nesting in your hair. We must be ruthless in starving sin of all that feeds it. Mortification is impossible otherwise.

3. *Pray.* Prayer alone obtains help from God. Promises that are not claimed are not normally fulfilled: 'you do not have, because you do not ask' (Jas. 4:2). The Spirit's help in mortification is gained only by constant believing prayer, as we claim the promise that sin shall not rule us, as we apply again and again to the Lord, who came and died and rose and lives to save us from sin, for 'grace to help in time of need' (Heb. 4:16). But if we ask and expect we shall not be disappointed. Says Owen: 'Set faith at work on Christ for the killing of thy sin...and thou wilt die a conquerer. Yea, thou wilt through the good providence of God live to see thy lust dead at thy feet.'

Our health
What all this has to say to you and me can be put thus.

Some of us need *correction*. We are children of an age that values kicks above character, self-gratification above self-control and emotional maturity above moral stature. Pleasures are regarded as more important than fidelity or honesty or altruism or service, and we plan harder for recreation than we do for righteousness. Not surprisingly, Christian folk catch this spirit (or it catches them) and in the church they seek a whirl of excitement, emotional 'highs', novelties, psychedelic therapies, thrilling intimacies of fellowship, shouting preachers, stirring songs, everything constantly on the boil; and they easily forget that God's priority is character rather than kicks, and his aim in dealing with us is our holiness, from which our happiness, in the sense of contentment with the way things are, flows as a by-product. But so it is, and the feverish state of mind that has just been described is not good health spiritually. Seeking holiness in Christ must come first, and the practice of mortifying sin, first by maintaining a daily crucifying of the flesh (Gal. 5:24) and then by watching and praying in order to drain the life out of the particular 'passions of the flesh that wage war against your soul' (1 Pet. 2:11), is an essential element in that quest. More Christlikeness of character is the only sure sign of spiritual progress, and without mortification that can hardly be. Mortifying sin is one of the first things that we must learn to put first in our life with God.

And then some of us need *direction*. We know that holiness is a priority; we seek to maintain our first repentance by daily consecration; we want to walk worthy of our calling each day of our lives. But we find in ourselves what, from the biblical standpoint, we must call habits of moral failure – jealousy, envy, greed, impatience, apathy, lust (heterosexual and homosexual), self-absorption, sloth apathy, indiscipline, festering resentment, discontent, arrogance, offhandness, and so on. What are we to do about it? Such habits are like running sores in our spiritual lives: they have to be broken and replaced with appropriate facets of the moral image of Jesus. But how?

There is no magic formula for instant replacement of unChristlike habits by their opposite. Joyous inward experiences of God's presence and love, fulfilling the promise of John 14:21–23, may strengthen your motivation for cleaving to God (*cf.* Rom. 12:1), and have been known to snuff out on the instant obsessive cravings (for alcohol, drugs, tobacco, gambling) that were fuelled by self-hatred: a fact which has sometimes led to these revelations of love being misconceived as experiences of sanctification. In fact, however, when the experience is over the need to seek character change still remains, and it is only by self-knowledge, self-discipline, self-watch and self-distrustful prayer in face of temptation and the recurring routines of sinful habit that headway here will be made. Gifted and electrifying people with flaws in their moral system are top-heavy, and riding for a fall: they should not be taken as role models. If we ourselves are conscious of being gifted, we too shall be tempted to think that public abilities will counter-balance personal shortcomings, but it is never so. As regular exercise is needed to maintain good physical health, so fighting and winning the battle for Christian character through the imitating of Christ and the mortifying of sin is the regular exercise by which alone good spiritual health is maintained. Paul really makes this very clear: so clear, that we are much to blame if we evade the issue.

'...You have died, and now the life you have is hidden with Christ in God. But when Christ is revealed – and he is your life – you too will be revealed in all your glory with him.

'That is why you must kill [mortify] everything in you that belongs only to earthly life: fornication, impurity, guilty passion, evil desires and especially greed... give all these things up: getting angry, being bad-tempered, spitefulness, abusive language and dirty talk; and never tell each other lies. You have stripped off your old behaviour with your old self, and you have put on a new self which will progress towards true knowledge the more it is renewed in the image of its creator; and in that image... there is only Christ: he is everything and he is in everything' (Col. 3:3–11, JB).

16

FELLOWSHIP

What does the word 'fellowship' suggest to you? A cup of tea in the church hall? Gossip in the porch after the service? Hiking with the youth club? A spell at a Christian holiday centre? Touring Scotland, or the Holy Land, with a coachful of churchpeople? We often say that we have had fellowship when all we mean is that we have taken part in some Christian social enterprise of this sort. But we ought not to talk in such terms. The fact that we share social activities with other Christians does not of itself imply that we have fellowship with them. To say this is not, of course, to deny that there may be a place for these activities. Our point is simply that to equate these activities with fellowship, and fellowship with them, is an abuse of Christian language.

And it is a dangerous abuse. It makes for self-deception. It fools us into thinking that we are thriving on fellowship when all the time our souls may be starving for lack of it. It is not a good sign when a person recognizes no difference between sucking sweets and eating a square meal. Equally, it is not a good sign when Christians recognize no difference between social activities in Christian company and fellowship. Fellowship is one of the great words of the New Testament: it denotes something that is vital to a Christian's spiritual health, and central to the church's true life. It is of the first importance, therefore, that we should be clear in our minds as to what Christian fellowship really is.

Fellowship features in the first description that the New Testament gives us of the life of the young church. 'They devoted themselves to the apostles' doctrine and *fellowship*' (Acts 2:42). Gossip, hikes, and tours? No; something of quite a different order, and on quite a different level, as the rest of the passage makes plain. We quote it more fully from the New English Bible, which has an illuminating paraphrase for 'fellowship' and brings out the force of the details strikingly: 'They met constantly to hear the apostles teach, and *to share the common life,* to break bread, and to pray. A sense of awe was everywhere...All whose faith had drawn them together held everything in common... With one mind they kept up their daily attendance at the temple, and, breaking bread in private houses, shared their meals with unaffected joy, as they praised God...' (Acts 2:42–47).

Here is a glimpse of fellowship as the New Testament understands it: and there is clearly a world of difference between this picture and most of the activities that we call 'fellowship' today. The truth is that the word 'fellowship' has been grievously cheapened. A great deal of 'fellowship', so-called, is not fellowship, but something far less, and the true reality of fellowship has largely vanished from our midst. This is one reason why even those parts of the modern church which remain doctrinally orthodox are often sluggish and feeble, compared with their counterparts of one or two centuries ago. Christ rebuked the Laodiceans (Rev. 3:17) for complacently supposing that they had all they needed when they were really in a state of spiritual bankruptcy. He would surely rebuke us in similar terms for talking so smugly about the happy fellowship we have when in fact lack of fellowship is one of our most glaring shortcomings.

For the people of God to recover the true meaning of fellowship is a crying need at the present time. A body in which the blood does not circulate well is always below par, and fellowship corresponds to the circulation of the blood in the body of Christ. The church gains strength through fellowship, and loses strength without it.

We must, then, labour to re-learn the true meaning of fellowship. How are we to set about it? What, essentially, is Christian fellowship?

The idea of fellowship
The Greek word translated 'fellowship' in our English Bible

expresses the idea of sharing, or having something in common with somebody else. (Hence the rendering of it as 'communion' in 1 Cor. 10:16; 2 Cor. 6:14; 13:14, AV, where RSV has 'participation', 'partnership', 'fellowship' respectively; hence also the paraphrase 'to *share* the *common* life' in the NEB version of Acts 2:42, quoted above.) Common participation takes a double form: it may exist either through your giving someone else a share of what you have, or through your receiving from him a share in what he has, or in what he is doing. In Christian fellowship, as we shall see, both forms of participation find a place.

Christian fellowship is two-dimensional; it is first vertical and then horizontal. The horizontal plane of fellowship, which is our immediate concern, presupposes the vertical for its very existence. The *vertical* dimension of fellowship was described by John when he wrote: 'our fellowship is with the Father and with his Son Jesus Christ' (1 Jn. 1:3). This fellowship is what makes a Christian; indeed, John's words afford a precise definition of a Christian. The man who is not in fellowship with the Father and the Son, however upright and pious he may be, is no Christian at all. The *horizontal* dimension of fellowship is the habitual sharing, the constant giving to and receiving from each other, which is the true and authentic pattern of life for the people of God.

Fellowship with God, then, is the source from which fellowship among Christians springs; and fellowship with God is the end to which Christian fellowship is a means. We should not, therefore, think of our fellowship with other Christians as a spiritual luxury, an optional addition to the exercises of private devotion. We should recognize rather that such fellowship is a spiritual necessity; for God has made us in such a way that our fellowship with himself is fed by our fellowship with fellow-Christians, and requires to be so fed constantly for its own deepening and enrichment.

When the faith of the Hebrew Christians was flagging, the apostolic writer urged them, among other things, to have more fellowship. 'Let us consider how to stir up one another ... not neglecting to meet together, as is the habit

of some, but encouraging one another...' (Heb. 10:24 r.)
It was a vital point in his message to them. For it will always
be the case that the church will flourish, and Christians will
be strong, only where there is fellowship. Nor is it merely of
the church on earth that this is true; heaven, the place for
the perfecting of the church, will be a place of fellowship at
its most free and joyful. But always, both here and hereafter, the fellowship practised by the redeemed will have as
its God-appointed goal the deepening of the fellowship
which each of them enjoys with the Redeemer. The first
truth to grasp about Christian fellowship is that it is not an
end in itself. Fellowship between Christians is for the sake
of fellowship with God.

Fellowship with God
Of the relationship of giving and taking that exists between
Christians and the first two Persons of the Trinity, we can
only speak briefly here. Suffice it to say that it is a two-sided
relationship, in which both the divine and the human parti-
cipants are active. God's fellowship with men covers all
that the Father and the Son have done, and do, and will do,
in order to share their glory with us sinners. Our fellowship
with God covers all the giving to him and taking from him
that we do in order to express our faith and repentance.
God gives himself to us as our Father on the basis of the
redemption wrought for us by his Son. We receive sonship
to God, and a title to all the blessings that sonship entails,
through taking the Lord Jesus Christ as our Saviour. 'He
who *receives* me,' said our Lord, 'receives him who sent me'
(Mt. 10:40). 'As many as *received* him [Christ],' John
assures us, 'to them gave he the right to become children of
God' (Jn. 1:12, RV).

This offered and appropriated sonship is the foundation
on which all our subsequent fellowship with God rests. Day
by day, as God's sons, we thankfully take the gifts that our
heavenly Father bestows – daily remission of sins, daily
reassurance from his promises, daily revelations of himself
from his Word. Day by day, we trustfully hand over to our
heavenly Father our various fears and failures, deliberately

unstrapping the burden of care from our own shoulders in order to cast it upon him. Such, in outline, is the taking and giving, the sharing with God, that constitutes the life of faith. With it go the giving and taking that make up repentance, the daily response to the daily summons – 'my son, *give* me your heart'; '*yield* yourselves to God';'*take* my yoke upon you, and learn from me'; '*take* up [your] cross daily, and follow me' (Pr. 23:26; Rom. 6:13; Mt. 11:29; Mk. 10:21). This is, so to speak, the structural shape of the Christian's fellowship with God; this, in essence, is the Christian life.

Fellowship between Christians

How does fellowship between Christians fit into this picture?

Christian fellowship is a family activity of God's sons. Like fellowship with the Father and the Son, it is a two-way traffic which involves both giving and taking on both sides. It is, first, a sharing with our fellow-believers the things that God has made known to us about himself, in hope that we may thus help them to know him better and so enrich their fellowship with him. The apostle John illustrates this side of Christian fellowship. He tells us that when he sat down to write his first epistle, his motive was that 'you may have fellowship with us'; and it is to explain the meaning of this wish that he adds the words already quoted – 'and our fellowship is with the Father and with his Son Jesus Christ' (1 Jn. 1:3). John is hoping to draw his readers into what he himself has come to know of fellowship with God. That is the 'fellowship with us' that he wants them to have.

This is one side of Christian fellowship; but there is another. Fellowship is, secondly, a seeking to share in what God has made known of himself to others, as a means to finding strength, refreshment, and instruction for one's own soul. In fellowship, one seeks to gain, as well as to give. The apostle Paul illustrates this side of the matter. He tells the Romans: 'I long to see you, that I may impart to you some spiritual gift to strengthen you.' But then, lest he should give the impression that he thinks of fellowship between himself and young churches as a one-way traffic only, he hastens to add – 'that is, that we may be mutually encouraged by each other's faith, both yours and mine' (Rom. 1:11 f.). The fellowship that Paul desires is to be a two-way traffic. Paul, great apostle though he is, is humble and realistic enough to acknowledge that he needs fellowship for his own encouragement, and to say outright that when he goes to minister to his fellow-Christians he does so in the hope, not merely that he will do them good, but that they will do him good. Some Christians of long standing are too proud to take help in spiritual things from their younger brethren; some ministers will not let themselves be helped by members of their congregations; but not so Paul! And this is the other side of Christian fellowship.

Thus, Christian fellowship is an expression of both love and humility. It springs from a desire to bring benefit to others, coupled with a sense of personal weakness and need. It has a double motive – the wish to help, and to be helped; to edify, and to be edified. It has a double aim – to do, and to receive, good. It is a corporate seeking by Christian people to know God better through sharing with each other what, individually, they have learned of him already.

The significance of fellowship

The above analysis makes three things plain.

First, fellowship is a *means of grace*. Through fellowship, one's soul is refreshed and fed, and by the effort to communicate one's knowledge of divine things one's own grasp of them is strengthened. To have God's children praying for you, caring for you as a fellow-believer, and sharing their experiences of trial and triumph with you brings vast enrichment; and your support of others in the way that others have supported you will mature you as well as benefiting them. Paul's constant pleas that Christians would pray for him as he prays for them (Rom. 15:30; 2 Cor. 1:11; Eph. 6:19; Col. 4:3; 1 Thes. 5:25; 2 Thes. 3:1 f.; Phm. 22; *cf.* Heb. 13:18) and James' injunction, 'confess your sins to one another, and pray for one another, that you may be healed' (5:16), confirm this. Christian fellowship is a means of grace that we neglect to our poverty and at our peril.

Second, fellowship is a *test of life*. Fellowship means opening one's heart to one's fellow-Christians. Where there is pretence or concealment, fellowship cannot exist. But the only man who is free to eschew pretence and concealment about himself when talking to his fellow-Christians is the man who is being open and honest in his daily dealings with God. A man who is not letting the light of God shine full on his whole life cannot have free fellowship with other believers; indeed, he will shrink from fellowship, lest his insincerities be detected. 'If we walk in the light, as he is in the light,' wrote John, 'we have fellowship with one another' – but not otherwise (1 Jn. 1:7).

Third, fellowship is a *gift of God*. The NEB translates Paul's benediction in 2 Corinthians 13:14 as follows: 'The grace of the Lord Jesus Christ, and the love of God, and *fellowship in the Holy Spirit,* be with you all' – and this is probably right. It is only where the Holy Spirit has been given, where men are spiritually alive and anxious to grow in grace themselves and help others to do the same, that fellowship becomes a possibility; and it is only as the Holy Spirit enables us to speak to others, and others to us, in such a way that Christ and the Father are made known through what is said, that fellowship is made a reality. When we seek to enjoy fellowship together, we should do so in prayerful dependence on the Holy Spirit, the third Person of the Trinity, whose office it is to reveal Christ to us; otherwise, our talk with each other will be empty and profitless, and the goal of fellowship – fuller acquaintance with our common Lord – will not be achieved.

The way of fellowship
When does fellowship become a reality?

The answer to this question is clear from what has been said already. Fellowship becomes a reality whenever two or more Christians, desiring to help each other to know God better, do in fact share with each other such knowledge of God as they individually possess. It may happen in many circumstances: in preaching, in prayer together, in private pastoral discussion, in group Bible study, in talk between friends over a meal, or between husband and wife round the fire. But what happens in every case is the same: the Lord's presence and power is realized, and he is known afresh, through the words of a fellow-Christian. For Christ's promise, 'where two or three are gathered in my name, there am I in the midst of them' (Mt. 18:20), applies no less to more informal acts of fellowship than it does to public worship, and it finds its fulfilment no less when two or more Christians meet to share spiritual things together than when a congregation gathers on a Sunday morning or evening.

What hinders fellowship? Four things, at least.

Obstacle one is *self-sufficiency*. There can be no fellowship where individuals do not see that they depend on each other for spiritual help. A spiritually self-sufficient attitude may reflect the deadness of the unconverted, to whom the whole realm of spiritual things seems unreal; or it may reflect the purblindness of sluggish Christians (*cf.* Heb. 5:12 ff.; Rom. 12:1–3) – who may yet be mature in years, and have been Christians of sorts for many of those years; or it may be the rationalized stance of one who through pride or guilt or conscious hypocrisy or all three is not willing to share his spiritual needs and ask for others' help. But whatever its source, self-sufficiency excludes fellowship from the start.

Obstacle two is *formality*. Some see their involvement in correct procedures in public worship, particularly at the Lord's Table, as the whole of Christian fellowship, and shrink from anything more intimate. Their idea has taken a beating in our time, particularly through the robust informalities of the charismatic movement, but there are places where it persists. Liturgical worship that is alive is certainly fellowship, but there is more to fellowship than liturgical worship, as is I hope clear by now.

Obstacle three is *bitterness,* which expresses itself in attitudes of sustained hostility. Hebrews 12:15 warns against the trouble that a 'root of bitterness' can cause. Bitterness seems most often to be due to wounded pride and defensive malice, to a sense of injustice, ill-treatment or betrayal, or to resentful jealousy at another's gifts or position or success. Jealousy in particular is regularly a hidden root of bitterness in controversy, in personal coolness, in gossip (well defined as the art of confessing other people's sins), in protest and in division. In true fellowship, where the goal is to make the other person greater for God, there is a proper place for criticism (criticism may be demanded by love, as parents know), but it will be constructive not destructive, offered gently and with restraint by one who is conscious of being a sinner himself, and who knows too how little criticism any of us can really accept and handle at any one time. Where bitterness motivates, however, criticism will be made in an arrogant, unbridled way that negates fellowship rather than furthers it.

Obstacle four is *élitism*, the superior attitude that produces cliques based on exclusiveness. This is a Satanic counterfeit of true fellowship, from which nothing excludes but unbelief. When 'super-keen' groups hive off on their own into associations in which minor peculiarities of belief, or the magnetic attraction of a leader, function as the bond, pride lives and fellowship dies.

This list of obstacles to fellowship could be elaborated, but there is surely no need. From what has been said there should be no difficulty in answering the question, why is there no fellowship here?, wherever that question may be asked. Let us move on. From what we have said, certain conclusions may be drawn.

The first is, that Christians today *need* fellowship. All Christians of every age do. None is spiritually self-sufficient; God does not make us so. Without fellowship, whether we are conscious of this or not, we shall be and remain feeble Christians. This is a law of the spiritual life. We have already quoted Wesley's wise and true saying, that there is nothing more unchristian than a solitary Christian.

The second is, that Christians today *lack* fellowship. We have many so-called 'fellowship' meetings, of different sorts, but the reality of fellowship is commonly absent, and, indeed, is rarely sought. That is because in our thinking we have substituted a secular, social idea of fellowship as a jolly get-together for the biblical, Trinitarian idea of fellowship as helping each other to draw nearer to the

Father and the Son through the power of the Holy Spirit. Hence we think we are enjoying fellowship when really we are not experiencing fellowship at all. We need a more realistic assessment of our situation in this respect.

The third is, that Christians today must *seek* fellowship. Lonely and isolated Christians, spiritually starved and discouraged Christians, and with them members of prosperous churches and busy Christian workers – all need fellowship, and all should make a point of endeavouring to get it. The Puritans used to ask God for one 'bosom friend', with whom they could share absolutely everything and maintain a full-scale prayer-partner relationship; and with that they craved, and regularly set up, group conversations about divine things. We should be wise to follow their example at both points. Both in history and in theology, fellowship and revival go together – indeed, a renewed spirit of fellowship among Christians is one aspect of revival. As we value the health of our own souls and of the Christian church, then, we must learn to prize fellowship, and labour to reinstate it in its proper place as a means of grace for all members of the body of Christ.

17
DEATH

'He passed, however, a not unsuccessful life in his profession, and the only Intruder he found himself unable to deal with was death.' So, at the close of his most powerful novel, Charles Williams bows out the nice young man who had no criterion of value save usefulness to himself. Williams' words would make an epitaph for many today, for they state very accurately how death hits the natural man. It does in truth come as an *intruder*, uninvited and not bargained for. And when a man sees it coming, panic rises. However brave or blasé a face he may put on it, inwardly he feels isolated, paralysed, drained of strength. He really is unable to cope with it.

Of all human experiences, said James Denney, the most universal is a bad conscience. If that is so, second in order of universality is surely the fear of death. The epistle to the Hebrews describes the redeemed as persons who 'through fear of death were subject to lifelong bondage' (Heb. 2:15). All the world knows death to be what is called in Job 'the king of terrors' (Jb. 18:14). All ages and cultures have found the thought of death traumatic: it shocks, upsets, unnerves. All the world over, people get embarrassed and rattled if you talk to them about dying. Everywhere, the experience of bereavement, or the death of a friend, shakes people to the core; everywhere, the expectation of dying casts invalids into apathetic despair. (That is why our doctors and hospitals staffs, often cruelly, try to hide from the dying their real condition.) Nineteen times the Bible calls the prospect of death its 'shadow', and this figure well brings out our feeling about it. We see death looming up ahead of us as a gross, dark threat, casting a shadow before it, streaking our sunniest moments already with chill and gloom. Daily we advance towards it; soon its shadow will engulf us completely, and life's sunshine will be over for ever. We shall have passed into the dark. As we contemplate that passage, we feel obscurely uneasy. What lies beyond the darkness? When this life stops – what starts? The question bothers people more than they are usually willing to admit.

Some, of course, resolutely shrug it off. To think about death, they say, is morbid; healthy-minded people will not do it. But it is doubtful whether their attitude is the wisest. For, in the first place, to reckon with death is no more than sober realism, since death is life's one and only certainty. The escapism which makes a man shut his eyes to the prospect of death is as stupid as it is neurotic and demoralizing. It is no more healthy-minded than is the so-called 'Victorian' attitude to sex. If we think it needful for mental and moral health to face the 'facts of life' concerning sex, we should remember that a much more fundamental fact of life is that death will sooner or later intervene to stop it, and we should not doubt the necessity of facing *this* fact if our outlook on life is to be a healthy one. Philip of Macedon was wise when he charged a slave to remind him every morning: 'Philip, remember that you must die.' Some of us could do with similar reminders.

In recent years the scientific community has studied death and dying intensely. The development of medical techniques for restarting hearts has displaced the old notion of a moment of death when the heart no longer beats in favour of the concept of a process of dying which becomes irreversible when electrical vibrations cease in the brain, twenty minutes or so after the heart stops. Folk have reported many kinds of experiences between the stopping and restarting of their hearts, and exponents of the occult have fastened on some of these as revelations of human destiny; but since none of them can tell us what happens when the dying process is complete and the brain can no longer support consciousness, the wise man will not treat them as decisive of anything. Nor will he imagine that the curiosity about death which all this has stirred up has done anything to lessen the traumatic effect of thinking about one's own exit from this world, into – what?

It seems clear that younger folk are better able to think straight about death than any other class of people. For when the sense of one's own individuality, and of life's limitless possibilities, has just crystallized out in one's mind, the real horror of approaching death strikes one more forcibly and painfully than it ever did before or ever will again. There are many between the ages of fifteen and twenty-five who have sometimes – lying awake, perhaps, at night, or out alone in the country – found themselves thinking: 'I want to live – I am just starting to live– but, oh horrors, I have got to *die*!' – and the thought hurts like a blow in the solar plexus. Members of this age-group see death as an unnatural evil, a cosmic outrage, making a mockery of all their new-born longings after truth, beauty and achievement. Doubt gnaws: is there any sense in pursuing worthwhile objectives, if at the end of your quest, or before it, you have to die?

As a rule, it is only in youth that this sense of the out-rageousness of death is strong. By middle age, youth's vision is blurred, and one simply resigns oneself to dying in due course, as a natural necessity (though one does not come to love death on that account). By old age, the vision is almost forgotten, and physical vitality falls so low that death may even be welcomed as a release. But the young adult sees death as a malevolent monstrosity, and resents it; and thereby he shows that his sense of reality is sharper than that of his elders. For death is in truth an unnatural evil, as we shall see in a moment.

The nature of death

When a person dies of disease or old age, we call it 'natural death', reserving 'unnatural death' for cases of accident and foul play. But Scripture confirms our instinctive feeling that, in the deepest sense, all death is unnatural. What is death? It is a dissolving of the union between spirit and body: 'the dust returns to the earth...and the spirit...to God who gave it' (Ec. 12:7). There is a back-reference here to the story of creation. As in the beginning God made man by breathing life into a thing of dust (Gn. 2:7), so now in death he partly un-makes him, severing the two realities which he originally joined together. This disintegration is, to man, unnatural in the highest degree. That is why sensitive people find dead bodies uncanny. It is sometimes said that the dead look peaceful, but this is hardly correct. What is true is that corpses look *vacant*. It is their evident emptiness that we find unnerving – the sense that the person whose body and face this was has simply *gone*.

Does death mean personal annihilation? Indeed no. Death is, in Paul's phrase, an 'unclothing' of a person, by dismantling his earthly 'tent' (2 Cor. 5:1 ff.), but it is not the end of his personal life. The Bible everywhere takes personal survival for granted. The Old Testament pictures the dead as going 'down' (a natural metaphor) to the place which it calls *Sheol* (Septuagint and Greek New Testament, *Hades*). The AV rendered both Sheol and Hades as 'hell', but this is misleading, since neither term implies anything as to the happiness or otherwise of the inhabitants of this place. (RV usually, and RSV invariably, retain the proper names in the text.)

Sheol is not, however, the ultimate abode of the dead. Scripture looks forward to an emptying of Hades when the dead are raised bodily for judgment at Christ's return (Jn. 5:28 f.; Rev. 20:12 f.; *cf.* Dn. 12:2 f.). Those whose names are written in the book of life (Rev. 20:12) will then be welcomed into endless bliss ('eternal life', Mt. 25:46; 'glory, honour, and peace', Rom. 2:10; a kingdom, Mt. 25:34; new Jerusalem, Rev. 21:2 – 22:5). But the rest will then undergo the extremest manifestation of divine displeasure ('unquenchable fire', Mt. 3:12; Mk. 9:43; Gehenna – which was the place of incineration outside Jerusalem – 'where the devouring worm never dies', Mk. 9:47 f., NEB; 'outer darkness', a place of 'wailing and grinding of teeth', Mt. 25:30, NEB; 'eternal punishment', Mt. 25:46; 'the eternal fire prepared for the devil and his angels', verse 41; 'wrath and fury... tribulation and distress', Rom. 2:8–9; 'eternal destruction and exclusion from the presence of the Lord',

2 Thes. 1:9; 'the lake that burns with fire and brimstone, which is the second death', Rev. 21:8, *cf.* 20:15).

Some hold that these texts imply the annihilation of those rejected – one searing moment in the fire, and then oblivion. But it seems clear that in reality the 'second death' is no more a cessation of being than is the first. For (i) the word rendered 'destruction' in 2 Thes. 1:9 (*olethros*) means, not annihilation, but *ruin* (*cf.* its use in 1 Thes. 5:3). (ii) The insistence in these texts that the fire, punishment and destruction are *eternal* (*aiōnios,* literally 'age-long'), and that the worm in Gehenna is *undying,* would be pointless and inappropriate if all that is envisaged is momentary extinction; just as it would be pointless and inappropriate to dwell on 'unending' pain resulting from an immediately fatal bullet wound. Either these words indicate the endlessness of torment, or they are superfluous and misleading. (iii) To the argument that *aiōnios* means only 'relating to the age to come', without any implications of endless duration, it seems sufficient to say that if in Matthew 25:46 'eternal' life means endless bliss (and surely it does), then the 'eternal' punishment mentioned there must be endless too. (iv) We are told that in the 'lake of fire' (the 'eternal fire prepared for the devil and his angels', Mt. 25:41) the devil will be 'tormented day and night for ever and ever' (Rev. 20:10). That any man sent to join him will endure a similar eternity of retribution is clear from the parallel language of Revelation 14:10 f.: 'he (the beast-worshipper) shall be tormented with fire and brimstone . . . the smoke of their torment goes up for ever and ever; and they have no rest, day or night.'

It seems plain that what these texts teach is not extinction, but the far worse prospect of an endless awareness of God's just and holy displeasure. Grievous as we may find it to contemplate, and sickening as we may find the Jewish apocalyptic imagery in which Christ and the apostles speak of it (this is, after all, the post-holocaust era), an endless hell can no more be removed from the New Testament than an endless heaven can. This is why physical death (the first death) is so fearful a prospect for Christ-less men; not because it means extinction, but precisely because it does *not* mean extinction, only the unending pain of the second death. The godless man dimly senses this, through God's general revelation (Rom. 1:32); no wonder, then, that he fears to die.

In the Old Testament, references to death denote on the surface, at any rate, only physical dissolution. But in the New Testament the concept of death is radically deepened. Death in the New Testament is seen primarily as a spiritual state, the state of mankind without Christ. As physical death means the separating of the spirit from the body, so spiritual death means a state in which man is separated from God, cut off from his favour and fellowship, 'dead through our trespasses' (Eph. 2:1, 5; *cf.* Mt. 8:22; Jn. 5:24; Rom. 8:6; Col. 2:13; 1 Tim. 5:6). As in the Bible 'life' repeatedly denotes the joy of fellowship with God (*cf.* 1 Jn. 5:12), so the state of being alienated from this 'life of God' (Eph. 4:18) is equated with 'death'. It is from spiritual death first and foremost that we need to be delivered.

Death and sin

Throughout the Bible, death in both its physical and its spiritual aspects is viewed as a penal evil, God's judgment upon sin (*cf.* Ezk. 18:4). Death, says Paul, is the 'wages' which are paid to sin's employees (Rom. 6:23). When God told Adam, 'in the day that you eat of it [the tree of knowledge] you shall die' (Gn. 2:17), the primary and explicit reference was to physical dissolution, as 3:19 makes clear. (The words 'in the day that' express *certainty* of sequence, not necessarily temporal *immediacy: cf.* the use of the same phrase in 1 Ki. 2:37. Adam did not die till long after, Gn. 5:5.). So when Paul says in 1 Corinthians 15:22 'in Adam all die', the context shows that he has in mind physical mortality alone, which Christ is to abolish by raising the dead.

But in Romans 5:12 ff., when he speaks of Christ delivering the 'many' who are his from the 'death' in which Adam had involved them, his reference is wider. For the deliverance he expounds is not physical resurrection merely (indeed, physical resurrection is not mentioned in the passage at all). It is, rather, present 'justification' (verses 16–19), leading to a restoration of 'life' (verses 17, 18, 21) – in other words, the healing of that vitiated relationship with God of which physical death was the proof and emblem. Implicit, therefore, in Genesis 2:17 we should find also a reference to the spiritual death which was pictured when God drove the man out of Eden (the place of fellowship), to prevent him eating any more of the tree of life.

What would have happened to man at the end of his probationary period on earth, if he had not sinned? Would he have died physically? Presumably no; not, at any rate, as he dies now. Perhaps God would just have 'taken' him, as he 'took' Enoch and Elijah (Gn. 5:24; 2 Ki. 2:1, 11). Some think we would have been physically transfigured, as Christ was (Mk. 9:2 ff.). But these are speculations, on a matter on which Scripture is silent, and questions which the Bible does not answer must be left unsolved.

The decisiveness of death

The world usually refers to physical death merely as an ending, the closing of a door on one's earthly life; but the New Testament sees it also as a beginning – the opening of a door into one's destiny, the new life in which one starts to reap what one has sown (cf. 2 Cor. 5:10; Gal. 6:7). In the Old Testament, it is true, we find the saints shrinking from the prospect of death, believing that in Sheol, though God was not absent (Ps. 139:8), they could not hope for such close and sweet fellowship with him as they had enjoyed on earth (cf. Pss. 88:10–12; 115:17; Ec. 9:5, 10; Is. 38:18; etc.). The New Testament seems to hint that the Old Testament saints were in fact kept waiting until Christ himself entered Sheol (the 'descent into hell' of the Creed: cf. Acts 2:27 ff.) before their fellowship with God in the celestial Zion became the complete and perfect thing that it is now (cf. Heb. 11:40 with 12:18–23).

However that may be, it is made clear in the New Testament that in these 'last days' the wheels of divine repayment are revolving from the moment of death on, and that each man at once finds himself experiencing in intensified form that relationship with God and (if in his lifetime he heard the gospel) with Jesus Christ which he chose to have during his life in this world – either to be *with* God and Christ, which now proves to be Paradise and joy (Lk. 23:43; Phil. 1:23; 2 Cor. 5:6–8; *cf.* Acts 7:55–59), or else to remain *without* both in the spiritual darkness of a self-willed and self-centred existence (*cf.* Jn. 3:19) – a condition which now, as one begins to realize what one has lost, proves to be agony (Lk. 16:23 ff.). For those with Christ, God in grace makes the new life one of increasing joy without any further pain (Rev. 7:15 ff.); for those without Christ, God in retributive justice makes the new life one of increasing pain without any further joy (Lk. 16:25). Already, therefore, our Lord's prediction is being verified: 'to every one who has will more be given; but from him who has not, even what he has will be taken away' (Lk. 19:26).

But it is too late to change; after death there is a 'great gulf' fixed between those whom God accepts and those whom he rejects (Lk. 16:26). The time of choice has passed. All that remains now is to receive the consequences of the choice already made; to a degree, in the 'intermediate state', more fully after the resurrection and final judgment (*cf.* Heb. 9:27). There is nothing arbitrary about the doctrine of eternal punishment: it is in essence a case of God respecting our choice, and continuing to us throughout eternity the spiritual condition which we chose to be in while on earth.

To many, this will come as grievous and unwelcome teaching; but we shall be wise not to ignore it, for a great deal of it comes directly from our Lord himself. A better reaction will be to set ourselves to live, as the saints before us have lived, *sub specie aeternitatis* – in the light of eternity. Well did the Psalmist pray, 'So teach us to number our days, that we may get a heart of wisdom' (Ps. 90:12). Well did Murray M'Cheyne paint a setting sun on the dial of his watch, to remind himself how short time is. It has been said with truth that we have all eternity to rejoice in victories won for Christ, but only a few brief hours here below in which to win them. All of us need a quickened sense of the shortness of our time, and of the eternal significance of the present moment.

Other views

'I have just read your article on Death and find it revolting.' So began a letter from a beloved Irish evangelist, now in glory, when the above paragraphs first appeared in print. Others may feel the same, and there may be nothing I can do about it, but let us see if some more exposition will help.

What alternatives are there to the view of the decisiveness of death that I have just set out? Only three: conditional immortality, post-mortem evangelism and universalism. Look at them.

Conditional immortality (the doctrine of the annihilation at judgment day of those rejected) was set aside above for biblical reasons. My evangelist friend reminded me that several distinguished British evangelicals who went through Cambridge University between the wars espoused conditionalism. That is true, but I do not think that it entitled him to affirm, as he did: 'You only quote from Scripture what suits your theory and ignore the rest.' 'The rest' is not text but interpretation. Let it be plainly said: there is no Bible passage out of which conditionalism can confidently be read. There are passages into which it can be read, and passages as we saw into which it can hardly be read, where special pleading is needed if conditionalism is not to fall. As one who is not interested in what Scripture can be made to mean, only in its *natural* meaning, I have to say that the special pleading I have met fails to convince.

In fact, the mainspring of conditionalism is not exegetical but theological. On the assumption that God's honour and glory does not require the continuance of the lost in misery after the judgment, it is felt that if God failed to annihilate them then he would be needlessly cruel. But the argument defeats itself: for on this assumption it is needlessly cruel for God to keep the lost in being in the misery of the intermediate state (on which see Lk. 16:23 ff.) until judgment day, and he ought to annihilate them at death –

which Scripture clearly shows that he does not do. In fact, however, righteous (that is, merited) judgment is not cruelty, and the biblical position is that God's appointment for the godless is righteous judgment (*cf.* Lk. 12:47 f.; Rom. 2:5–16), making for his praise (*cf.* Rev. 16:5–7; 19:1–3).

Post-mortem evangelism, embracing all who never heard the gospel preached 'intelligently', was affirmed by my evangelist friend. But there is no clear Scripture for this. The mystery verses, 1 Peter 3:19 f., cannot be pressed into service, for (i) the 'spirits in prison' are at least as likely to be fallen angels as fallen men (*cf.* Gn. 6:1–4; Jude 6); (ii) the statement that Christ preached to spirits who disobeyed in Noah's day more naturally implies that the preaching was not to others than that it was; (iii) 'preached' (Greek, *kēryssō*), with the message unspecified, does not imply an offer of life any more naturally than it does a bare proclamation of Jesus' triumph. So the verses will not prove universal post-mortem evangelism, nor will any other passage. And clear texts speak against this notion, notably those which view this life as decisive for one's future (2 Cor. 5:10; Gal. 6:7; *etc.*)

In any case, those who did not hear the gospel presented 'intelligently' still had light from God in their consciences, which they either heeded or disregarded, either setting themselves to seek the God of whom they had inklings or not. We may safely say (i) if any good pagan reached the point of throwing himself on his Maker's mercy for pardon, it was grace that brought him there; (ii) God will surely save anyone he brings thus far (*cf.* Acts 10:34 f.; Rom. 10:12 f.); (iii) anyone thus saved would learn in the next world that he was saved through Christ. But what we cannot safely say is that God ever does save anyone this way. We simply do not know. All we are sure of is that 'the wrath of God is revealed from heaven against all ungodliness and wickedness of men who by their wickedness suppress the truth', and that Paul does not hesitate to echo the psalmist's generalization, 'none is righteous, no, not one' (Rom. 1:18; 3:10, *cf.* 9–18). Nor does God owe any presentation of the gospel, let alone an 'intelligent' one, to any man.

Universalism, the third of the alternatives, is usually stated as an optimistic form of 'second-chance' teaching: all whom God made and who did not turn to him in this life he will meet in Christ after death and lead to love him, even if he has to send them to a purgatorial gehenna for a time to bring them to their senses. But this was clearly not Christ's own view (see Mt. 12:32; 26:24), nor is it the necessary or even natural meaning of any single text taken in its context.

One of fiction's great detectives laid it down that when you have eliminated all the impossibilities what remains, however improbable, must be true. Similarly, the theologian knows that when you have eliminated all unscriptural options what remains, however unpalatable, must be God's truth. I do not say that the position I have set forth concerning eternal loss is pleasant or comfortable to live with; I urge only that it is actually taught by Christ and by the New Testament, and must be reckoned with accordingly.

The conquest of death

If you cannot make sense of death, you cannot make sense of life either; and no philosophy that will not teach us how to master death is worth twopence to us. As this point the philosophers retire beaten – and the gospel comes into its own. For the mastering of death is, from one point of view, its central theme – the theme which John Owen summed up as *the death of death in the death of Christ.*

For Christ's resurrection was no mere temporary resuscitation, as were the raisings of Lazarus, and Jairus' daughter, and the widow's son of Nain. 'Christ being raised from the dead *will never die again*; death *no longer has dominion* over him...he lives to God' (Rom. 6:9 f.). 'I died, and behold *I am alive for evermore,* and I have the keys of Death and Hades' (Rev. 1:18). His rising proclaimed and guaranteed both present forgiveness and justification for his people (Rom. 4:25; 1 Cor. 15:17), and also their present co-resurrection with him into newness of spiritual life (Rom. 6:4–11; Eph. 2:1–10; Col. 2:12 f.; 3:1–11). This spiritual co-resurrection will be matched when Christ returns by a physical transformation of us if alive (Phil.

3:21), or re-clothing of us if dead (*cf.* 2 Cor. 5:4 f.; 1 Cor. 15:50–54): and that will mean the final destruction of death, as a hostile and destructive intruder into God's world (1 Cor. 15:26, 54f.).

Meanwhile, the dread of physical death, which sprang from the sense that death was the door into suffering and judgment (Heb. 2:15), has for the Christian been abolished: death's 'sting' has been drawn (1 Cor. 15:55 f.), through the knowledge that one's sins are forgiven and that 'neither death, nor life,...nor things to come,...nor anything else in all creation, will be able to separate us from the love of God in Christ Jesus our Lord' (Rom. 8:38 f.). Physical death is now 'sleep' (*i.e.* rest and refreshment, Rev. 14:13; not unconsciousness) 'in Jesus' (1 Cor. 15:18, 51; 1 Thes. 4:13 ff.; Acts 7:60): a 'sleep' brought on by Christ's coming to receive to himself those for whom he has been preparing a place (Jn. 14:2 f.). They 'depart' to 'be with Christ', which 'is far better' (Phil. 1:23).

A Christian may rightly think of his death-day as a date in Jesus' diary: when the appointed time comes the Saviour will be there to lead his servant into the light of his own nearer presence and closer communion. Dying, therefore, however hard and hurtful in physical terms, becomes a journey into joy. A play in London some years back had the striking title, *Happy Death-day,* and for the believer so in deed it will be. Fellowship with Christ, and with God through Christ, once begun here on earth, never ends: through death, through the 'intermediate state' between death and resurrection, and for ever after, Christ is with his people: and that is life eternal. Thus he verifies his promise, proclaimed to Martha as she mourned for Lazarus: 'I am the resurrection and the life; he who believes in me, though he die, yet shall he live, and whoever lives and believes in me shall never die' (Jn. 11:25 f.).

So death is conquered; and, with Mrs. Margaret Baxter,[1]

---

[1] These verses come from a poem written by Richard Baxter and printed in his *Poetical Fragments* (1681), under the title 'The Covenant and Confidence of Faith', with the following note: 'This Covenant my Dear Wife in her former sickness subscribed with a cheerful will. Joh. xii. 26.'

the Christian may calmly and joyfully say:

> *Lord, it belongs not to my care*
>   *Whether I die or live;*
> *To love and serve thee is my share,*
>   *And this thy grace must give.*
>
> *If life be long, I will be glad*
>   *That I may long obey;*
> *If short – yet why should I be sad*
>   *To soar to endless day?*
>
> *Christ leads me through no darker rooms*
>   *Than he went through before;*
> *He that into God's kingdom comes*
>   *Must enter by this door.*
>
> *Then shall I end my sad complaints*
>   *And weary sinful days,*
> *And join with the triumphant saints*
>   *That sing Jehovah's praise.*
>
> *My knowledge of that life is small,*
>   *The eye of faith is dim;*
> *But it's enough that* Christ knows all,
>   And I shall be with him.

Be prepared

Three centuries ago a story went round about a student's visit to Thomas Goodwin, the Puritan president of Magdalen College, Oxford. In the dark study Goodwin opened the conversation by asking if his visitor was ready to die. The lad fled. The story was told for laughs then, as it would be now; but it ought to be said that if it really happened, Goodwin was asking a proper pastoral question that should not be made fun of, whatever we might think of his technique. For however old or young you are, one secret of inner peace and living to the full is to be realistically prepared for death – packed up, we might say, and ready to go. It is not absurd for us to remind each other of that fact.

Yesterday's Christians knew it well. They looked on all

life as preparation for death and eternity, and hence took (not themselves, but) each present moment very seriously. Mediaeval and Puritan instruction on the art of dying turns out to be an approach to the art of living; Ken's words, 'live each day as if thy last,' are always what North Americans call the bottom line. Living this way, yesterday's Christians undoubtedly got more out of life than most moderns do. Today, as we have seen, healthy-mindedness is defined in terms not of thinking about death but of not thinking about it, and even Christians who harp on Christ's second coming seem unaware that readiness for that and for death are two sides of the same coin, two facets of the same theme – namely, the end of this world for you and me, because Christ has come for us. This is all retrograde, and a return to the older wisdom would be much to our advantage.

How may Christians live their lives packed up and ready to go? There is no mystery about it; common sense should tell us. Be wholly committed to Christ's service each day. Don't touch sin with a barge-pole. Keep short accounts with God. Think of each hour as God's gift to you, to make the most and best of. Plan your life, budgeting for seventy years (Ps. 90:10), and understanding that if your time proves shorter that will not be unfair deprivation but rapid promotion. Never let the good, or the not-so-good, crowd out the best, and cheerfully forgo what is not the best for the sake of what is. Live in the present; gratefully enjoy its pleasures and work through its pains with God, knowing that both the pleasures and the pains are steps on the journey home. Open all your life to the Lord Jesus and spend time consciously in his company, basking in and responding to his love. Say to yourself often that every day is one day nearer. Remember that, as George Whitefield said, man is immortal till his work is done (though God alone defines the work), and get on with what you know to be God's task for you here and now.

Said Paul: 'The time has come for me to be gone. I have fought the good fight to the end; I have run the race to the finish; I have kept the faith; all there is to come now is the crown of righteousness reserved for me, which the Lord, the righteous judge, will give to me on that Day; and not only to me but to all those who have longed for his Appearing' (2 Tim. 4:6–8, JB).

Urged Peter: 'Make every effort to add to your faith goodness; and to goodness, knowledge; and to knowledge, self-control; and to self-control, perseverance; and to perseverance, godliness; and to godliness, brotherly kindness; and to brotherly kindness, love...make your calling and election sure. For if you do these things, you will never fall, and you will receive a rich welcome into the eternal kingdom of our Lord and Saviour Jesus Christ' (2 Pet. 1:5–7, 10 f., NIV).

That's the way.

INDEX OF BIBLICAL PASSAGES

217